Warman's

Bottles

FIELD GUIDE

3rd Edition

Michael Polak

Values and Identification

Published by

Krause Publications, a division of F+W Media, Inc.
700 East State Street • Iola, WI 54990-0001
715-445-2214 • 888-457-2873
www.krausebooks.com

ISSN 2153-8913
ISBN-13: 978-1-4402-1240-6
ISBN-10: 1-4402-1240-6

Designed by Katrina Newby
Edited by Dan Brownell

Printed in the United States of America

DEDICATION

Warman's® Bottles Field Guide, 3rd Edition, is dedicated to all the bottle clubs and organizations that continue to promote interest in and having fun with the hobby of bottle collecting.

PHOTO CREDITS

Bob Kay
Bob Moore
Bob Snyder
Bud Hastin (*Avon Collector's Encyclopedia*)
Collector Books/Schroeder Publishing
David Graci
David Spaid
Frank Bartlett
Gary & Vickie Lewis
International Assoc. of Jim Beam Bottle &
    Specialties Club
Jeff Wichmann (American Bottle Auctions)
Jennifer Tai
John Tutton
Michael & Lori Eckles (Showtime Auction
    Services)
Jim Hagenbuch (*Antique Bottle & Glass Collector
    Magazine*, Glass Works Auctions)
Norman C. Heckler (Norman C. Heckler and
    Company, Auctions)
Rick Sweeney
Rick Wiener
Samia Koudsi
Steve Ritter (Steve Ritter Auctions)
Willy Young

ACKNOWLEDGMENTS

Bob Kay: Thanks for your contribution of pricing inputs on miniature bottles and your support of the project.

Bud Hastin *(Avon Collector's Encyclopedia)*: Thanks for the great photographs and your help with the Avon collectibles pricing.

Collector Books/Schroeder Publishing: Thank your for the contribution of Avon photographs.

David Graci: Thanks for your contribution of photographs and background information on soda and beer bottle closures.

David Spaid: Thanks for your help with understanding the world of miniature bottles and your support of the project.

Gary and Vickie Lewis: Thanks for your contribution of photographs of ACL soda bottles and your overall support of the project.

Jacque Pace Polak: A special thank you to my wife for her continued patience and invaluable moral support.

Jim Hagenbuch (Antique Bottle & Glass Collector & Glass Works Auctions): Thank you for the great assortment of photographs, pricing input, and overall support of the project.

John Tutton: Thank you for your contribution of photographs of milk bottles and your overall support of the project.

Michael & Lori Eckles (Showtime Auction Services): Thank you for your contribution of various photographs and your overall support of the project.

Norm Heckler (Heckler Auctions): Thank you for your contribution of photographs and your support of the project.

Steve Ritter (Steve Ritter Auctioneering): Thanks for your help in obtaining the ACL soda bottle photographs and your pricing input.

Rick Sweeney: Thanks for your help and understanding with the pricing input for applied color label soda bottles.

Violin Bottle Collectors Association and members: Thanks for all of your help with the contribution of photographs and an overall understanding of violin bottles. A special thank you to Bob Linden, Frank Bartlett, Samia Koudsi, and Bob Moore for their time and effort in providing photographs, pricing data, and resource information.

Jeff Wichman (American Bottle Auctions): Thanks for your great assortment of Western bottle photographs and overall support of the project.

Rick Wiener: Thanks for all the photos you provided for the 3rd edition of the field guide.

CONTENTS

INTRODUCTION

Welcome to the third edition of *Warman's® Bottles Field Guide* and the fun hobby of antique bottle collecting. Once again, a special thank you to all my readers for your support in making the second edition a huge success. In order to make the third edition the best informative reference and pricing guide available, I have provided the beginner and veteran collector with a broader range of detailed information and data. For the third edition, there are 300 new photos and five new chapters on the fastest growing segments of bottle collecting: crocks and stoneware; food and pickle bottles; ginger beer bottles; mineral water bottles; and soda fountain syrup dispensers. Plus, I've added an informative new feature: "The Top Ten Bottle Collecting Destinations." The book is divided into four color-coded sections: Reader Advice (blue), Old Bottles (Pre-1900) (red), New Bottles (Post-1900) (violet) and Reader Resources (green).

Interest in bottle collecting continues to grow, with new bottle clubs forming throughout the United States and Europe. More collectors are spending their free time digging through old dumps, foraging through old ghost towns, digging out old outhouses (that's right), exploring abandoned mine shafts, and searching out their favorite bottle or antique shows, swap meets, flea markets, or garage sales.

In addition, the Internet has expanded extensively, with many new auction sites offering collectors numerous opportunities and resources without even leaving the house. Many bottle clubs now have Web sites providing even more information for the collector. Having more resources available is always a good thing for the hobby.

Most collectors, however, still look beyond the type and value of a bottle to its origin and history. I find that researching the history of bottles has at times proved to be more interesting than finding the bottle itself. I enjoy both pursuits for their close ties to the rich history of the United States and the early methods of merchandising.

My goal has always been to enhance the hobby of bottle collecting for both the beginner and expert collectors and to help them experience the excitement of antique bottle collecting, especially the thrill of making that special find. I hope the third edition of *Warman's® Bottles Field Guide* continues to bring an increased understanding and enjoyment of the hobby of bottle collecting.

For a more in-depth study of bottle collecting, I recommend my full-length book *Antique Trader® Bottles Identification and Price Guide*, 6th Edition. With 52 categories of bottles containing thousands of price listings, the sixth edition covers far more pricing and reference information than can be included in this field guide. The sixth edition contains a number of chapters not included in this field guide, such as twenty-nine more categories of bottles and a number of chapters to aid more extensive research, such as "Bottles: History and Origin" (which also explains the various ways antique glass bottles were made), "Digging for Bottles," "Bottles Clubs," "Auction Companies," and "Museums Research Resources."

If you would like to provide feedback regarding this third edition of the field guide, or would just like to talk about bottles, I can be contacted at my e-mail address: bottleking@earthlink.net, or through my Web site: www.bottlebible.com.

Good bottle hunting and have fun with the hobby of bottle collecting!

BOTTLE COLLECTING NEWS AND MARKET UPDATE

There isn't a shortage of exciting news about events in the world of antique bottle collecting. The hobby is strong and continues to gain popularity, bringing an overall greater awareness to a wide spectrum of antique collectors. Recent auctions have demonstrated this excitement and popularity.

American Bottle Auctions, Sacramento, California, concluded a bottle auction on May 8, 2009, that resulted in 302 lots bringing in total sales of $220,875, with an average of $751 per bottle. The highlight of this auction was $26,880 paid for a Sachem's Bitters in pure green, the most ever paid for this specific variation. Then, during another American Bottle auction that concluded on August 21, 2009, 260 lots brought in total sales of $250,000. The highlight of this auction was a medium chocolate amber California Clubhouse Whiskey bottle, circa 1872-1874, that sold for $30,240. This bottle, only one of nine known examples, featured a fancy monogram in the center of the bottle, and a stunning embossing pattern. Following this auction, Jeff Wichmann, owner of ABA, stated, "The results of this auction told me that the antique bottle market is very strong despite a weak economy." Further evidence is the results of an auction conducted by Glass Works Auction, East Greenville, Pennsylvania, on October 19, 2009, when a medium amber log-cabin, 9-1/8" tall bitters bottle, American Life Bitters/ P.E. Iler, circa 1865-1875, sold for $26,000. Another highlight in this auction was a rare Franktown Glass Works, Pittsburg, Pennsylvania Wormser Flask, circa 1859-1870, Union Clasped Hands, Eagle with Banner, that sold for $19,000. Yes, the antique bottle market is indeed very strong.

Another great example is a new exhibition, *Pottery with a Past: Stoneware in Early America*, on display at Colonial Williamsburg's DeWitt Wallace Decorative Arts Museum in Williamsburg, Virginia. These pottery artifacts are significant because, during the first half of the seventeenth century, stoneware was the only method for storing liquids and food products, thus fulfilling an important role in history. The exhibit, which will remain through January 2, 2011, spans the early 1600s to the early 1800s, and includes more than 300 intact objects and archaeological fragments recovered from sites in New England, the Middle Atlantic, and the Southern colonies. For additional information, call (800) 447-8679.

Crocker Farm Auctions conducted an auction on March 21, 2009, in which a decorated two-gallon 13-inch keg-formed cooler sold for $103,500 to Leigh Keno, one of the Keno brothers seen regularly on the *Antiques Road Show* series. The cooler was inscribed "Albany, August 7 1817," stamped "Boynton," and decorated with fish and a crested bird.

Want to learn about the art of glass making, and take a cruise at the same time? Here's your chance. The Corning Museum of Glass in Corning, New York, is noted for its live, narrated glassblowing demonstrations. Now, the *Hot Glass Show* will also be available on Celebrity Cruise's newest ship, the *Celebrity Solstice*. The ship will have a permanent glass studio run by the museum on the top deck. In addition, there will be glass sculptures and art exhibits throughout the ship as a decorative motif, with finished glass products being sold on the ship.

How many times have you admired 1930-era seltzer bottles, especially in the various colors of blue and green, and thought how neat it would be to own one. Well, in 1997, Russell Johnson of Cody, Wyoming, was at a flea market in Buenos Aires, Argentina, and noticed a man selling numerous antique seltzer bottles. He brought one back and showed it to some of his peers in the interior design industry, and they wanted more. Johnson started a business relationship with that seller, and now the bottles are cleaned, refurbished, and recreated as pendant lamps, jars, votive candle holders, wine chillers, spoon holders, or just sold as is. For more information, visit his Web site at www.artthang.com.

While we're on the subject of refurbishing old bottles for new uses, Dr. Pepper soda bottles are now being featured on AMC's new hit series *Mad Men*. The Dr. Pepper Museum, located in

Waco, Texas, received a request for some 1960s Dr. Pepper bottles for use in various scenes in the series. But *Mad Men* is not the only series using the bottles. The recent Indiana Jones movie *Indiana Jones and the Kingdom of the Crystal Skull* used a mint-green rust-covered Dr. Pepper vending machine along with various dinner-type accessories. Mary Beth Webster, collections manager at the museum, said "Who would have ever thought there was all this stuff?" I say, who would have ever thought it would be put back to good use again?

And finally, how about a front and back bar that sold for $302,500 during an auction conducted by Showtime Auction Services on October 4, 2008. The mahogany bar, made around 1893 by Brunswick, Balke & Collender Co., also included an original matching liquor cabinet with adjustable shelves. Mike Eckles, co-owner with his wife Lori of Showtime Auction Services, said that "We've only seen two of these bars in 25 years, and only one with a matching original liquor cabinet."

As you can see, antique bottle collecting is truly strong and continues to include all aspects of antique collecting, increasing the interest and fun in antique bottle collecting.

TOP TEN BOTTLE COLLECTING DESTINATIONS

Whenever I attend a bottle show and sign books, I am constantly amazed at the range of questions that collectors ask. But they invariably ask where they can actually see antique bottles and learn about their history. To answer that question, I have compiled the following ten bottle collecting destinations that will not only be educational and informative, but also a lot of fun.

Corning Museum of Glass
One Museum Way
Corning, NY 14830
(800) 732-6845
www.cmog.org

The Corning Museum of Glass has one of the world's best collections of art and historical glass, with more that 45,000 objects from 3,500 years of glassmaking history. There are hands-on exhibits, live narrated glassblowing demonstrations, and a unique try-it-yourself glassmaking program. Visitors can also purchase glass treasures from around the world in the 18,000 square-foot glass market.

Museum of American Glass at Wheaton Village
1501 Glasstown Road
Millville, NJ 08332
(800) 998-4552
www.wheatonarts.org/museumamericanglass

The museum's collection has expanded to over 12,000 pieces and contains the most comprehensive exhibit of American glass in the world. The collection is arranged chronologically beginning with glass from the first successful glass factory in America dating from 1739 to contemporary art glass. Displays are changed throughout the year, and special exhibits are presented regularly.

National Bottle Museum

76 Milton Ave,
Ballston, Spa, NY 12020
(518) 885-7589
www.crisny.org/not-for-profit/nbm

The museum does a superb job of preserving the history of our nation's first major industry, bottle making, with one entire wall on the first floor displaying 2,000 bottles of many colors shapes, and forms. The museum has access to collections from all over the United States and frequently updates its exhibits.

Ohio Glass Museum

124 w. Main Street,
Lancaster, OH 43130
(740) 687-0101
www.ohioglassmuseum.org

The museum, located in the heart of the downtown historic district, reflects the importance of glass in the history and development of Lancaster County from 1888 to present. Because of the abundance of natural resources in the area, the glass industry quickly expanded there. Educational and artistic displays guide the visitor through the development and production of industrial glass as well as pressed, blown, and art glass.

The Sandwich History Glass Museum

Rt. 130 & Tupper Road at 129 Main St.
Sandwich, MA 02563
(508) 888-0251
www.sandwichglassmuseum.org

Incorporated in 1637, Sandwich, Mass., is the oldest town on Cape Cod, where glass manufacturing began in the mid-1820s when American manufacturers began to experiment with pressed glass. Featuring 5,000 pieces of glass produced from 1825 to 1888, the museum collects, preserves, and interprets the history of the town of Sandwich and its involvement in American glass production. It also offers a 20-minute glass blowing demonstration every half hour when molten glass is drawn from a furnace, blown, and pressed into exquisite shapes.

Biedenharn Coca-Cola Museum

1107 Washington Street
Vicksburg, MS 39183
(601) 638-6514
www.biedenharn
    coca-colamuseum.com

Located in a restored 19th century candy store with a soda fountain, this is where the first bottle of Coca-Cola was produced in 1894. The museum features a wide variety of exhibits covering the beginnings of Coca-Cola, the process used to bottle the first Coca-Cola, a reproduction of bottling equipment, and an excellent collection of Coca-Cola bottles.

New Bern North Carolina Museum

256 Middle Street
New Bern, NC 28560
(252) 636-5898
www.pepsistore.com

Located in the original location where Caleb Bradham invented Pepsi-Cola in his pharmacy in 1898, the museum offers exhibits with Pepsi history and memorabilia.

Dr. Pepper Museum

300 South 5th Street
Waco, TX 76701
(254) 757-1025
www.drpeppermuseum.com

Housed in the 1906 Artesian Manufacturing and Bottling Company Building in downtown Waco, Texas, the museum is listed in the National Register of Historic Places and is known as the "Home of Dr. Pepper." The museum details the history and significance of Dr. Pepper and other soft-drink memorabilia, and conducts tours of the bottling room.

Central Nevada Museum

1900 Logan Field Road
Tonopah, NV 89049
(775) 482-9676
www.tonopahnevada.com/centralnevadamuseum.html

Located in Tonopah, Nevada, "The Queen of the Silver Camps" displays a large collection of bottles from local mining camps, as well as photos, exhibits, and other artifacts representing the area's mining, ranching, and pioneering heritage.

The Bottle Tree Ranch

24266 National Trails Hwy,
Oro Grande, CA 92368

The Bottle Tree Ranch, on historic Route 66 between Victorville and Barstow, is a fascinating exhibit of how owner and artist Elmer Long integrates antique bottles with sculpture and local artifacts such as Route 66 and Coca-Cola signs, elk horns, and miner's picks.

THE BEGINNING COLLECTOR

The first thing to understand about antique bottle collecting is that there aren't set rules. Your finances, spare time, storage space, and preferences will influence your approach. As a collector, you need to think about whether to specialize and focus on a specific type of bottle or group of bottles or become a maverick collector who acquires everything. The majority of bottle collectors that I have known, including me, took the maverick approach as new collectors. We grabbed everything in sight, ending up with bottles of every type, shape, and color.

Now after 30 years of collecting, I recommend that beginners only do a small amount of maverick collecting and focus on a specific group of bottles. Taking the general approach gave me a broader background of knowledge about bottles and glass, but specializing provides the following distinct advantages:

- More time for organization, study, and research
- The ability to become an authority in a particular area
- The opportunity to trade with other specialists who may have duplicate or unwanted bottles
- The ability to negotiate a better deal by spotting underpriced bottles

Specialized collectors will still be tempted

by bottles that don't quite fit into their collection, so they will cheat a little and give in to the maverick urge. This occasional cheating sometimes results in a smaller side collection, or turns the collector back to being a maverick. Remember, there are no set rules except to have fun.

Starting a Collection

What does it cost to start a collection and how do you know the value of a bottle? The beginner can do well with just a few pointers. Let's start with buying bottles, instead of digging for bottles. This is a quicker approach for the new bottle collector.

What Should I Pay?

Over the years, I've developed a quick method of buying bottles by grouping them into three categories:

Low End or Common Bottles

These bottles have noticeable wear and are never embossed. The labels are typically missing or not visible. In most cases, the labels are completely gone. The bottles are dirty and not easily cleaned. They have some scrapes but are free of chips. These bottles are usually clear.

Average Grade/Common Bottles

These bottles show some wear and labels may be visible but are usually faded. They are generally clear or aqua and free of scrapes or chips. Some of these bottles may have minimal embossing, but not likely.

High End and Unique Bottles

These bottles can be empty or partially or completely full, and have the original stoppers and labels or embossing. Bottles can be clear but are usually green, teal blue, yellow, or yellow green with no chips or scrapes and very little wear. If it has been stored in a box, the bottle is most likely in good or excellent condition. Also, the box must be in very good condition.

Price ranges will be discussed briefly since there is a "Determining Bottle Values" section. Usually, low-end bottles can be found for $1 to $5, average from $5 to $20, and high end from $20 to $100, although some high-end bottles sell for $1, 000 or more. Any bottles above $100 should be closely examined by an experienced and knowledgeable collector.

As a general rule, I try not to spend more than $2 per bottle for low-end bottles and $5 to $7 for average. It's easier to stick to this guideline when you've done your homework, but sometimes you just get lucky. As an example, during a number of bottle and antique shows, I have found sellers who had grab bags full of bottles for $2 a bag. I never pass up a bargain like this because of the lure of potential treasures. After one show, I discovered a total of nine bottles, some purple, all earlier than 1900 in great shape, with embossing, for a total cost of 22 cents per bottle. What could be better than that? Well, I found a Tonopah, Nevada, medicine valued at $100.

In the high-end category, deals are usually made after some good old horse trading and bartering. But, hey, that's part of the fun. Always let the seller know that you are a new collector with a limited budget. It really helps. Bottle sellers will almost always help new collectors get the best deal on a limited budget.

Is It Old or New?

Collectors should also know the difference between old and new bottles. Quite often, new collectors assume that any old bottle is an antique, and if a bottle isn't old it isn't collectible. With bottle collecting, that isn't necessarily the case. In the antique world, an antique is defined as an article more than 100 years old, but a number of bottles listed in this book that are less than 100 years old are just as valuable—and perhaps more so—than those that by definition are antiques.

The number and variety of old and antique bottles is greater than the new collectible items in today's market. On the other hand, the Jim Beams, Ezra Brooks, Avons, recent Coke bottles, figurals, and miniature soda and liquor bottles manufactured more recently are very desirable and collectible and are manufactured for that purpose. If you decide you want to collect new bottles, the best time to buy is when the first issue comes out on the market. When the first issues are gone, the collector market is the only available source, which limits availability and drives up prices considerably.

For all collectors, books, references guides, magazines, and other similar literature are readily available at libraries, in bookstores, and on the Internet.

Beware Reproductions and Repairs

I want to emphasize the importance of being aware of reproductions and repaired bottles. Always check bottles, jars, and pottery carefully to make sure that there have been no repairs or special treatments. It's best to hold the item up to the light or take it outside with the dealer to look for cracks, nicks, or dings. Also, look for scratches that may have occurred during cleaning. Also check the closures. Having the proper closure can make a big difference in the value of a bottle, so it's important to make sure the closure fits securely, and the metal lid is stamped with the correct patent dates or lettering. If you need help, ask an experienced collector, and if you have any doubt about a bottle's authenticity, request that the dealer provide a money-back guarantee.

Now, check out those antique and bottle shows, flea markets, swap meets, garage sales, and antique shops. Pick up those bottles, ask plenty of questions, and you will be surprised by how much you'll learn and how much fun you'll have.

BOTTLE BASICS

New bottle collectors need to learn certain facts such as age identification, grading, labeling, glass imperfections, and peculiarities.

Age

The common methods of determining age are mold seams, lips/tops, stoppers/closures, and color variations.

IDENTIFYING BOTTLE AGE BY MOLD SEAMS

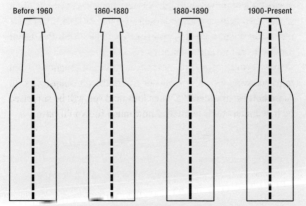

Before 1860: Seams extend to just over the shoulders.
1860-1880: Seams go most of the way up the neck of the bottle.
1880-1890: Seams continue through the top but not through or over the lip.
1900-present: Seams extend the full length of the bottle and over the lip.

Mold Seams

Prior to 1900, bottle manufacturing was done by either a blowpipe (free blown) to 1860 or with a mold to 1900. The mouth or lip was formed last and applied to the bottle after completion (applied lip). The applied lip can be identified by the mold seam that runs from the base up to the neck, and near the end of the lip. For machine-made bottles, the lip is formed first and the mold seam runs over the lip. The closer the seam extends to the top of the bottle, the more recent the bottle.

On bottles manufactured before 1860, the mold seams end low on the neck or at the shoulder. Between 1860 and 1880, the mold seam stops right below the mouth and makes it easy to detect where the lip was separately formed. Around 1880, the closed mold was utilized, in which the neck and lip were mechanically shaped, and the glass was severed from the blowpipe with the ridge being evened off by hand sanding or filing. This mold seam usually ends within one-quarter inch from the top of the bottle. After 1900, the seam extends clear to the top.

Lips and Tops

One of the best ways to identify bottles manufactured prior to 1840 is by the presence of a "sheared lip." This type of lip was formed by cutting or snipping the glass free of the blowpipe with a pair of shears that left the lip with a stovepipe look.

Above are just four examples of the myriad types of lips
and tops created on antique bottles.

Around 1840, bottle manufacturers began to apply a glass
ring around the sheared lip forming a "laid-on-ring" lip.
Between 1840 and 1880, numerous variations of lips or tops were
produced using a variety of tools.

After 1880, manufacturers started to pool their processing
information, resulting in more evenly finished and uniform tops.
As a general rule, the more uneven and crude the lip or top, the
older the bottle.

Glass stoppers 1850-1900.

Closures/Stoppers

The Romans used small stones rolled in tar as stoppers, and for many centuries there was little advancement. For most of the 15th and 16th centuries, the closure consisted of a sized cloth tied down with heavy thread or string. The stopper beneath the cover was made of wax or bombase (cotton wadding). Cotton wool was also dipped in wax and used as a stopper along with coverings of parchment, paper, or leather. Corks and glass stoppers were used in great numbers, with the cork sometimes being tied or wired down for effervescent liquids. When the "closed mold" came into existence, the shape of the lip was more accurately controlled, making it possible to invent capping devices.

On July 23, 1872, British inventor Hiram Codd invented a bottle made with a groove inside the neck and was granted Patent No. 129,652. A glass marble was inserted and then a ring of cork or rubber was fitted into the groove. When an effervescing liquid was used, the pressure of the gas forced the marble to the top of the neck, sealing the bottle. A second patent, Patent No. 138,230, issued April 29, 1873, contained an interior lug, ball holding element. Interestingly, many young boys broke these bottles to get the marble.

Hiram Codd interior ball stopper, Patent #129,652, July 23, 1872. Carbonation pushed the glass ball to the top of the neck, forming a tight seal.

Charles G. Hutchinson stopper, Patent #213,992, April 8, (year uncertain). A wire loop was pulled upward to seat a rubber gasket in the neck of the bottle. Carbonation helped keep it in place.

From 1879 to the early 1900s, the Hutchinson stopper was a common bottle closure after Patent No. 213,992 was issued on April 8, 1879. Hutchinson's concept used a heavy wire loop to control a rubber gasket that stayed inside the neck of the bottle. After filling the bottle, the gasket was pulled up against the shoulders and was kept in place by the carbonation. The Hutchinson stopper was easily adaptable to a number of other bottle types.

Until the invention of the crown cap in 1892, the lightning stopper was the best closure for beer bottles. The lightning stopper was a porcelain or rubber plug anchored to the outside of the bottle by a permanently attached wire. The wire formed a bar that controlled the opening and closing of the bottle.

The lightning stopper, designed to hold carbonated beverages, was eventually replaced by the crown cap.

William Painter crown cap, Patent #468,226, Feb. 2, 1892.

In 1892, William Painter patented the crown cap, which consisted of metal and a cork gasket crimped over the mouth of the bottle. This cap revolutionized the soft drink and beer bottling industry. By 1915, all major bottlers had switched to the crown-type cap. Finally, in 1902, threads were manufactured on the outside of the lip to enable a threaded cap to be screwed onto the mouth of the bottle. This wasn't a new idea. Early glass blowers produced bottles with inside and outside screw caps long before the bottle-making machines. Early methods of production were so complex, however, that screw-topped bottles produced before the 1800s were considered specialty bottles. They were expensive to replace and today are considered rare and quite collectible. The conventional screw-top bottle did not become common until after 1924, when the glass industry standardized the threads.

Dumfries Ale (English). The bottle's inside threads were sealed with a rubber stopper. This device was unpopular because the rubber interacted with the contents, distorting its color and taste.

In 1875, some glass manufacturers introduced an inside screw-neck whiskey bottle using a rubber stopper. This invention wasn't popular because the alcohol interacted with the rubber, which discolored the whiskey and made it bitter.

The following list is a portion of the brands of embossed whiskeys that featured the inside threaded neck and the approximate dates of manufacture:

WHISKEY COMPANY	DATE OF CIRCULATION
Adolph Harris	1907-1912
Chevalier Castle	1907-1910
Crown (squatty)	1905-1912
Crown (pint)	1896-1899
Donnelly Rye	1910-1917
Old Gilt Edge	1907-1912
Roth (aqua)	1903-1911
Roth (amber sq.)	1898-1909
Roth (amber fluted shoulder)	1903-1911
Roth (amber qt.)	1903-1911
Rusconi-Fisher	1902-1915
Taussig (clear)	1915-1918

Glass Color

Another effective method of determining age is the color of the glass. Producing colored and clear glass were major challenges for all glass manufacturers. Prior to 1840, intentionally colored or colorless glass was reserved for fancy figured flasks and vessels. Bottle color was essentially considered unimportant until 1880, when food preservation packers began to demand clear glass for food products. Because most glass produced prior to this time was green, glass manufacturers began using manganese to bleach out the green tinge created by the iron content. Only then did clear bottles become common.

Iron slag was used up to 1860 and produced a dark olive green or olive amber glass that has become known as black glass and was used for wine and beverage bottles that needed protection from light. Colors natural to bottle glass are brown, amber, olive green, and aqua.

Blue, green, and purple were produced by metallic oxides added to the glass batch. Cobalt was added for blue glass; sulfur for yellow and green; manganese and nickel for purple; nickel for brown; copper or gold for red; and tin or zinc for milk-colored glass (for apothecary vials, druggist bottles, and pocket bottles).

The Hocking Glass Company discovered a process for making a brilliant red glass described as copper-ruby. The color was achieved by adding copper oxide to a glass batch as it was cooling and then immediately reheating the batch before use. Since these bright colors were expensive to produce, they are very rare and sought after by most collectors. Many bottle collectors think purple is the most appealing color and therefore is prized above others. The iron contained in sand caused glass to take on color between green and blue. Glass manufacturers used manganese that counteracted the aqua to produce clear glass. But when exposed to ultraviolet light from the sun, the manganese in the glass oxidizes and turns the glass to purple. The longer the glass is exposed to the sunlight, the deeper the purple color. Glass with manganese content was most common in bottles produced between 1880 and 1914. Because Germany was the main producer of manganese, the supply ceased at the beginning of World War I. By 1916, the glass making industry began to use selenium as a neutralizing agent. Glass produced between 1914 and 1930 is most likely to change to an amber or straw color.

Imperfections

Imperfections and blemishes also provide clues to how old a bottle is and often add to the charm and value of an individual piece. Blemishes usually show up as bubbles or "seeds" in the glass. In the process of making glass, air bubbles form and rise to the surface where they pop. As the fining out (elimination process) became more advanced around 1920, these bubbles or seeds were eliminated.

Another peculiarity of the antique bottle is the uneven thickness of the glass. Often the base has a thick side that slopes to paper thinness on the opposite edge. This imperfection was eliminated with the introduction of the Owens bottle-making machine in 1903.

In addition, the various marks of stress and strain, sunken sides, twisted necks, and whittle marks (usually at the neck, where the wood mold made impressions in the glass) also give clues to indicate that a bottle was produced before 1900.

Labeling and Embossing

While embossing and labeling were a common practice in the rest of the world for a number of centuries, large American bottle manufacturers with good financial backing began embossing with custom molds around 1810. Smaller, less lucrative companies did not begin embossing until about 1850. The inscriptions included information about the contents, manufacturer, distributor, slogans, or other messages advertising the product.

Manufacturers produced raised lettering using a plate mold, sometimes called a slug plate, fitted inside the casting mold. This plate created a sunken area and has resulted in these bottles being of a special value to collectors. Irregularities such as a misspelled name add to the value of the bottle, as will any name embossed with hand etching or other method of crude grinding. These bottles are very old, collectible, and valuable.

Inscription and embossing customs came to an end with the introduction of paper labels and the production of machine-made bottles beginning in 1903. In 1933, with the repeal of prohibition, the distilling of whiskey and other spirits was resumed under new strict government regulations. One of the major regulations was that the following statement was required to be embossed on all bottles containing alcohol: "Federal Law Forbids Sale or Re-Use of this Bottle." This regulation was in effect until 1964 and is an excellent method of dating spirit bottles from 1933 to 1964.

DETERMINING BOTTLE VALUES

Collectors and dealers typically use rarity, age, condition, and color to determine bottle values. These factors are consistent with the criteria I have used over the years.

Supply and Demand

As with any product, when demand increases and supply decreases, prices increase.

Condition

Mint: An empty or full bottle (preferably full) with a label or embossing. The bottle must be clean and have good color, with no chips, scrapes, or wear. If the bottle comes in a box, the box must be in perfect condition too.

Extra Fine: An empty or full bottle with slight wear on the label or embossing. The bottle must be clean with clear color, and no chips or scrapes. There is usually no box, or the box is not in very good condition.

Very Good: The bottle shows some wear, and the label is usually missing or not very visible. Most likely there is no embossing and no box.

Good: The bottle shows additional wear and label is completely absent. The color is usually faded and the bottle is dirty and has some scrapes and minor chips. Most likely there is no box.

Fair or Average: The bottle shows considerable wear, the label is missing, and embossing is damaged.

Rarity

Unique: A bottle is considered to be unique if only one is known to exist. These bottles are the most valuable and expensive.

Extremely Rare: Only 5 to 10 known specimens.

Very Rare: Only 10 to 20 known specimens.

Rare: Only 20 to 40 known specimens.

Very Scarce: No more than 50 bottles in existence.

Scarce: No more that 100 bottles in existence.

Common: Common bottles, such as clear 1880 to 1900 medicine bottles, are abundant, easy to acquire, usually very inexpensive, and great bottles for the beginning collector.

Historic Appeal, Significance, and Geography

For example: territorial bottles (bottles made in regions that had not yet been admitted to the Union) vs. bottles made in states admitted to the Union.

Embossing, Labeling and Design

Bottles without embossing are common and have little dollar value to many collectors. Exceptions are bottles handblown before 1840, which usually don't have embossing.

Embossing describes the name of the contents, manufacturer, state, city, dates, trademarks, and other valuable information. Embossed images and trademarks can also increase the value of the bottle.

Labeling found intact with all the specific information about the bottle also increases the value of the bottle.

Age

While age can play an important role in the value of a bottle, there's not always a direct correlation. As stated in "The Beginning Collector" chapter, the history, rarity, and use of a bottle can be more important than age to a collector.

Color

Low Price: clear, aqua, amber

Average Price: milk glass, green, black, basic olive green

High Price: teal blue, cobalt blue, purple (amethyst), yellow, yellow green, puce

Unique Features

The following characteristics can also significantly affect value: pontil marks, whittle marks, glass imperfections (thickness and bubbles), slug plates, and crudely applied tops or lips.

Even with the above guidelines, it's important to consult more detailed references, especially concerning rare and valuable bottles. See the bibliography and the Web site listing at the back of this book. Remember, never miss a chance to ask other collectors and dealers for advice and assistance.

BOTTLE SOURCES

Collectible bottles can be found in a variety of places and sometimes where you would least expect them. Excluding digging, the following sources are good potential places for finding all types of bottles.

The Internet

In the 30 years that I've been collecting, I've never seen anything impact the hobby of bottle collecting as much as the Internet. Go to the Internet, type in the words "antique bottle collecting," and you'll be amazed at the amount of data instantly at your fingertips. Numerous Web sites throughout the United States, Canada, Europe, and Asia provide information about clubs, dealers, antique publications, and auction companies. These sites have opened up the entire world and are convenient and inexpensive resources for collectors and dealers.

Flea Markets, Swap Meets, Thrift Stores, Garage Sales & Salvage Stores

For the beginner collector, these sources will likely be the most fun (next to digging) and yield the most bottles at the best prices. As a rule, the majority of bottles found at these sources will fall into the common or common-but-above-average category.

Flea Markets, Swap Meets, and Thrift Stores: Target those areas where household goods are being sold. It's a good bet they will have at least some bottles.

Garage Sales: Focus on the older areas of town, since the items will often be older, more collectible, and more likely to fall into a rare or scarce category.

Salvage Stores or Salvage Yards: These are great places to search for bottles because these businesses buy from companies that salvage old houses, apartments, and businesses. A New York company discovered an untouched illegal prohibition-era distillery complete with bottles, unused labels, and equipment. What a find!

Local Bottle Clubs and Collectors

By joining a local bottle club or working with other collectors, you will find more ways to add your collection, gather information, and do more digging. Members usually have quantities of unwanted or duplicate bottles, which they will sell very reasonably, trade, or sometimes even give away, especially to an enthusiastic new collector.

Bottle Shows

Bottle shows not only expose new collectors to bottles of every type, but provide the opportunity to talk with experts in specialized fields. In addition, there are publications relating to all aspects of the hobby. There is always something new to learn and share and, of course, bottles to buy or trade. Look under the tables at these shows, since great bargains may be lurking where you least expect them.

Auctions

Auction houses are a great source of bottles and glassware. When evaluating auction houses, try to find one that specializes in antiques and estate buyouts. They usually publish catalogs with bottle descriptions, conditions, and photographs, which can also be used as a reference source. I recommend, however, that you first visit an auction to learn how the process works before you decide to participate. When buying, be sure of the color and condition of the bottle, and terms of the sale. These guidelines also apply to all Internet auctions. Use caution and follow these general rules:

Buying at Auctions

• Purchase the catalog and review all of the items in the auction. Before a live auction, a preview is usually held to inspect the items.
• After reviewing the catalog and making your choice, phone or mail your bid. A 10 percent to 20 percent buyer's premium is usually added to the sale price.
• Callbacks allow bidders to increase the previous high bid on certain items.
• The winning bidder receives an invoice in the mail. After payment clears, the item will be shipped.
• Most auction houses have a return policy, as well as a refund policy, for items that differ from the description in the catalog.

Selling at Auctions

- Evaluate the auction venue before consigning any merchandise. Make sure the auction venue is legitimate and has not had any problems with payments or quality of products.
- Package the item with plenty of bubble pack, insure it, and mail the package by certified mail, signed receipt requested.
- Allow 30 days to receive payment and be aware that most firms charge 15 percent commission fee on the sales price.

Estate Sales

An estate sale can be a great source for bottles if the home is in a very old neighborhood or section of the city that has historical significance. These sales are a lot of fun, especially when the people running the sale let you look over and handle the items to be able to make careful selections. Prices are usually good and are always negotiable.

Knife and Gun Shows

Bottles at knife and gun shows? Quite a few gun and knife enthusiasts are also great fans of the West and keep an eye open for related artifacts. Every knife and gun show I've attended has had at least 10 dealers with bottles on their tables (or under the tables) for sale. And the prices were about right, since they were more interested in selling their knives and guns than the bottles. Plus, these dealers will often provide information on where they made their finds, which you can put to good use later.

Retail Antique Dealers

This group includes dealers who sell bottles at or near full market prices. Buying from a dealer has advantages and disadvantages. Dealers usually have a large selection and will provide helpful information and details about the bottles, and it's a safe bet that the bottles for sale are authentic.

It can be very expensive to build a collection this way. However, these shops are a good place to browse and learn,

General Antique and Specialty Shops

The primary difference between general and retail antique shops is that general shops usually have lower prices and a more limited selection than retail shops. This is partly because merchants in general shops are not as well informed about bottles and may overlook critical characteristics. Knowledgeable collectors can find great opportunities to acquire quality underpriced bottles at a general shop.

BOTTLE HANDLING

While selling bottles and listening to buyers at various shows, I am inevitably asked questions about cleaning, handling, and storing bottles. Some collectors believe that cleaning a bottle diminishes its collectible value and desirability. Leaving a bottle in its natural state, as it was found, can be special. Others prefer to remove as much dirt and residue as possible. The choice rests with the owner. The following information will provide some help with how to clean, store, and take care of those special finds.

Bottle Cleaning

First, never attempt to clean your new find in the field. In the excitement of the moment, it's easy to break the bottle or otherwise damage the embossing. With the exception of soda and ale bottles, glass bottles manufactured before 1875 usually have very thin walls. Even bottles with thicker walls should be handled very carefully.

The first step is to remove as much loose dirt, sand, or other particles as possible with a small hand brush or a soft-bristled toothbrush followed by a quick warm water rinse. Then, using a warm water solution and bleach (stir the mixture first), soak the bottles for a number of days (depending upon the amount of caked-on dirt). This should remove most of the excess grime. Also, adding some vinegar to warm water will add an extra sparkle to the glass. Other experienced collectors use cleaning

Don't clean bottles in the field. Wait until you get home and can clean them carefully to avoid damaging them. Courtesy of Rick Wiener.

mixtures such as straight ammonia, kerosene, Lime-A-Way, Mr. Clean, and chlorine borax bleach. Do not use mixtures that are not recommended for cleaning glass, never mix cleaners, and do not clean with acids of any type. Mixing cleaners has been known to release toxic gasses and poisonous vapors and fumes.

After soaking, the bottles may be cleaned with a bottle brush, steel wool, an old toothbrush, any semi-stiff brush, Q-tips, or used dental picks. At this point, you may want to soak the bottles again in lukewarm water to remove any traces of cleaning materials. Either let the bottles air-dry or dry them with a soft towel. If the bottle has a paper label, the work will be more painstaking since soaking is not a cleaning option. I've used a Q-tip to clean and dry the residue around the paper label.

Never clean your bottles in a dishwasher. While the hot water and detergent may produce a very clean bottle, these older bottles were not designed to withstand the extreme heat of a dishwasher. As a result, the extreme heat, along with the shaking, could crack or even shatter the bottles. In addition, bottles with any type of painted label may also be subjected to severe damage.

A better option is to consult a specialist who will clean your rare bottles with special tumbling, or cleaning machines. These machines work on the same principle as a rock tumbler with two parallel bars running horizontally acting as a "cradle" for the cleaning canisters. The key to the machine cleaning process is the two types of oxides that are used: polishing and cutting. The polishing oxides include aluminum, cerium, and tin, which remove stains and give the glass a crystal clean and polished appearance. The polishing oxides do not harm the embossing. The cutting oxides such as silicon carbide remove the etching and scratching. There are many individuals who are in the business of cleaning bottles with these machines, or you can also purchase the machines for personal use.

Bottle Display

Now that you have clean, beautiful bottles, display them to their best advantage. My advice is to arrange your bottles in a cabinet rather than on wall shelving or randomly around the house. While the last two options are more decorative, the bottles are more susceptible to damage. When choosing a cabinet, try to find one with glass sides that will provide more light and better viewing. As an added touch, a light fixture sets off a collection beautifully. If you still desire a wall shelving arrangement, make sure the shelf is approximately twelve inches wide, with a front lip for added protection. This can be accomplished with round molding. After the bottle is placed in its spot, draw an outline around the base of the bottle and then drill four 1/4-inch holes for pegs just outside the outline. The pegs will provide stability for the bottle. If you have picked up any other goodies from your digging, like coins or gambling chips, scatter them around the bottles for a Western flavor.

Bottle Protection

Because of earthquakes, especially in northern and southern California, bottle collectors across the country have taken added steps to protect their valuable pieces.

Since most of us have our collections in some type of display cabinet, it's important to know how to best secure it. First, fasten the cabinet to the wall studs with brackets and bolts. If you are working with drywall and it's not possible to secure the cabinet to a stud, butterfly bolts will provide a tight hold. Always secure the cabinet at both the top and bottom for extra protection.

Next, lock or latch the cabinet doors. This will prevent the doors from flying open. If your cabinet has glass shelves, be sure to not overload them. In an earthquake, the glass shelving can break under the stress of excess weight.

Finally, it's important to secure the bottles to the shelves with materials such microcrystalline wax, beeswax, silicone adhesive, double-sided foam tape, adhesive-backed Velcro spots or strips. These materials are available at local home improvement centers and hardware stores. One of the newest and most commonly used adhesives is called Quake Hold. This substance, which is available in wax, putty, and gel, is similar to the wax product now used extensively by numerous museums to secure their artwork, sculptures, and various glass pieces. It is readily available to the general public at many home improvement stores and antique shops.

Bottle Storage

The best method for storing bottles you've chosen not to display is to place them in empty liquor boxes with cardboard dividers (which prevent bottles from knocking into each other). As added protection, wrap the individual bottles in paper prior to packing them in the boxes.

Recordkeeping

Last but not least, it's a good idea to keep records of your collection. Use index cards detailing where the bottle was found or purchased, including the dealer's name and price you paid. Assign a catalog number to each bottle, record it on the card, and then make an index. Many collectors keep records with the help of a photocopy machine. If the bottle has embossing or a label, put the bottle on the machine and make a copy of it. Another method is to make a pencil sketch by applying white paper to the bottle and rubbing over the embossing with a No. 2 pencil. Then, type all the pertinent information on the back of the image and put it in a binder. When it comes to trading and selling, excellent recordkeeping will prove to be invaluable.

OLD BOTTLES: PRE-1900

The bottles in this section have been categorized by physical type and/or by the original contents of the bottle. For most categories, the trade names can be found in alphabetical order if they exist. Note that in the case of certain early bottles, such as flasks, a trade name does not appear on the bottle. These bottles have been listed by subject according to the embossing, label, or other identification on the bottle.

Since it is impossible to list every bottle available, I've provided a representative selection of bottles in various price ranges and categories, rather than listing only the rarest or most collectible pieces.

The pricing shown reflects the value of the particular bottle listed. Similar bottles could have higher or lower values than the bottles specifically listed in this book, but the following listings provide collectors with an excellent starting point for determining a reasonable price range.

BARBER BOTTLES

Starting in the mid-1860s and continuing to 1920, barbers in America used colorful decorated bottles filled with various tonics and colognes. The end of these unique and colorful pieces came when the Pure Food and Drug Act of 1906 restricted the use of alcohol-based ingredients in unlabeled or refillable containers.

Very early examples have rough pontil scars and numerous types of ornamentation such as fancy pressed designs, paintings, and labels under glass. The bottles were usually fitted with a cork, metal, or porcelain-type closure. Since the value of barber bottles is very dependent upon the painted or enameled lettering or decoration, it is important to note that any type of wear such as faded decoration or color, faded lettering, or chipping will lower their value.

Ticoulet & Beshorman – Sac. Ca, medium amber, quart, smooth base, tooled top, American 1900-1910 . . . . **$30-40**

Advertising Barber Bottle – Uno Tonique For The Hair Refressing and Pleasing Made by Fred Dolle, Chicago ILL. Opalescent milk glass, light mint green background, 9-3/8", pontil-scarred base, rolled lip, extremely rare, American 1885-1925 . . . . **$400-500**

August Kern / Barber Supply / St. Louis – Bay Rum (floral decoration), Milk glass, 9-1/8", smooth base, tooled mouth, American 1885-1925 . . . . **$250-300**

Bay Water – Early Labeled Barber Bottle, Aqua, 9-5/8", open pontil, applied mouth, American 1840-1860 . . . . **$85-160**

Barber Bottle – Art Nouveau Style Cameo Decoration – Vegederma, Deep purple amethyst, white enamel, 8", pontil-scarred base, tooled mouth, American 1885-1925 . . . . **$375-450**

Barber Bottle – Buerger Bros. Supply Co. – Since 1885 Denver Colorado – Not For Sale, Used in Barber Show at Pueblo about 1885, Deep turquoise blue with cut glass fluted sides, neck ring and mouth, 10", polished pontil, applied mouth, American 1883-1885 . . . . **$200-300**

Barber bottle, opalescent milk glass with cherub decoration, 7-1/2", pontil-scarred base, sheared and tooled lip, American 1885-1925, **$200-250.**

Barber bottle, opalescent turquoise blue with white coral decoration, 7-1/8", polished pontil base, rolled lip, American 1885-1925, **$200-300.**

Barber Bottle – Cameo Mary Gregory, Clear glass with light amber flashing, 8-1/2", coinspot pattern, pinkish white enamel, smooth base, tooled lip, rare color and pattern, American 1885-1925 .... **$195-350**

Barber Bottle – (cherubs reading a song book decoration), Opaque milk glass, multicolored enamel decoration, 8-1/8", pontil-scarred base, sheared and tooled lip, American 1885-1925 .... **$175-200**

Barber Bottle – (cherub with dove and cage decoration), Milk glass, 7-3/4", ground pontil, rolled lip, American 1885-1925 .... **$175-200**

Barber Bottle – Crème De Rose Broyer Baume Italiene, France Italian Parfum C, Paris Messian (Label), Deep yellowish green, vertical rib-pattern with orange, white, and gold enamel floral decoration, 6-7/8", pontil-scarred base, tooled lip, American 1885-1925 .... **$175-200**

Barber Bottle – Hair Oil – E. Berninghaus Cincinnati O Trade Mark Climax, Opalescent milk glass, 8-3/4", pontil-scarred base, applied lip, American 1885-1925 .... **$250-300**

Barber Bottle – Herringbone Pattern – Corset Waist Form, Opalescent cranberry with white, 7-1/4", smooth base, tooled mouth, very rare, American 1885-1925 ..... $400-700

Barber bottle, opalescent cranberry red with coral decoration, 6-7/8", polished pontil base, tooled lip, American 1885-1925, **$200-300.**

Barber bottle, clear glass with coin-spot pattern milk-glass overlay, 7-1/8", polished pontil base, rolled lip, American 1885-1925, **$200-300.**

Barber Bottle – (Mary Gregory boy with butterfly net decoration), Medium yellowish green, 8", pontil-scarred base, rolled lip, scarce color, American 1885-1925 . . . . **$250-350**

Barber Bottle – (Mary Gregory girl playing tennis decoration), Cobalt blue with white, 8", pontil-scarred base, rolled lip, American 1885-1925 . . . . **$200-300**

Barber Bottle – Palm Tree, Frosted clear glass, green and while enamel decoration, 8", smooth base, tooled mouth, extremely rare (only two known examples), American 1885-1925 . . . . **$500-800**

Barber Bottle – Shampoo, Opalescent blue gray milk glass, multicolored enamel decoration of ski lodge, pontil-scarred base, rolled lip, American 1885-1925 . . . . **$250-350**

Barber Bottle – (floral decoration), Deep cobalt blue, 7-5/8", rib-pattern with white and gold enamel, pontil-scarred base, tooled mouth, American 1885-1925 . . . . **$80-100**

Barber Bottle – (foxhunt decoration), Milk glass with multicolored enamel, 7-1/2", pontil-scarred base, tooled mouth, American 1885-1925 . . . . **$140-180**

Barber Bottle – Bay Rum (Grist Mill decoration), Deep purple amethyst, 7-3/4", rib-pattern with white enamel, pontil-scarred base, rolled lip, American 1885-1925 . . . . **$300-450**

Barber bottle, light apple green with thumb-spot pattern, white yellow and orange enamel floral decoration, 8-1/8", polished pontil base, tooled lip, American 1885-1925, **$150-200.**

Barber bottle, medium cobalt blue, 8-1/4", white and orange floral and butterfly enamel decoration, polished-pontil base, tooled lip, American 1885-1925, **$250-350.**

Barber Bottle – Stag Decoration, Cobalt blue, 8", rib-pattern with multicolored enamel, pontil-scarred base, tooled lip, American 1885-1925 . . . . **$250-350**

Barber Bottle – Hair Tonic (windmill decoration), Deep purple amethyst, rib-pattern with white enamel, pontil-scarred base, rolled lip, American 1885-1925 . . . . **$300-400**

Barber Bottle – Hobnail Pattern, Yellow amber, 6-7/8", polished pontil, rolled lip, American 1885-1925 . . . . **$125-150**

Barber Bottle – Hobnail Pattern, Turquoise blue, 6-7/8", polished pontil, rolled lip, American 1885-1925 . . . . **$125-150**

Barber Bottle, Fiery opalescent cranberry red glass with pink overlay and coin spot pattern, melon rib sides, 8-1/2", smooth base, rolled lip, American 1885-1925 . . . . **$175-250**

Barber Bottle, Medium emerald green with white enamel decoration, 7-3/8", pontil-scarred base, tooled mouth, American 1885 1925 . . . . **$175-250**

Barber Bottle, Turquoise blue, rib-pattern with white and gold floral decoration, bulbous form, 8", pontil-scarred base, tooled mouth, American 1885-1925 . . . . **$170-200**

Barber Bottle, Clear glass with ruby red flashing, rib-pattern with yellow and silver floral decoration, 7-7/8", pontil-scarred base, rolled lip, American 1885-1925 . . . . **$250-300**

Barber bottle, medium pink amethyst, 6-7/8", rib pattern with yellow, white, and red floral decoration, open pontil, sheared and tooled lip, American 1885-1925, **$150-200.**

Barber bottle, opalescent robin egg blue, 8-5/8", white, green, and maroon floral enamel decoration around a house with trees, open pontil, rolled lip, American 1885-1925, **$250-350.**

Barber Bottle, Purple amethyst, 7-1/2", rib-pattern with yellow enamel fleur-de-lis decoration, pontil-scarred base, tooled mouth, rare and unusual decoration, American 1885-1925 . . . . **$350-450**

Barber Bottle, Deep purple amethyst, 7-1/8", vertical rib-pattern, white and gold fleur-de-lis and diamond enameled decoration, pontil-scarred base, tooled mouth, American 1885-1925 . . . . **$130-190**

Brillantine Barber Bottle, Cobalt blue rib pattern with orange, yellow, and white enamel decoration, 4-3/8", sheared and ground lip, original metal screw cap on metal dispenser, American 1885-1925 . . . . **$150-200**

Cremex / Shampooing / Vase / Registered Design, Cobalt blue, 7-3/4", smooth base, tooled lip, bent neck with finger grooves on back to prevent from slipping, American 1885-1925 . . . . **$180-250**

Personalized Barber Bottle – Adam S. Eberhard – Tonic (multicolored with rose decoration), Opaque milk glass, 9-1/2", smooth base (W.T. & CO.), ground lip, American 1885-1925 . . . . **$200-300**

Personalized Barber Bottle – H. Hildebrand – Bay Rum (multicolored floral decoration), Milk glass, 8-3/4", smooth base, tooled mouth, American 1885-1925. . . . . **$300-400**

Personalized Barber Bottle – J. Kaufmann – Tonic (two deer running across a field near the woods with mountains in the background), Milk glass, 10-1/4", smooth base, ground lip with original screw cap, American 1885-1925 . . . . **$600-800**

Personalized Barber Bottle – C.V. Wolf – (lighthouse and ship decoration), Milk glass, 9-5/8", smooth base (W.T. & CO), ground lip with original pewter screw cap, American 1885-1925 . . . . **$375-475**

Personalized Barber Bottle – Thos. L. Kirk (running horse decoration), Milk glass, 9-1/2", smooth base, ground lip, original pewter screw cap, American 1885-1925 . . . . **$400-600**

Personalized Barber Bottle – Wm. F. Stolte – Tonic (sailing boat surround by flowers), Opaque milk glass, 9-1/2", smooth base (W.T. & CO.), ground lip, American 1885-1925 . . . . **$450-550**

Personalized Barber Bottle – W.T. Hillborn – Bay Rum (dancer decoration), Milk glass, 9-5/8", smooth base (W.T. & CO), ground lip with original pewter screw cap, American 1885-1925 . . . . **$375-475**

T. Noonan & CO / Barbers / Supplies / Boston, Mass, Deep cobalt blue, 8", smooth base, tooled mouth, American 1885-1925 . . . . **$90-120**

BEER BOTTLES

Attempting to find an American beer bottle made before the mid-19th century is a difficult task. Until then, most bottles used for beer and spirits were imported. The majority of these imported bottles were black glass pontiled bottles made in three-piece molds and rarely embossed. There are four types of early beer bottles:

1. Porter (most common): 1820 to 1920
2. Ale: 1845 to 1850
3. Early lager (rare): 1847 to 1850
4. Late lager: 1850 to 1860

In spite of the large amount of beer consumed in America before 1860, beer bottles were very rare and all have pontiled bases. Most beer manufactured during this time was distributed and dispensed from wooden barrels, or kegs, and sold to local taverns and private bottlers. Collectors often ask why various breweries did not bottle the beer they manufactured. During the Civil War, the federal government placed a special tax on all brewed beverages that was levied by the barrel. This taxing system prevented the brewery from making the beer and bottling it in the same building. Selling the beer

to taverns and private bottlers was much simpler than erecting another building just for bottling. This entire process changed after 1890 when the federal government revised the law to allow breweries to bottle the beer straight from the beer lines.

Along with the brewing processes, the federal government also revised guidelines for bottle cleanliness. The chart below show the age and rarity of beer bottles.

YEAR	RARE	SCARCE	SEMI-COMMON	COMMON
1860-1870	X			
1870-1880		X		
1880-1890			X	
1890-1930				X

Embossed bottles marked "ale" or "porter" were manufactured between 1850 and 1860. In the late 1860s, the breweries began to emboss their bottles with names and promotional messages. This practice continued into the 20th century. It is interesting to note that Pennsylvania breweries made most of the beer bottles from the second half of the 19th century. By 1890, beer was readily available in bottles in most of the country.

The first bottles used for beer in the United States were made of pottery, not glass. Glass did not become widely used until after the Civil War (1865). A wholesaler for Adolphus Busch named C. Conrad sold the original Budweiser beer from 1877 to 1890. The Budweiser name was a trademark of C. Conrad, but in 1891, it was sold to the Anheuser-Busch Brewing Association.

Before the 1870s, beer bottles were sealed with cork stoppers. Late in the 19th century, the lightning stopper was invented. It proved a convenient way of sealing and resealing blob top bottles. In 1891 corks were replaced with the crown cork closure invented by William Painter. The closure made use of a thin slice of cork within a tight-fitting metal cap. Once these were removed, they couldn't be used again.

Until the 1930s, beer came in green glass bottles. After Prohibition, brown glass came into use, since it was thought to filter out the damaging rays of the sun and preserve freshness.

Albion – Burnell & Co. – S.F. – Brewery, Medium green, half-pint, smooth base, crown top, American 1920-1930 .... **$550-650**

A.G. Boehm / 78-82 Essex St. / Lawrence / Mass / Registered – This Bottle / Not To Be Sold, Orange amber, 9-3/8", smooth base, tooled blob mouth, American 1885-1900 ..... **$70-100**

A. G. Van Nostrano / Charlestown / Mass. / Bunker Hill Lager (inside banner) / Bunker Hill / Breweries / Established 1821 / Registered August Stoehr / Milwaukee / Lager / Manchester, N.H. – This Bottle / Not To / Be Sold, Medium amber, 9-5/8", smooth base, tooled mouth, original lightning-style closure, American 1885-1900............... **$90-110**

August Reinig / 2107 / Germantown / Ave / Philada. – This Bottle / Not To / Be Sold, Yellow with olive tone, 9-1/2", smooth base (1A), tooled blob mouth, American 1885-1900 .... **$70-100**

August Stoehr / Milwaukee / Lager / Manchester, N.H. – This Bottle / Not To / Be Sold, Medium yellow olive, 9", smooth base (No. 2), tooled mouth, original lightning closure, American 1885-1900 .... ,,,,,,,,,, **$90-130**

B & CO / (monogram inside diamond) A. Bierweiler & CO / Boston / Mass. / Registered, Medium golden yellow amber, mug-base, 9-1/4", smooth base, tooled mouth, American 1885-1900 .... **$90-140**

Ogdens porter, blue aqua, 7", American 1840-1860, **$150-200.**

J.B. Edwards - Columbia Pa, brown stout, emerald green, 6-1/4", American 1840-1860, **$375-475.**

O.G.M. Gaines - Columbia Pa - brown stout, blue green, 6-3/8", **$350-450.**

Dr. Cronk's / Compound / Sarsaparilla Beer, blue aqua, 8-5/8", American 1840-1860, **$400-600.**

Bay View – Brewing Co – Seattle Wash., Medium green, 9", quart, smooth base, tooled top, American 1890-1905 ....**$175-225**

Beer Steam Bottling Co. – (monogram WG & Son in diamond) – Wm Goeppert & Son – San Francisco, Medium amber, quart, smooth base, applied top, rare, American 1882-1884 .... **$700-800**

Buffalo Brewing Co. – (monogram BBC) – S.F. Agency, Medium green, pint, 7-1/2", smooth base, applied top, American 1885-1900 .... **$250-300**

Buffalo BR'G CO. – Sacramento – This Bottle Not To Be Sold, Medium amber, quart, smooth base, applied top, American 1885-1900 .... **$95-110**

C. Conrad & Cos. – Original Budweiser U.S. – Patent No. 6376, Aqua, 9", quart, smooth base, applied top, American 1890-1905 .... **$100-150**

C.D. Postel – (monogram wheat stalks T.M.) – S. F. Cal., Deep amber, quart, smooth base, applied top, American 1884................................... **$500-600**

C.D. Postel – (monogram wheat stalks T.M.) – S. F. Cal., Medium amber, quart, smooth base, applied top, American 1884................................... **$2,500-3,000**

C.D. Postel – (monogram wheat stalks T.M.) – S. F. Cal., Dark amber, quart, smooth base, applied top, American 1884................................... **$1,300-1,500**

Chas D. Kaier / KDK (monogram) Mahanoy City / PA – This Bottle / Not To / Be Sold, Medium green, 9-3/8", smooth base (Putnam 26), applied blob type mouth, American 1880-1890 . . . . **$250-350**

Chas Joly / No. 9 / So Seventh St / Philadelphia – This Bottle / Not To / Be Sold, Medium olive green, 9-1/2", smooth base, tooled mouth, American 1885-1900 . . . . **$70-100**

Chicago Lager Beer – Chicago Brewing – S.F., Medium amber, quart, smooth base, applied top, American 1887-1990 . . . . **$45-55**

Colombia Weiss Beer Brewery – St. Louis Mo. – This Bottle Is Never Sold, Medium amber, 8-7/8", smooth base, tooled top, American 1885-1900 . . . . **$65-90**

Coors, Light amethyst, pint, smooth base, tooled top, American 1910-1920. . . . . **$75-110**

Consumers – (monogram CBCo.) Bottle Co., Deep amber, half-pint, smooth base, tooled top, American 1885-1900 . . . . **$85-95**

Consumer's – (monogram CBCo,) Bottling Co. – S.F. CAL., Medium amber, quart, smooth base, tooled top, American 1885-1900 . . . . **$300-400**

E. Wagner / Trade W (inside cross) Mark / Manchester / N.H. – The Property / Of / E. Wagner / Not Sold, Light to medium yellow with olive tone, 9-1/8", smooth base, tooled mouth, original lightning style closure, American 1885-1900 . . . . **$90-140**

E.A. Olendorf / Sarsaparilla Lager (in slug plate) / This Bottle / Is Never Sold, medium orange amber, 9-1/4", American 1885-1895, **$250-300.**

E.N. Lewis / Sarsaparilla / Beer, deep blue aqua, 6-3/4", American 1865-1880, **$200-300.**

E. Wagner / Trade W (inside cross) Mark / Manchester / N.H. – The Property / Of / E. Wagner / Not Sold, Light to medium yellow with olive tone, 9-3/8", smooth base, tooled mouth, original lightning style closure, American 1885-1900 .... **$90-140**

F.J. Kastner / FJK (diamond monogram inside) Newark N.J. – This Bottle / Not To / Be Sold, Medium golden yellow with amber tone, 9-3/8", applied mouth, American 1885-1900 .... **$90-140**

F. Jacob Jockers / 803-805 / Dickinson St / Phila, PA. / Registered – Contents 12-1/2 Oz, Light to medium cobalt blue, 9", smooth base, tooled mouth, few tall blob beers were made in cobalt blue, American 1885-1900 .... **$150-250**

F.O. Brandt – Healdsburg CAL., Medium amber, quart, smooth base, tooled top, scarce, American 1885-1900 ..... **$100-125**

Geo. Braun Bottler – (monogram GB) – 2210 Pine St. S.F., Dark amber, half-pint, smooth base, tooled top, American 1885-1900 .... **$75-85**

Golden Gate Bottling Works – Chas. Roschmann – San Francisco (reverse side – Trade – photo of bear – Mark), Medium amber, half-pint, smooth base, tooled top, American 1885-1900 .... **$150-200**

H. Clausen & Son / Brewing Co / 888-890 – 2nd Ave / New York / Phoenix Bottling – This Bottle / Not To / Be Sold, Medium olive green, 9-1/8", smooth base, tooled mouth, American 1885-1900 .... **$125-200**

H. Koehler & Co / Fidelio / Beer / New York, Deep amber, 8-5/8", smooth base, tooled mouth, American 1885-1900 . . . . **$70-100**

Hoosac Bottling Works / JLG (monogram) Hoosick Falls. N.Y. – This Bottle / Not To / Be Sold, Medium amber, 9-1/8", smooth base, tooled mouth, American 1885-1900 . . . . **$80-120**

Honolulu Brewing Co. – Honolulu – H.T., Light green, quart, smooth base, tooled top, American 1890-1905 . . . . . **$85-100**

J.B. Cueno – San Francisco, Medium amber, pint, smooth base, tooled top, American 1885-1900 . . . . **$150-200**

J. Gahn / Trade (motif of mug) Mark / Boston / Mass – Milwaukee / Lager Beer, Medium yellow amber, 9-3/8", smooth base, tooled mouth, American 1885-1900 . . . . **$60-80**

J. Proll Bottling Works – Bottling – U.S. Lager – S.F. CAL, Medium amber, pint, smooth base, tooled mouth, rare, American 1885-1905 . . . . **$375-425**

John Wieland's – Export Beer – SF, Medium amber, 5-3/4" (sample size), smooth base, tooled top, American 1895-1905 . . . . **$250-325**

John Wieland's – Export Beer – S.F., Deep amber, pint, smooth base, tooled top, American 1895-1905 . . . . **$100-125**

Lynch Bros / Plymouth, PA – This Bottle / Not To / Be Sold, Medium citron green, 9-1/4", smooth base, tooled mouth, original lightning-style closure, rare colored blob top beer, American 1885-1900 . . . .**$125-175**

Mirasoul – Bros – S.F., Medium amber, pint, smooth base, tooled top, American 1885-1905 . . . .**$45-55**

National Bottling Works (Trade Mark – eagle) San Francisco, CA – Not To Be Sold, Amber, 9", smooth base, tooled mouth, American 1895-1901 . . . . **$175-200**

National Brewing Co. – San Francisco, Medium amber, quart, smooth base, tooled top, American 1885-1900 . . . . . . **$55-65**

Pacific Bottling Co. (monogram J) – S.F., Light amber, quart, smooth base, tooled top, American 1885-1900 rare **$135-145**

Philadelphia Bottling Co. – (monogram eagle In nest) – Lager Beer – Lang Bros' Props' – 1318 S. F. Scott St., Medium amber, quart, smooth base, applied top, American 1886-1889 . . . .**$1,000-1,200**

Phillips Bros. / Champion / Bottling Works / Trade (motif of two boxers) Mark / Registered / Baltimore MD. U.S.A. / This Bottle Is Registered / Not To / Be Sold, Amber, 9-1/8", smooth base, tooled mouth, American 1885-1900 . . . . **$70-100**

Registered / The W.H. Cawley Co. / Somerville / Dover / Flemington / NJ / This Bottle / Not To Be Sold, Light green, 9", smooth base (C), tooled mouth, lightning-style closure, American 1885-1800 . . . . **$70-100**

Registered / Wagner and Matthes / Lawrence, Mass. / Registered, Deep amber, 9-1/4", smooth base, tooled mouth, American 1885-1900 . . . . **$70-100**

Richmond – Bottling Works, Light amber, half-pint, smooth base, tooled top, American 1885-1900 . . . . **$75-85**

Richmond – Bottling Works, Clear, half-pint, smooth base, tooled top, American 1885-1905 . . . . **$90-100**

Robert Portner / Brewing Co / Trade / Tivoli / Mark / Alexandria, VA – This Bottle / Not To / Be Sold, Deep olive green, 9-3/8", smooth base, applied blob mouth, American 1885-1900 . . . . **$100-150**

Santa Clara – County – Bottling Co. – San Jose, Dark amber, quart, smooth base, tooled top, American 1885-1900 . . . . **$50-60**

Santa Fe Bottling Co. – C.V. & CO. – S.F., Medium amber, pint, smooth base, tooled top, American 1885-1900 rare **$50-60**

Schlitz Milwaukee Lager Howe & Streeter – Manchester, N.H., Brilliant yellow, 9", smooth base, tooled top, American 1885-1900 . . . . **$150-200**

Schroeder's / B.W.B. Co / St. Louis, MO., Yellow green, 9-1/8", smooth base, tooled mouth, original porcelain stopper and wire lightning-style closure, American 1885-1900 .... **$60-90**

Schroeder's / B.W.B. Co / St. Louis, MO., Yellow green, 10", smooth base, tooled mouth, original porcelain stopper and wire lightning-style closure, American 1885-1900 .... **$60-90**

S.F. Stock Brewing – S.F.S.B. – San Francisco, CAL., Medium amber, pint, smooth base, tooled top, American 1885-1900 .... **$400-500**

Sunset Bottling – (monogram SBCo.) – San Francisco, CAL., Amber, pint, smooth base, tooled top, American 1880-1900 .... **$75-85**

Tacoma Bottling Co. – S.F. CAL., Dark amber, half-pint, smooth base, tooled top, American 1885-1905 .... **$45-55**

Tettner & Thoma Weiss Beer – Brewery – St. Louis, Medium amber, pint, smooth base, tooled top, American 1885-1890 .... **$60-85**

Union Brewing and Malting Co. – S.F. CAL., Medium amber, pint, smooth base, applied top, American 1885-1900 .... **$45-55**

BITTERS

Bitters have long been a favorite of bottle collectors. Because of their uniqueness, they were saved in great numbers, giving the collector of today great opportunities to build a special and varied collection.

Bitters, which originated in England, were originally a type of medicine made from bitter tasting roots or herbs, giving the concoction its name. During the 18th century, bitters were added to water, ale, or spirits with the intent to cure all types of ailments. Because of the pretense that those mixtures had some medicinal value, bitters became popular in America since Colonists could import them from England without paying the liquor tax. While most bitters had low alcohol content, some brands were as much as 120 proof, higher than

most hard liquor available at the time. As physicians became convinced that bitters did have some healing value, the drink became socially acceptable, promoting use among people who normally weren't liquor drinkers.

The best known among the physicians who made their own bitters for patients was Dr. Jacob Hostetter. After his retirement in 1853, he gave permission to his son David to manufacture it commercially. Hostetter Bitters was known for its colorful, dramatic, and extreme advertising. While Hostetter said it wouldn't cure everything, the list of ailments it claimed to alleviate with regular use covered almost everything: indigestion, diarrhea, dysentery, chills and fever, liver ailments, and pains and weakness that came with old age (at that time, a euphemism for impotence). Despite these claims, in 1888 David Hostetter died from kidney failure that should have been cured by his own bitters formula.

One of the most sought after bitters is the Drakes Plantation Bitters that first appeared in 1860 and received a patent in 1862. The Drakes Bitters is shaped like a log cabin and can be found in a four-log and a six-log variant with colors in various shades of amber, yellow, citron, puce, green, and black. Another interesting characteristic of the Drake bitters is the miscellaneous dots and marks, including the "X" on the base of the bottles, that are thought to be identification marks of the various glass houses that manufactured the bottles.

Most of the bitters bottles—over 1,000 types—were manufactured between 1860 and 1905. The more unique shapes called "figurals" were in the likeness of cannons, drums, pigs, fish, and ears of corn. Others were round, square, rectangular, barrel-shaped, gin-bottle shaped, twelve-sided, and flask-shaped. The embossed varieties are also the oldest and most valuable.

The most common color was amber (pale golden yellow to dark amber brown), then aqua (light blue), followed by green or clear glass. The rarest and most collectible colors are dark blue, amethyst, milk glass, and puce (a purplish brown).

Baker's / Orange Grove – Bitters, Medium to deep strawberry puce, 9-5/8", roped corners, smooth base, applied tapered collar mouth, American 1865-1875. . . . .**$1,000-1,500**

Bell's / Cocktail / Bitters / Jas. M. Bell & Co / New York, Medium copper puce, 10-1/2", lady's leg form, smooth base, applied mouth, American 1865-1880. . . . . **$400-500**

Bissell's / Tonic Bitters / Patented. Jany, 21. 1868 – O.P. Bissel / Peoria Ill, Bright yellow amber, 9", smooth base (L & W), applied sloping mouth collar, American 1868-1875. **$275-375**

Bourbon Whiskey / Bitters, Medium copper puce, 9-1/4", barrel form, smooth base, applied mouth, American 1865-1875 . . . .**$375-475**

Brophy's Bitters (in a crescent moon and star) Trade Mark / Nokomis / Illinois, Aqua, 7-3/8", smooth base, tooled lip, American 1880-1890 . . . . **$100-150**

Burdock / Blood Bitters – Foster Milburn & Co – Buffalo, N.Y., Aqua, 4-1/8", smooth base, tooled lip, rare sample, American 1890-1900 bitters $90-140, C. Gautiers / Native / Wine Bitters, Yellow olive green, 9-7/8", flowerpot-form bottle, smooth base (Washington, D.C. Patented 1867) applied mouth, rare, American 1867-1875 . . . . **$400-600**

C. Sandhegers / Famous / Stomach Bitters / Cincinnati / Ohio (inside an etched wine glass) Trade Mark, Clear, 10-1/8", smooth base, tooled lip, American 1890-1900 . . . . **$200-300**

The Fish Bitters - W.H. Ware - Patented 1866, greenish yellow, 11-1/2", smooth base, applied top, American 1866-1875, **$9,000-11,000.**

The Fish Bitters - W.H. Ware - Patented 1866, amber, 11-1/2", smooth base, applied top, American 1866-1875, **$350-450.**

C.C. Seely's / Strengthening / Stomach Bitters / Pittsburgh, PA, Medium amber, 9-3/8", rectangular form with indented chamfered corner panels on three sides, red iron pontil, applied mouth, extremely rare, American 1845-1860 . . . . **$10,000-15,000**

Colton's Stomach Bitter – Back Bar Bottle, Black olive amber, 11-3/4", smooth base, applied ring mouth, American 1870-1880 . . . . **$450-550**

Cooley's / Anti- / Dispeptic / Or / Jaundice / Bitters, Blue aqua, 6-1/4", oval form with chamfered corner indented front panel and 8-paneled roof, open pontil, applied tapered collar mouth, American 1840-1860 . . . . **$1,000-1,500**

Curtis & Perkins / Wild Cherry / Bitters, Aqua, 6-3/4", open pontil, applied mouth, American 1840-1860 . . . . **$75-120**

XXX / Dandelion / Bitters, Clear, 6-7/8", smooth base, tooled lip, American 1890-1900 . . . . **$85-110**

Dr. A.W. Coleman's – Anti Dyspeptic / And / Tonic Bitters, Deep olive green, 9-1/2", smooth base, applied sloping collar mouth, American 1855-1865 . . . . **$1,500-1,700**

Dr. Blake's – Aromatic / Bitters – New York, Aqua, 7", open pontil, applied mouth, American 1840-1860 . . . . . . **$150-200**

Dr. Corbett's – Renovating – Shaker Bitters, Aqua, 9-1/2", open pontil, applied double collar mouth, American 1840-1860 . . . . **$1,400-1,800**

Dr. De Andries – Sarsaparilla / Bitters – E.M. Rusha / New Orleans, Yellow amber, 9-3/4", smooth base, applied sloping collar mouth, American 1855-1865 .... **$1,800-2,000**

Dr. Flint's – Quaker Bitters – Providence, R.I. – Paper Label reads: Dr. H. S. Flint & Co. – Celebrated – Quaker – Root and Herb – Choice – Bitters – "Try This and Thou Shalt Be Benefitted", Aqua, 9-1/2", smooth base, applied mouth, American 1872-1880 .... **$1,400-1,600**

Dr. Geo. Pierce's – Indian / Restorative / Bitters – Lowell, Mass, Blue aqua, 7-5/8", open pontil, applied mouth, American 1840-1860 .... **$250-350**

Dr. J. Boveedods – Imperial // Wine Bitters – New York, Aqua, 10-1/8", smooth base, applied double collar mouth, American 1855-1865 .... **$400-500**

Dr. J. Henry Salisbury / Hinsdale, N.Y. / 1869 – Mountain Herb and / Root Bitters / I.S.P. – I.N., Deep amber, 9-3/4", smooth base, applied mouth, rare, American 1869-1875 ... **$600-800**

Dr. Jacob's Bitters – S.A. Spencer – New Haven, CT, Bluish aqua, 10", open pontil, applied mouth, American 1840-1860 .... **$275-325**

Dr. Loew's Celebrated / Stomach Bitters & / Nerve Tonic – The / Loew & Sons Co / Cleveland, O, Medium yellow lime green, 9-1/2", fluted neck and shoulder, smooth base, tooled lip, American 1890-1900 .... **$300-400**

Atwood's Jaundice Bitters - Moses Atwood - Georgetown Mass, yellow amber, 6-1/8", 12-sided, smooth base, applied top, American 1875-1885, **$1,400-1,600.**

Greeley's Bourbon Whiskey Bitters (label with full-color scene of a beautiful girl in a grassy field) medium topaz, 9-1/4", smooth base, applied top, American 1865-1875, **$4,000-5,000.**

Dr. Loew's Celebrated / Stomach Bitters & / Nerve Tonic – The / Loew & Sons Co / Cleveland, O, Medium yellow lime green, 3-7/8", fluted neck and shoulder, smooth base, tooled lip, sample size, American 1890-1900 . . . . **$375-475**

Dr. XX / Lovegood's – Family – Bitters, Deep amber, 9-3/8", cabin form, smooth base, applied tapered collar mouth, American 1865-1875 . . . . **$1,000-1,500**

Dr. M. Pearl & Co – Peruvian Bark / Bitters – New Orleans, LA, Medium apple green, 10-1/8", smooth base, applied mouth, extremely rare, American 1870-1880 . . . . **$850-950**

Dr. Mampe's / Oshkosh, Wis, Aqua, 7-1/4", smooth base, tooled lip, American 1890-1900 . . . . **$75-100**

Dr. Marcus – Universal / Bitters – Philada, Bluish aqua, 8-1/8", open pontil, applied mouth, extremely rare, American 1840-1860 . . . . **$550-750**

Dr. Renz's / Herb Bitters, Deep yellow amber, 10", smooth base, applied mouth, American 1855-1870 . . . . **$600-800**

Dr. Rcnz's / Herb Bitters, Medium to deep amber, 10-1/8", smooth base, applied mouth, American 1855-1870 . . . . **$650-750**

Dr. S.B. Hartman & Co. – Mishler's Herb Bitters – Table Spoon Graduation, Medium yellow copper topaz, 9", smooth base (Stoeckels Grad Pat. Feb. 11, 66) applied collar mouth, American 1865-1875 . . . . **$350-450**

Dr. Shepards / Compound / Wahoo Bitters / Grand Rapids, Mich, Ice blue, 7-1/2", smooth base, applied mouth, American 1865-1875 . . . . **$200-275**

Dr. Skinner's / Celebrated / 25 Cent Bitters / So Reading, Mass, Aqua, 8-1/2", rectangular with wide beveled corner panels, pontil-scarred base, applied double collar mouth, American 1840-1860 .... **$175-375**

Dr. Skinner's / Celebrated / 25 Cent Bitters / So Reading, Mass – Label reads: Dr. W.M. Skinner's Celebrated Bitters, For Sale at the Doctor's Laboratory, South Reading, Mass, Aqua, 8-3/4", rectangular with wide beveled corner panels, pontil-scarred base, applied double collar mouth, American 1840-1860 .... **$250-350**

Dr. Walkinshaw's – Curative Bitters – Batavia, N.Y., Amber, 10", smooth base, applied mouth, American 1865-1875 .... **$1,400-1,600**

Dr. Washington's / American / Life Bitters, Medium amber, 9-1/4", smooth base, tooled lip, extremely rare, American 1880-1890 .... **$200-300**

Dr. Wheeler's / Tonic / Sherry Wine Bitters – Established / 1849 (inside a shield) – Boston, Bluish aqua, 9-1/2", roped corners, smooth base, applied mouth, American 1865-1875 .... **$6,000-7,500**

Dr. Whitney's / Bitters – Olean, N.Y. / U.S.A., Amber, 7-1/4", semi-oval form, smooth base, tooled lip, extremely rare form, American 1885-1895 .... **$300-400**

Dr. Wise's / Olive Bitters / Cincinnati / O, Clear, 9-3/4", smooth base, tooled lip, American 1890-1910 rare **$300-400**

Dr. Zabriskie's – Bitters – Jersey City / N.J., Clear moonstone glass, 6", pontil-scarred base, tool flared-out lip, extremely rare, American 1845-1860 . . . . **$700-1,000**

Drs. Lowerre & Lyon's / Restorative Bitters, Bluish aqua, 8-3/4", open pontil, applied mouth extremely rare, American 1840-1860 . . . . **$800-1,100**

Doctor / Fischs Bitters – W. H. Ware / Patented 1866, Yellow amber, 11-5/8", fish form, smooth base, applied mouth, American 1866-1875 . . . . **$300-400**

E. Dexter Loveridge / Wahoo Bitters / (bird with arrow) E. Dexter Loveridge / Wahoo Bitters – DWD – 1863 – XXX – PATD, Medium amber, 10-1/8", smooth base, applied ring lip, American 1860-1870 . . . . **$700-800**

EDW. Brehr – Thuringer – Aromatic / Stomach / Bitters, Deep yellow olive green, 8-3/4", open pontil, applied mouth, American 1845-1860 . . . . **$1,500-2,000**

Established / 1845 / Schroeder's / Bitters / Louisville / And Cincinnati – Embossed on Metal Neck: Schroeder's Cocktail Bitters Co, Amber, 5-1/4", lady's leg, smooth base, tooled lip rare sample size, American 1890-1900 . . . . **$1,500-1,900**

Established / 1845 / Schroeder's / Bitters / Louisville / Henry H. Shufeldt & Co / Peoria, Ill / Sole Owners, Amber, 11-5/8", lady's leg, smooth base, tooled lip rare, American 1890-1900 . . . . **$800-1,200**

Fritz Reuter Bitters (reverse of bottle same), Milk glass, 9-7/8", tapered gin form, smooth base, applied mouth, American 1880-1895 . . . . **$350-450**

Geo. Benz / & / Sons / Appetine / Bitters / St. Paul, Minn, Deep amber, 8-1/8", smooth base (Pat. / Nov 23 / 1897), tooled lip, American 1897-1900 . . . . **$150-200**

Germania (motif of a seated lady) Bitters – label reads: Germania Brand Magen Stomach Bitters, Luhenthal Bros. & Co., Cleveland, Ohio, Milk glass, 9-5/8", tapered gin form, smooth base, applied mouth, rarest of tapered milk glass bitters bottles, only three or four known examples, American 1880-1895 . . . . **$450-450**

Hart's / Star Bitters / (Letters O-B-L-P-C and the date "1868" inside a star) Philadelphia / PA, Clear glass, 9-1/8", fish form, smooth base, tooled lip, American 1880-1890 . . . . . **$400-600**

Hartwig Kantorowicz / Posen / Ham / Burg / Ger / Many, Milk glass, 3-7/8", case gin form, smooth base, applied mouth, rare sample bitters, American 1890-1900 . . . . **$150-200**

Hartwig Kantorowicz / Posen / Ham / Burg / Ger / Many, Milk glass, 5-3/8", case gin form, smooth base, applied mouth, American 1890-1900 . . . . **$200-250**

Hartwig Kantorowicz / Posen / Ham / Burg / Ger / Many, Milk glass, 9-1/8", case gin form, smooth base, applied mouth, American 1890-1900 . . . . **$200-250**

Gilbert's Sasparilla Bitters, N.A. Gilbert & Co., Enosburgh Falls VT., light amber, 9-1/8", smooth base, applied top, American 1875-1885, **$900-1,100.**

Romaine's Crimean Bitters - Patented 1863, medium tobacco amber, 10", smooth base, applied top, American 1863-1875, **$900-1,200.**

Harvey's – Prairie – Bitters – Patented, Medium amber to yellow amber, 9-3/4", smooth base, applied sloping collar mouth, whiskey barrel corners and a corncob domed top, one of the top five or six most desirable bitters bottles, American 1860-1870 . . . . **$15,000-20,000**

Herb's / Pure / Wild (Tree) Cherry / Bark / Bitters / Wertz & Field / Reading, Pa (Label under glass), Amber, 8", smooth base (H.M. Co.), tooled lip, American 1885-1900 . . . . **$3,000-3,500**

Herkules Bitter (GA monogram) 4 FL. OZ, Bright medium green, 4-1/8", smooth base, tooled liprare sample bitters bottle, three or four known examples, American 1885-1900 . . . . **$1,400-1,600**

Hertrich's Gesundheits Bitter / Hans / Hertrich / Hof / Erfinder U. Allien / Destillateur – Gesetzlich Geschutzt, Olive green, 12", smooth base, applied double collar mouth, German 1880-1890 . . . . **$375-475**

Honi Soit Qui Mal Y Pense (in banner) Royal Pepsin / Stomach Bitters / L & A Scharff / Sole Agents / St. Louis, U.S. & Canada, Amber, 7-1/2", smooth base, tooled mouth, American 1890-1900 . . . . **$150-250**

Hops / & / Malt / Bitters (on all four roof and shoulder panels) Hops & Malt / Trade (sheaf of grain) Mark / Bitters, Medium amber, 9-1/2", semi-cabin form, smooth base, applied sloping color mouth, American 1875-1885 . . . . **$400-600**

E. Dexter Loveridge Wahoo Bitters, Patd 1863 XXXDWD (with embossed bird), 11", smooth base, applied top, American 1863-1875, **$2,000-2,500.**

Ohas. Nichols J. & Co. Props, Dr. Chandler's Jamaica Ginger Root Bitters, medium yellow green, 11", smooth base, applied top, American 1860-1880, **$8,000-9,000.**

Isaac D. Lutz / Reading, PA – Label under glass reads: Lutz's / German / Stomach / Bitters / Reading, Pa. / Registered, Amber, 7-3/4", smooth base, tooled lip, American 1885-1900 . . . .**$3,000-4,000**

Keystone Bitters, Orange amber, 9-3/4", barrel form, smooth base, applied tapered collar mouth, American 1865-1875 . . . . **$700-900**

Khoosh – Bitters, Yellow olive, 8-1/4", smooth base, applied double collar mouth, English 1880-1900 . . . . **$120-140**

King Solomon's Bitters – Seattle Wash – Label reads: King Solomon Stomach Bitters, Amber, 8-3/8", smooth base, tooled mouth, American 1890-1900 . . . . **$350-450**

Koehler & Hinrichs / Red Star / Stomach Bitters / St. Paul, Minn., Yellow amber, 11-1/2", fluted panels around shoulder and about base, smooth base, tooled lip, American 1900-1905 . . . . **$500-600**

Laughlin / Smith & Co. – Old Home / Bitters – Wheeling, W. VA, Deep yellow amber, 10", semi-cabin form, smooth base, applied mouth, American 1865-1875. . . . .**$1,700-1,900**

Lediard's – Celebrated – Stomach Bitters, Teal blue, 10-1/8", smooth base, applied sloping double collar mouth, American 1860-1875 . . . .**$1,800-2,000**

Litthauer Stomach Bitters / Invented 1864 By / Josef Loewenthal, Berlin, Milk glass, 9-1/2", case gin form, smooth base, applied mouth, American 1875-1890. . . . . **$200-275**

Lohengrin / Bitters / Adolf Marcus / Von Buton / Germany, Front Label reads: Lohengrin, Celebrated Stomach Bitters, Smaller Label Under Embossing Reads: Adolf Marcut, Tucker Hardy Co., Sole Distributors, Chicago, Milk glass, 9-3/8", tapered gin form, 9-3/8", smooth base, applied mouth, rare, American 1880-1895 . . . . **$800-1,200**

Malabac Bitters – M. Cziner Chemist, Yellow amber, 11-3/4", lady's leg, smooth base (This Bottle Not To Be Sold), applied double collar mouth, blown in three-piece mold, rare, American 1870-1880 . . . . **$500-700**

Mills Bitters / A.M. Gilman / Sole Proprietor, Medium yellow amber, 11-1/4", lady's leg, smooth base, applied ring lip, American 1870-1890 . . . .**$2,000-2,5000**

Morning (Star) Bitters / Inceptum 5869 – Patented / 5869, Medium amber, 7-3/8", oval form, smooth base, tooled mouth, American 1865-1875 . . . . **$200-300**

Moulton's Olorosa Bitters / Trade (motif of pineapple) Mark, Blue aqua, 11-1/4", fluted neck, shoulder and side at base panels, smooth base, applied mouth, American 1865-1880 . . . . **$300-400**

National / Bitters, Medium amber, 12-1/4", ear-of-corn form, smooth base, applied mouth, American 1865-1875 . . **$400-500**

N.W. Med. Co. / Bitters, Medium amber, 7-3/8", oval form, smooth base, tooled mouth, extremely rare, American 1880-1895 . . . . **$200-300**

Old Dr. Solomon's – Great Indian Bitters, label reads: Old Doctor Jas. M. Solomon's Great Indian Wine Bitters, Aqua, 8-3/4", smooth base, applied mouth, American 1870-1880 . . . . **$400-600**

Old Dominion, Vegetable Bitter (Capitol Building) E.W. Mills, Fredericksburg, Va (label only), Clear glass, 6", flask, smooth base, tooled lip, American 1890-1910 . . . . **$250-300**

Parhan's – German Bitters / For The Cure Of / Dyspepsia – Liver Complaint – Prepared By / Dr. C. Parham / Philada, Aqua, 6-3/8", open pontil, applied ring mouth, extremely rare bitters/cure combination, American 1840 -1860 . . . . **$2,500-3,000**

Pat'd 1884 / Dr. Petzold's / Genuine / German / Bitters / Incpt 1862, Amber, 10-1/4", semi-cabin form, smooth base, tooled mouth, American 1885-1895 . . . . **$200-275**

Pat'd 1884 / Dr. Petzold's / Genuine / German / Bitters / Incpt 1862, Yellow amber, 8", semi-cabin form, smooth base, tooled mouth, American 1885-1895 . . . . **$400-500**

Pepsin / Calisaya Bitters – Dr. Russel Med. Co., Deep green, 4-5/8", smooth base, tooled lip, American 1895-1905 . . . . . . **$150-200**

Pepsin / Calisaya Bitters – Dr. Russel Med. Co., Light green, 8-1/8", smooth base, tooled lip, American 1895-1905 . . . . . . **$150-200**

Peruvian / Bitters – W & K, Yellow amber, 9-1/4", smooth base, applied mouth, American 1875-1885 . . . . **$100-130**

Botanic (motif of sphinx) Bitters
– Herzberg & Bros – New York, yellow
amber, 9-7/8" American 1870-1880,
$400-600.

Baker's Orange Grove Bitters,
emerald green, 9-5/8" smooth base,
applied top, American 1860-1880,
$13,000-16,000 (rare in this color).

Philadelphia / Hop / Bitters (African man holding a bottle), Deep blue aqua, 9-3/8", semi-cabin form, smooth base, applied mouth, Australian 1880-1890 . . . . **$275-375**

R.B. Samuels – Century Stomach Bitters – Back Bar Bottle, Dark olive green, 12-1/4", inscribed pewter label in a fancy recessed panel, smooth base, applied ring mouth, American 1870-1880 . . . . **$400-500**

Royal Pepsin / Stomach Bitters / L & A Scharff / Sole Agents / St. Louis, U.S. & Canada (rampart lion and unicorn on either side of shield), Reddish amber, 9", smooth base, tooled double collar mouth, American 1885-1900 . . . . **$100-150**

Russ / Stomach / Bitters / New York, Medium yellow amber, 10-1/8", lady's leg, iron pontil, applied ring mouth, American 1860-1865 . . . . **$5,000-6,000**

Sanborn's / Kidney / and / Liver / Vegetable / Laxative / Bitters, Amber, 10", smooth base, tooled lip, American 1890-1900 . . . . **$80-120**

Sazerac Aromatic Bitters (monogram PHD & CO), Milk glass, lady's leg, 11-3/4", smooth base, applied mouth, American 1865-1875 . . . . $275 375

Schroeder's / Bitters / Louisville, KY, Medium amber, 9", lady's leg, smooth base (S.B. & G. CO), tooled lip, blown in four-piece mold, American 1885-1895 . . . . **$400-600**

Sharp's – Mountain Herb – Bitters, Medium amber, 9-3/4" smooth base, applied sloping collar mouth, scarce bitter, American 1870-1880 . . . . **$250-350**

Simon's Centennial Bitters – Trade Mark, Blue aqua, 10-1/8", bust of George Washington, smooth base, applied double collar mouth, American 1876, manufactured to capitalize on the 1876 Centennial **$700-900**

St / Drake's / 1860 / Plantation / X / Bitters – Patented / 1862, Medium olive yellow, 9-7/8", 6-log cabin, smooth base, applied tapered mouth, American 1862-1870 .... **$1,000-1,500**

Smyrna / Stomach / Bitters – Prolongs Life / Dayton, Ohio, Medium amber, 9", smooth base, tooled lip, rare, American 1880-1895 .... **$400-700**

The Great Tonic / Caldwells / Herb Bitters, Yellow amber, 12-1/4", triangular form, iron pontil, applied mouth, American 1865-1875 .... **$300-400**

The Great Tonic / Caldwells / Herb Bitters, Yellow amber, 12-1/2", triangular form, smooth base, applied mouth, American 1865-1875 .... **$275-375**

The Royal – Bitters – Geo. A. Clement / Niagara, Ont, Deep blue aqua, 8-3/8", oval with strap sides form, smooth base, applied double collar mouth, very rare, Canadian 1875-1885 .... **$800-900**

Thos A. Hurleys – Stomach / Bitters – Louisville, KY, Yellow amber, 10-1/2", smooth base, applied mouth, extremely rare, American 1865-1875 .... **$900-1,300**

Travelers – Walking Man With Cane – Bitters – 1834 / 1870, Yellow amber, 10-1/2", smooth base, applied tapered collar mouth, American 1865-1875. .... **$3,500-5,000**

Yerba Buena – Bitters, S.F. Cal. label reads: Dr. Warren's Yerba Buena Bitters, The Greatest Medical Discovery of the Age, H. Williams & Co. Proprietors, San Francisco, Ca, Yellow amber, 8-1/4", strap sided, smooth base, applied mouth, American 1880-1890 . . . . **$650-850**

W.C. Bitters / Brobst & Rentschler / Reading, PA., Yellow amber, 10-3/4", barrel form, smooth base, tooled lip, American 1885-1895 . . . . **$500-700**

W.L. / Richardson's – Bitters – South / Reading – Mass, Blue aqua, 7", open pontil, applied mouth, American 1840-1860 . . . . **$275-375**

Weis / Bros. / Knickerbocker / Stomach / Bitters (all on applied shoulder seal), Orange amber, 12-1/8", lady's leg, smooth base, tooled mouth, American 1885-1895 . . . . **$2,000-3,000**

Zingari / Bitters – F. Rahter, Medium amber, 12-1/4", lady's leg, smooth base, applied ring mouth, American 1865-1875 . . . . **$275-375**

CROCKS AND STONEWARE

Although crocks are made of pottery rather than glass, many bottle collectors also have crock collections, since they have been found wherever bottles are buried. Crock containers were manufactured in America as early as 1641, and were used extensively in the sale of retail products during the 19th and early 20th centuries. Miniature stoneware jugs were often used for advertising, as were some stoneware canning jars. Storeowners favored crocks since they kept beverages cooler and extended the shelf life of certain products. Crocks appeal to collectors because of their interesting shapes, painted and stenciled decorations, lustrous finishes, and folk art value. In addition, molded stoneware shouldn't be considered mass produced, since a great deal of detailed design and handwork had to be done on each crock.

In the late 1800s, the discovery of disease-causing bacteria prompted many medicine makers to seize a profitable if not unethical opportunity. An undocumented number of fraudulent cures were peddled to gullible and unsuspecting customers. The most infamous of these so-called cures were produced and sold in pottery containers by William Radam. He was given a patent for his "Microbe Killer" in 1886 and stayed in business until 1907, when the Pure Food and Drug Act ended his scheme. His "cure" was nothing more than watered down wine (wine comprised only 1 percent of the total contents.)

With the invention of the automatic bottle machine in 1903, glass bottles became cheaper to make and hence more common. This contributed to the steady decline of production and use of pottery crocks and containers.

Advertising Stoneware Jug – Firm of Matthews M'F'Rs of Carbonated Beverage, Sirups & C 333 East 26th Street N.Y., Gray pottery with cobalt slip over lettering, 9", handled, smooth base, American 1880-1900 . . . . **$175-250**

One Quart Ovoid Cream Pot, Medium gray, 6-1/2", brushed flower design, smooth base American 1870, Shenfelder Factory **$700-1,000**

One-Half Gallon Advertising Jug – Storrs & Curtis / Syracuse / N.Y., Dark brown, 7", smooth base, American 1880 . . . . **$200-400**

One-Half Gallon Canning Jar, Dark gray, 8", accent stripes at base and rim, 4-teardrop brushed blue design in the center, smooth base, American 1860 . . . . **$100-175**

E. Swasey & Co., Portland, Me, three 1 gallon brown & white bristol glazed advertising jugs, 5-1/2" to 8-1/2", American 1900, **$80-90 for all.**

Relief panel of man smoking a pipe, Amsterdam, tan, 7", American 1900 / unsigned & undecorated ovoid jug, "P. Mas" in script ink on bottom, tan, 6-1/2", American 1840, **$20-30 for both.**

One-Half Gallon Canning Jar, Dark gray, 8-1/2", brushed blue accents stripes at top and bottom, accented with 10 graduated teardrops in middle, smooth base, American 1860 .... **$150-220**

One Gallon Advertising Stoneware Jug – Quintard & Thompson / Ship Chandlers & Grocers / No. 28 South St. N. York, Dark brown, 9" beehive-shape form, smooth base, American 1870 .... **$100-140**

One Gallon Cake Crock – Moore, Nichols & Co. – Williamsport, Gray, 5-1/2", dotted flower decoration, blue accents at handles, smooth base, American 1878 .... **$200-400**

One Gallon Ovoid Jug – P. Pugler & Co. – Buffalo, NY, Light cream, 11", brushed flower and stem decoration, smooth base, American 1850. .... **$1,500-1,700**

One Gallon Preserve Jar with Stoneware Lid – Cowden & Wilcox, Gray, 9-1/2", man in the mood design in blue, American 1870 .... **$6,000-8,000**

One Gallon Preserve Jar – Hamilton & Jones – Greensboro PA, Dark gray, 9-1/2", name in blue stencil on front, smooth base, American 1870. .... **$75-100**

One Gallon Saltglaze Stoneware Jug, Brownish, 10-1/2", bullet-head form, handled, stamped "J.B. Caire & Co./Pokeepsie, N.Y." on shoulder above a cobalt skip flower and number 1, smooth base, American 1865-1880 .... **$200-300**

One Gallon Stoneware Jug – J. & E. Norton Bennington, VT, Cream, 10-1/2", one-of-a-kind decoration of a large plump strawberry, smooth base very rare, possibly a special order, American 1855. . . . . **$500-1,000**

One Gallon Stoneware Pitcher, Gray, 10-1/2", thick blue vine and flower design at the midsection and neck, smooth base, American 1850. . . . .**$1,200-1,400**

One and One-Half Gallon Ovoid Crock – Liberty Forev Warne & Letts – 1807 S. Amboy – N. Jersey, Cream, 10", blue filled scallop design above the name, blue accents under the ears, accented with impressed dental molding around the rim, smooth base, American 1807 . . . . **$20,000-24,000**

One and One-Half Gallon Jar – F.B. Norton Sons – Worcester Mass, Cream, 10-1/2", dove design, smooth base, American 1886. . . . . **$700-1,000**

One and One-Half Gallon Preserve Jar, Medium brown, 12", cylinder shape, four flower drapes around the shoulder, smooth base, American 1850 . . . . **$60-120**

Two Gallon Cake Crock, Gray, 6", blue drape design repeated in the front and back, blue accents at the applied ears, smooth base, American 1850 . . . . **$150-250**

Two Gallon Cream Pot – G. Haidle & Co. – Union Pottery – Flemington, N.J., Cream, 9-1/2", swan on a lake with "Old Scotch" in blue, American 1870 . . . . **$800-1,000**

J. Norton & Co, Bennington Vt., tan with dotted floral spray, 2 gallon preserve jar, 12'', American 1861, **$250-325.**

Two Gallon Ovoid Crock, Cream, 13", blue accented lollipop flower outline at shoulder, smooth base, American 1830 .... **$150-175**

Two Gallon Ovoid Jug – Paul Cushman, Dark cream, 14", maker's mark in large letters impressed at shoulder, smooth base, American 1807 .... **$1,000-1,400**

Two Gallon Saltglaze Stoneware Crock – F.H. Cowden Harrisburg 2, Gray pottery with cobalt spitting flower decoration, 11-1/4", close handles, smooth base, American 1881-1888 .... **$200-300**

Two Gallon Saltglaze Stoneware Crock – F.H. Cowden Harrisburg 2, Gray pottery with cobalt stenciled decoration, 11-3/4", close handles, smooth base, American 1881-1888 .... **$150-200**

Two Gallon Stoneware Jug – C. Crolius Manufacturer – Wells, New York, Cream, 13", brushed blue accents at the handle, smooth base, American 1830 .... **$1,300-1,500**

Two Gallon Stoneware Jug – Brewer & Halm Havana, Cream, 13-1/2", dotted tulip and leaf decoration, back is splattered with cobalt blue, smooth base, American 1852 ..... **$350-450**

Two Gallon Stoneware Jug – Somerset Pottery Works, Cream, 14-1/2", blue double flower and vase decoration, smooth base, American 1870. .... **$200-250**

Three Gallon Saltglaze Stoneware Crock – E. L. Farrar / Iperville, Q, Cobalt blue slip flower on front, 10-1/4", smooth base, Canadian 1860-1880 .... **$100-150**

E.A. Gowen & Son, Oysters & Clams, Locust Street Market, Dover, N.H., tan and brown glaze, 1/2 gallon, 8-1/2", American 1900 / G.M. Long & Co, Wholesale & Retail Dealers in Sea Food, Foot of State Street, New London, Conn, 1 quart, tan, 6", American 1900, **$150-200 for both.**

Three Gallon Blue and White Stoneware Cooler – The Robinson Clay Products Co., Akron, Ohio, Raised decoration of a man pondering at a well with a cabin, tree trunk, as, and tree in background, on the other side a cornucopia of flowers, 12-1/4", smooth base, American 1890-1910 . . . . **$200-250**

Three Gallon Blue and White Stoneware "Ice Water" Cooler, Raised decoration of flower and leafs with flowers on the back side, 16", original metal faucet, American 1890-1910 . . . . . . **$300-400**

Three Gallon Stoneware Crock, Dark gray pottery with cobalt flower decoration on both sides, 12-7/8", close handles, smooth base, American 1825-1845 .... **$200-275**

Four Gallon Advertising Crock – Philbrick & Spaulding / 23 Washington St / Haverhill, Cream, 11-1/2", impressed name is framed with a double feather design, smooth base, American 1870 .... **$100-150**

Four Gallon Crock – Tyler & Co – Troy NY, Cream, 11-1/2", design of a shore bird with snowflakes, smooth base, American 1860. .... **$3,000-4,000**

Four Gallon Ovoid Crock – Thomas D. Chollar – Cortland, Gray pottery, 13-1/2", brushed cobalt blue flower design, smooth base, American 1845 .... **$200-300**

Four Gallon Water Cooler – Cortland, Cream, 17-1/2", double handled, four bud potted flower fills the front, blue accents at the handle and drain hole, smooth base, American 1870 .... **$1,500-3,000**

Five Gallon Advertising Jug – 1/2 Gallon / M. Farrell & Co. / 95 Haverhill St., Cream, 9-1/2", patriotic hand incised eagle design with a banner (1872) in its mouth, smooth base, rare, American 1872. .... **$1,700-1,900**

Five Gallon Ovoid Crock, Cream, 16", design of cobalt blue birds in a flower tree on front and Germanic-style tulips on back, double handled, smooth base, American 1840 .... **$40,000-43,000**

T.F. Reppert, Greensboro PA, 1 gallon canning jar, gray, 9-1/2",
American 1880, **$175-200.**

Gay's Distilled Water, Insures Health, Fort Myers, Florida, Bristol glaze cooler with chrome spout, 3 Gallon, 11-1/2" American 1900, **$40-50.**

Quinn's / Quality / Quantity / Rye Whiskey / Kansas City, Mo, Largest Mail Order Grocer & Liquor Merchant in the West, canteen shape, 1-1/2 Gallon, 13", dark brown glaze, American 1900, **$40-50.**

Five Gallon Handled Advertising Jug – E. A. Buck & Co / Blackstone St / Boston, Mass, Cream, 17-1/2", fancy chicken in light blue pecking at corn, smooth base, American 1880. . . . . **$700-1,000**

Five Gallon Saltglaze Stoneware Jug – 5 Poland Mineral Spring Water, Hiram Ricker & Sons, Proprietors, South Poland, ME, None Genuine Unless Sealed with the Trademark, Dark gray pottery with cobalt glaze over wording, 18-1/4", handled with a hand-tooled internal pour spout, smooth base, very rare American 1880-1895 . . . . **$400-700**

Six Gallon Crock – Adam Caire – Pokeepsie, N.Y., Gray, 13-1/2", bird on a dotted stump design, large crow's foot and glazed spider in front the of left ear, smooth base, American 1880 . . **$300-400**

Unsigned spittoon with a brushed plume design, Albany glaze, 7", American 1870 (attributed to F. B. Norton), **$175-225.**

Sixteen Gallon Crock – Thompson Williams Co., Morgantown, W. VA, Gray pottery with cobalt stencil and decoration, 24", closed ear handles, smooth base, very rare, American 1880-1895 . . . .**$2,500-3,000**

Saltglaze Advertising Crock – H. J. Heinz Co., Cream, 5-1/2", impressed and blue accented logo on front, tooled blue accent bands on top and bottom, smooth base, American 1880-1890 . . . . **$350-450**

Saltglaze Stoneware Crock – Thomas D. Chollar, Cortland, Gray pottery with cobalt fern decoration, 9", closed handles, smooth base, American 1832-1842 . . . . **$90-120**

Wm. White & Son, Wholesale, Straight Whiskey House, 18-22 Armory St., Manchester, N.H, tan, 9" / Whiskey In This Jug Was Distilled 1869, Maryland, tan, 8" / Barnabas Clarke, Wines & Liquors, 148-153 Kneeland 8th, Boston, American 1869-1900, **$75-90 for all.**

Saltglaze Stoneware Crock – Goodwin & Webster, Cream pottery, 12-5/8", sailing ship on front, close handles, smooth base, American 1820-1840 .... **$6,000-8,000**

Saltglaze Stoneware Jug, Cobalt blue wash with impressed swan, 11", smooth base, American 1880-1890 .... **$200-300**

Saltglaze Stoneware Handled Jug – Goodale / Stedman / Hartford, Gray pottery, 14", incised leaf and upper body of a bald naked man, light cobalt blue across name, ringed neck, American 1822-1825 .... **$1,500-2,000**

Stoneware Crock – G.A.R. Buckingham Post No 12, Nov 21, 1883, Medium brown glaze, 2-3/4", lid, smooth base, American 1863-1870 .... **$275-375**

Stoneware "Bullet Head" Jug, Dark brown with incised swirled lines decoration around shoulder, 18-5/8", smooth base, handled, American 1820-1840 .... **$200-300**

Stoneware Fruit Jar – Los Angeles (motif of olive on branch) Olive Growers Ass'n – Los Angeles, CAL, Two-tone with medium brown on top, cream on bottom half, quart size, wire bail, top reads "THE WEIR PAT MAR. 1, 1892," smooth base, American 1892............................. **$300-400**

Stoneware Poison Jug – "It Kills Bed Bugs / Roaches / National Mining & Milling Co., Baltimore, Md", Cream with blue lettering, 6-3/4", cylindrical handled jug, smooth base rare, American 1880-1890 .... **$1,000-2,000**

FIRE GRENADES

The fire grenades is a highly prized item among bottle collectors and represents one of the first modern improvements in firefighting. A fire grenade is a water-filled bottle about the size of a baseball. Its use was simple. It was designed to be thrown into a fire, where it would break and—hopefully—extinguish the flames. The fire grenades worked best when the fire was spotted immediately.

The first American patent on a fire grenade was issued in 1863 to Alanson Crane of Fortress Monroe, Virginia. The best known manufacturer of these specialized bottles, the Halden Fire Extinguisher Co., Chicago, Illinois, was awarded a patent in August 1871.

The grenades were manufactured in large numbers by companies with names as unique as the bottles themselves: Dash-Out, Diamond, Harkness Fire Destroyer, Hazelton's High Pressure Chemical Firekeg, Magic Fire, and Y-Burn. The fire grenade became obsolete with the invention of the fire extinguisher in 1905. Many of these grenades can still be found with the original closures, contents, and labels.

Acme – Fire / Ext'r – Pat'd / June 29th / 1869, Yellow amber, 6", smooth base, sheared and ground lip, very rare, American 1880-1895 ....**$2,500-3,000**

American / Fire / Extinguisher / Co. / Hand Grenade, Clear glass, 6-1/8", smooth base, tooled lip, original light blue contents, rare, American 1870-1895.....................**$600-900**

Babcock / Hand Grenade / Non-Freezing / Manufactured By American LA France Fire Engine Co. / Elmira N.Y., Light aqua, 7-1/2", smooth base, sheared and tooled lip, extremely rare, American 1880-1895 ....**$3,500-3,800**

Barnum's / Hand Fire / Ext. – Diamond – Pat'd / June 26th / 1869 – Diamond, Blue aqua, 6", smooth base (diamond), tooled lip, original contents, American 1885-1900.........**$3,000-3,300**

Barnum's / Hand Fire / Ext. – Diamond – Pat'd / June 26th / 1869 – Diamond, Yellow amber, 6-1/8", smooth base (diamond), tooled lip, original contents, rare, American 1870-1895 ....**$2,000-2,500**

C. & NW. RY (Chicago & Northwest Railroad), Clear glass, 17-3/4", tube-style grenade, smooth rounded base, rough and sheared ground lip, American 1885-1900.........**$250-500**

California Fire Extinguisher (walking bear in panel), Medium amber, 6-5/8", horizontal rib pattern with label panel on reverse, smooth base, applied mouth, American 1885-1900, only fire grenade made in California **$5,500-6,500**

Diamond – Fire / Ext'r – PAT'D / June 29th / 1869 – Diamond, Yellow amber, 6", smooth base, tooled lip, American 1870-1895 . . . .**$1,500-2,500**

Du Progres – Grenades – Extinctives – Grenades, Medium yellow amber, 5-1/8", pontil-scarred base (TC 2367), tooled lip, rare, German 1880-1900 . . . .**$175-200**

Fire Grenade – Label only reads: Patented Aug. 8th 1871 / Liquid / Patented Sept. 19th 1876 / and / February 5th 1878 / Improved 1881, Deep cobalt blue, 6-1/8", smooth base, sheared and ground lip, American 1870-1895 . . . .**$500-600**

Fire Grenade – PAT NOV / 28, 1884, Yellow amber, 6-1/4", smooth base, sheared and ground lip, original neck seal and contents, Canadian 1884-1895 . . . .**$250-300**

Fire Grenade – PSN (monogram), Amber, 7", smooth base, rough sheared lip, American 1870-1895 . . . .**$400-500**

Flagg's / Fire / Extinguisher – Pat'd Aug. 4th 1868, Yellow amber, 5-7/8", smooth base, rough sheared lip, American 1870-1895 . . . .**$1,000-1,300**

Flagg's / Fire / Extinguisher – Pat'd Aug. 4th 1868, Yellow amber, 6-1/2", smooth base, sheared and ground lip, rare specimen of the two Flagg variants with the horizontal Pat'd Aug 4th 1868 embossing, American 1870-1895 . . . .**$1,500-2,000**

Francaise / Grenade, Bright lime green, 6-5/8", rib pattern and below center band, smooth base (GF/14) sheared and ground lip, original contents, extremely rare, French 1889-1900 . . . . **$800-1,200**

Grenade / L.B., Medium turquoise blue, 5-1/8", vertical rib pattern, smooth base, sheared and ground lip, original contents, French 1880-1900 . . . . **$700-800**

Grenade / Unic / Extingtrice (embossed on four indented circular panels), Orange amber, 5-1/2", vertical rib pattern, smooth base, sheared and ground lip, French 1880-1900 . . . . **$350-450**

Hand / (letter "H" inside a shield) Grenade, Deep cobalt blue, 6-1/4", raised hobnails around entire grenade, smooth base (RD No 421256) sheared and ground lip, extremely rare due to hobnails, English 1880-1900 . . . . **$2,500-3,000**

Harden's Improved – Grenade Fire – Extinguisher PAT – Oct 7th 1884, Cobalt blue, 2-1/2", smooth base (2) rough sheared and ground lip, American 1885-1900 . . . . **$120-160**

Harden's Hand / Extinguisher / Grenada / Patented, Medium cobalt blue, 4-7/8", footed smooth base, rough sheared and ground lip, original contents, scarce in this color and size, American 1885-1900 . . . . **$140-180**

Harden's Hand / Fire / Extinguisher / Grenada – Patented, Turquoise blue, 5-1/8", footed smooth base, rough sheared and ground lip, original contents, American 1885-1900 . . . . **$150-200**

Harden's Improved / Hand Grenade / PAT'D OCT / NO. 1 / 1884 / Fire Extinguisher (on two of three sections), Three-section grenade: two sections are clear glass, the third section is amber, 3-7/8", smooth bases, referred to as a cluster grenade and is considered the most rare of all fire grenades, American 1885-1900 . . . . **$700-900**

Hardens Hand / Fire / Extinguisher / Grenade – Aug. 8. 71 / Patd Aug 14. 83 – star (inside star), turquoise blue, 6-5/8", smooth base, rough-sheared mouth, American 1871-1895, **$150-250.**

Hayward's / Hand / Fire / Grenade - Patented / Aug / 8 /1871 – S F Hayward / 407 / Broadway / N.Y., clear glass, 6-1/4", "4" on smooth base, tooled mouth, American 1871-1885, **$250-350.**

Harden's Improved – Grenade Fire-Extinguisher PAT OCT 7th 1884 (embossed on both sections) Label reads: Throw This Genade so as to Break it / and Deliver its Contents into the Fire / Harden's / Nest / Grenade / Fire / Extinguisher / Manufactured / At / 247 / So. Canal St. / Chicago, Ill, Two clear glass sections held together by copper wire, 4-7/8", "No. 3" on one base and 97% orange and black label on other, both sections have rough and sheared lips, grenade is rarely seen with original wire and label, American 1885-1900 . . . . **$1,500-1,700**

Harden's Hand / Fire / Extinguisher / Grenada – Patented / No 1 / Aug 8, 1871 / Aug 14, 1883, Turquoise blue, 6-1/4", footed base (2), rough sheared and ground lip, American 1885-1900 . . . . **$80-150**

Harden's Hand / Fire / Extinguisher / Grenada – Patented / No 1 / Aug 8, 1871 / Aug 14, 1883, Turquoise blue, 6-1/4", footed base, rough sheared and ground lip, original contents, 97% – Label reads: "How To Use," American 1885-1900 . . . . **$250-350**

Harden's Hand / Fire / Extinguisher – Patented (original contents and top of mouth label reads: Semper Paratos (grenade) Trade Mark, Turquoise blue, 6-1/4", footed base, rough sheared and ground lip, American 1885-1900 . . . . **$80-120**

Hayward's / Hand / Fire / Grenade – Patented / Aug / 8 / 1871 – S.F. Hayward / 407 / Broadway / N.Y. (in diamond panel) – Original red lettering on black background label reads: In case of fire throw or break the grenade so that the contents will be scattered over the flames, Yellow amber, 6", smooth base (3), tooled lip, original contents, American 1877-1895 . . . . **$400-500**

Hazelton's / High Pressure / Chemical / Fire Keg, Yellow amber, keg form, 11", smooth base, tooled lip, original contents, metal neck band and handle, American 1885-1900 . . . . . . **$400-500**

Hazelton's / High Pressure / Chemical / Fire Keg – Label on base reads: In Case of Fire Break Keg Upon the Flames, Frank R. Hazelton, Concord, N.H. Patent Applied For, Orange amber, 11-1/8", barrel form, smooth base, tooled mouth, American 1885-1900 . . . . **$350-450**

Healy's Hand Fire – Extinguisher, Olive yellow, 10-3/4", smooth base, tooled lip, American 1880-1895 . . . . **$800-1,000**

Imperial / Hand D.R.P. Granate (inside a belt) / Fire / Feverloscher, Medium yellow green, 6-1/2", smooth base, sheared and ground lip, European 1885-1900 . . . . . **$180-220**

Little Giant / Fire Extinguisher – Label reads: The Automatic Fire Extinguisher, Buffalo, N.Y. Directions – Place this extinguisher where fire is most likely to occur. The fuse will ignite and break it., Aqua pint, 6-1/2", smooth base, tooled mouth, American 1885-1900 . . . . **$1,800-2,200**

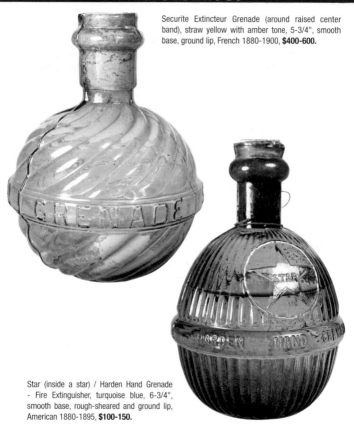

Securite Extincteur Grenade (around raised center band), straw yellow with amber tone, 5-3/4", smooth base, ground lip, French 1880-1900, **$400-600.**

Star (inside a star) / Harden Hand Grenade - Fire Extinguisher, turquoise blue, 6-3/4", smooth base, rough-sheared and ground lip, American 1880-1895, **$100-150.**

P.R.R. (Pennsylvania Railroad Fire Grenade), Clear glass, 7-1/8", horizontal rib pattern, original contents, rare, American 1880-1895 . . . .**$1,600-1,800**

Pronto Fire Extinguisher – The Allen Corporation, New York, Stops Fire Quick (label only), Amber, 11", ABM lip, American early 20th Century. **$50-75**

Pyrolite Fluid Fire Extinguisher, Pull Cork Dash Contents on Fire, by C.J. Cross M'F'G'Co. New York (label only), Aqua, 11", smooth base (Pyrofite on side of base), tooled lip, American 1900-1920 . . . . **$75-100**

Pyrolite Fluid Fire Extinguisher, Pull Cork Dash Contents on Fire, by C.J. Cross M'F'G'Co. New York (label only), Clear, 11", smooth base (Pyrofitc on side of base), ABM lip, American 1900-1920 . . . . **$75-100**

Pyrolite Fluid Fire Extinguisher, Pull Cork Dash Contents on Fire, by C.J. Cross M'F'G'Co. New York (label only), Amber, 11", smooth base (EXO 5 on side of base), ABM lip, American 1900-1920 . . . . **$75-100**

Securite – Extincteur – Grenade, Yellow copper amber, 5-5/8", twisted rib pattern above and below center band, smooth base, sheared and ground lip, very rare, fewer than five known examples, French 1880-1900. . . . . **$400-600**

Sinclair & Co, Hand Grenade, 19 Elson St. London (label only), Deep cobalt blue, 7-1/4", smooth base (tool), sheared and ground lip, original monogram impressed neck seal and contents, English 1880-1900 . . . . **$375-475**

(Star inside an embossed star) / Harden Hand Grenade – Fire Extinguisher, Deep yellow green, 6-1/4", smooth base, sheared and ground lip, original neck plug and contents, very rare in this color, American 1880-1895. . . . . **$800-1,200**

(Star inside an embossed star) / Harden Star Hand Grenade – Fire Extinguisher, Clear glass with some aqua, 6-3/4", smooth base (10490), rough sheared and ground lip, original contents, English 1885-1900 . . . . **$450-550**

(Star inside an embossed Star) / Harden Hand Grenade – Fire Extinguisher, Turquoise blue, 6-3/4", smooth base, rough sheared and ground lip, American 1885-1900 . . . . . **$225-325**

(Star inside an embossed star) / Harden Hand Grenade – Fire Extinguisher, Clear glass, quart, 8-1/4", smooth base (May 27, 84), sheared and tooled lip, American 1885-1900 . . **$600-900**

(Star inside an embossed star) / Harden Grenade / S.P. Rinkler, Deep cobalt blue, 17-3/4", tubular grenade, smooth base (RD / NO.60064), tooled lip, original contents and metal pull ring, English 1885-1900. . . . . **$800-1,200**

The / Harden / Star (inside a star) / Tubular / Grenade, Clear glass, 17-3/4", tubular grenade, smooth round bottom, sheared and tooled lip, original contents and cast iron wall mounts, American 1885-1900 . . . . **$900-1,100**

The Imperial Grenade (inside a belt) / Fire / Extinguisher, Medium yellow green, 6-1/2", smooth base, rough sheared lip, part original contents and red neck foil, English 1885-1900 . . . . **$250-300**

The Kalamazoo / Automatic And / Hand Fire Extinguisher, Cobalt blue, 11-1/8", smooth base, tooled lip, American 1880-1895 . . . . **$400-500**

The Royal Grenade / Fire / Extinguisher – Patent Applied For / June 1884, Medium cobalt blue, 5-1/4", four circular raised panels and overall raised hobnail pattern, smooth base, sheared and ground lip, extremely rare, Canadian 1884-1895 . . . .**$2,500-3,500**

Unembossed Fire Grenade, Yellow amber, 6-1/8", smooth base, rough sheared lip, original contents, rare, Canadian 1885-1895 . . . .**$1,500-1,800**

Vertical Rib Pattern Fire Grenade, Deep olive green, 6-3/4", vertical rib pattern around entire grenade, smooth base has grooves for a metal rack, outward rolled lip, rare, American 1885-1890 . . . . **$350-450**

W. D. Allen – Manufacturing – Company – Chicago – Illinois (crescent moon), Cobalt blue, 8-1/8", melon sided, smooth base, ground lip, rare, American 1880-1895 . . . .**$3,000-3,600**

Whiz Fire Extinguisher – The R.M. Hollingshead Co, Camden, N.J. (label only), Amber, 11", ABM lips, American early 20th Century **$50-75**

FLASKS

Flasks have become a most popular and prized item among collectors due to the variety of decorative, historical, and pictorial depictions on many pieces. The outstanding colors have a major effect on the value of these pieces, more so than most other collectible bottles.

American flasks were first manufactured by the Pitkin Glasshouse in Connecticut around 1815, and quickly spread to other glasshouses around the country. Early flasks were freeblown and represent some of the better craftsmanship with more intricate designs. By 1850, approximately 400 designs had been used. Black graphite pontil marks were left on the bottles because the pontils were coated with powdered iron, allowing the flask's bottom to break away without damaging the glass. The flasks made between 1850 and 1870, however, had no such markings because of the widespread use of the newly invented snapcase.

Since flasks were intended to be refilled with whiskey or other spirits, more time and effort was expended in manufacturing than most other types of bottles. Flasks soon became a popular item for use with all types of causes and promotions. Mottos frequently were embossed on flasks and included a number of patriotic sayings and slogans. George Washington's face commonly appeared on flasks, as did Andrew Jackson's and John Quincy Adams's, the candidates for the presidential elections of 1824 and 1828. Events of the time were also portrayed on flasks.

One of the more controversial flasks was the Masonic flasks, which bore the order's emblem on one side and the American eagle on the other side. At first, the design drew strong opposition from the public, but the controversy soon passed, and Masonic flasks are now a specialty items for collectors.

Another highly collectible flask was the Pitkin-type flasks named for the Pitkin Glassworks, where it was exclusively manufactured. While Pitkin-type flask and ink bottles are common, Pitkin bottles, jugs, and jars are very rare. German Pitkin flasks are heavier and straight-ribbed, while the American patterns are swirled and broken-ribbed with unusual colors such as dark blue.

Because flasks were widely used for promoting various political and special interest agendas, they represent a major historical record of the people and events of those times.

A Merry Christmas – And Happy New Year (label under glass with Santa Claus), Clear, 6", smooth base, screw top with cap, ground lip American 1905-1915 . . . . **$1,000-1,300**

A Merry Christmas – Cooking Good Stuff – Happy New Year (label under glass), Clear, 6", smooth base, screw top with pewter cap, ground lip American 1905-1915 . . . . . . **$550-650**

A. Livingston – Wholesale and Retail – Carson City, Nev, Clear, pint, smooth base, tooled top, rare, American 1885-1905 . . . . **$1,000-1,300**

A.M. Smith's – A.D. 1892 249 Hen. Av. – Minneapolis Minn. – California Wine Depot, Clear, 4-1/2", pumpkinseed form, smooth base, tooled top, American 1880-1895 . . . . . **$100-160**

H.C. Heidtmann – Becker's – Reno, Nev, Clear, half-pint, coffin flask form, smooth base, tooled top, American 1900-1918 . . . . **$650-850**

Baltimore / Anchor / Glass Works – Bird Above Flames / Resurgam, Yellow amber, pint, smooth base, applied double collar mouth, scarce color, American 1865-1870, Baltimore Class Works, Baltimore, Maryland **$500-800**

Bininger's / Travelers / Guide / A.M. Bininger & Co / No 19 Broad St NY, Medium golden amber, 6-7/8", teardrop flask, smooth base, applied double collar mouth, American 1860-1875 . . . . **$600-800**

Bust of Man in Military Uniform – Falcon with Crown, Cobalt blue, pint, pontil-scarred base, sheared and tooled mouth, European 1840-1860 . . . . **$180-250**

Bust of Columbia – Eagle / B&W, Blue aqua, pint, open pontil, sheared and tooled lip, American 1835-1845 . . . . . . **$400-600**

Bust of Washington – Tree, GWA85-028, Cobalt blue, calabash, open pontil, applied mouth, extremely rare, one of three known examples, American 1855-1860 . . . . **$17,000-22,000**

But For Joe (in banner) Woman on a Bicycle, Blue aqua, pint, smooth base, applied ringed mouth, American 1875-1885 . . . . **$200-250**

Columbus / (bust of Columbus coming out of a barrel) on a Barrel – (rooster), Pale aqua, 5-3/4", half-barrel form, smooth base, tooled lip, rare, American 1890-1900 . . . . **$300-400**

Columbian Exposition / Bust of Columbus / 1893 / A.E. Bros & Co – Pennsylvania / Pure Rye / Baker Whiskey, Amber, 6-3/4", pumpkinseed form, smooth base, tooled mouth, rare, American 1893-1895 . . . . **$1,500-1,700**

Eagle / C.T. Bond (in circle) – C.T. Bond / Merchant & Trader / New Albany / Miss, Yellow with amber tone, half-pint, smooth base, applied ringed mouth, extremely rare, one of two known examples, American 1865-1875 . . . . **$5,500-6,500**

Eagle / Granite / Glass Co – Eagle / Stoddard N.H., Deep amber, pint, pontil-scarred base, sheared and tooled mouth, American 1850-1860 . . . . **$300-400**

Frank Abadie – Wholesale Liquors – Eureka, Nev, clear, pint, smooth base, tooled top, American 1880-1886, **$1,000-1,600.**

Eagle – New London / (anchor) Glass Works (historical flask), Brilliant yellow olive, pint, large red iron pontil mark, applied double collared mouth, rare color and rare iron pontil, American 1856-1860, New London Glass Works, New London, Connecticut **$2,000-4,000**

Eagle – Morning Glory, Blue aqua, pint, pontil-scarred base, sheared and tooled lip, American 1830-1840 . . . . . **$500-600**

Eagle (embossed) – Louisville / KY / Glass Works, Dark amber, half-pint, vertically ribbed flask, smooth base, applied top with ring, American 1860-1865. . . . .**$1,500-3,000**

Exchange – Flood & Barks Prop. – Tel. Main 187 – Bakersfield, Clear, pint, pumpkinseed form, smooth base, tooled top, American 1885-1895 . . . . **$100-160**

Frank Abadie – Wholesale Liquors – Eureka, Nev, Clear, pint, smooth base, tooled top, American 1884 -1886 . . . . **$100-160**

G. Lewis – Liquor – Co. – Silver State – Victor, Colo, Clear, half-pint, smooth base, tooled top, American 1880-1895 . . . . **$700-1,000**

Geo. W. Robinson / Dog's Head / No 8 Main St / Wheeling W. VA, Blue aqua, strap-sided pint, smooth base, applied mouth, American 1870-1880 . . . . **$150-200**

Geo. W. Robinson / No 75 / Main St. W. VA, Blue aqua, strap-sided quart, smooth base, applied mouth, American 1870-1880 . . . . **$140-180**

Label under glass whiskey flask, white silhouette of Victorian woman with embossed eagle on back, clear, 5-1/4", smooth base, screw-top lip, American 1900-1920, **$100-125.**

Grotesque Face – Two Men Talking, Cobalt blue, half-pint, pontil-scarred base, sheared and tooled lip, rare, European 1850-1860 . . . . **$500-800**

Henry Chapman & Co. – Sole Agents – Montreal, Golden amber, 5-3/4", teardrop form, smooth base, ground lip, American 1870-1885 . . . . **$75-100**

In Silver We Trust / Bust Of Bryan / Bryan 1896 Sewall – United Democratic Ticket / We Shall Vote / American Eagle / 61 to 1, Medium amber, half-point, 5-1/4", smooth base, tooled lip, rare political flask made for the Presidential election of 1896, American 1896. . . . . **$600-800**

Isabella / Anchor / Glass Works – Factory, Blue aqua, quart, open pontil, sheared and tooled lip, American 1855-1865 . . . . **$325-425**

J.R. & Son – Scroll Flask, Pale Ice blue, pint, scroll in a corseted form, pontil-scarred base, sheared top, American 1830-1840, John Robinson and Son Manufacturers, Pittsburgh, Pennsylvania **$350-750**

Label Under Glass Pocket Flask – Photograph of Gentlemen – Compliments of J.P. Haddox – Winchester, VA, Clear, 5", smooth base, screw top lid with cap, American 1885-1915 . . . . **$1,500-1,600**

Label Under Glass Pocket Flask – Victorian Man and Woman Holding Hands, Clear, 5", smooth base, screw top lid with cap, American 1885-1915 . . . . **$450-550**

Label under glass whiskey flask, pink with image of Victorian woman, clear, 5-1/4",
smooth base, screw-top lip, American 1900-1920, **$350-400.**

Label Under Glass Pocket Flask – Photograph of Victorian Woman, Clear, 5", smooth base, screw top lid with cap, American 1885-1910 . . . .**$1,700-1,900**

Label Under Glass Pocket Flask – Photograph of Beautiful Woman – For Fine Old Rye Whiskey, Clear, 5", smooth base, screw top lid with cap, American 1885-1910
. . . . **$600-800**

Label Under Glass Pocket Flask – Photograph of Naval Officer – Remember The Maine, Clear, 5-1/4", smooth base, screw top lid with cap, American 1885-1915 . . . . **$600-800**

Label Under Glass Pocket Flask – Photograph of Provocative Posing Woman, Clear, 5-3/4", smooth base, screw top lid with cap, American 1885-1910 . . . .**$1,700-1,900**

Label Under Glass Pocket Flask – Kaiser Wilhelm I. Denkmal A.D. Wittekinberg B / Perta Building, Clear, 5-3/4", smooth base, screw top lid with cap, American 1885-1920
. . . . **$90-110**

Label Under Glass Pocket Flask – Photograph of Provocative Posing Woman, Clear, 6", smooth base, screw top lid with cap, American 1880-1905 . . . .**$1,500-1,700**

Label Under Glass Pocket Flask – Photograph of Provocative Woman in Attire, Clear, 6", smooth base, screw top lid with cap, American 1885-1910 . . . .**$1,100-1,300**

Label Under Glass Pocket Flask – Beautiful Woman Lifting Up Her Dress, Clear, 6", smooth base, screw top lid with cap, American 1885-1920 . . . .**$1,300-1,400**

Label Under Glass Pocket Flask – Beautiful Victorian Woman Holding Roses, Clear, 6", smooth base, screw top lid with cap, American 1885-1915 . . . . **$600-800**

Label Under Glass Pocket Flask – G.W. Schmidt / Merry Christmas / (pretty woman in Victorian dress) / Happy New Year / Pittsburgh, Pa, Clear glass, 6-1/4", horizontal side ribbing, smooth base, sheared and tooled lip, original metal screw cap and neck chain, extremely rare, American 1885-1910 . . . . **$700-900**

Label Under Glass Pocket Flask – Theodore Roosevelt (Stars & Stripes background), Clear, 6-1/2", smooth base, screw top lid with cap, American 1885-1920 . . . . **$450-550**

Layfayette – Liberty Cap Portrait Flask, Brilliant aquamarine, half-pint, pontil-scarred base, sheared mouth, extremely rare, American 1824-1825 Coventry Glass Works, Coventry, Connecticut **$5,000-10,000**

Liberty / Eagle – Willington / Glass / Co / West Willington / Conn, Olive amber, half-pint, smooth base, applied double collar mouth, American 1855-1875 . . . . **$200-250**

M. Heims – 139 – Washington St. Indianapolis, Clear, half-pint, pumpkinseed form, lattice design, smooth base, tooled top, American 1895-1905 . . . . **$100-120**

Label under glass whiskey flask, image of Oto Wallin, Waukegan, Il, gentleman merchant with son, clear, 5-1/4", smooth base, screw-top lip with cap, American 1900-1930, **$200-300.**

Label under glass military whiskey flask, depiction of clock with playing cards, "It's a long time between drinks, U.S." embossed on back, clear, 5", smooth base, screw top lip with cap, American 1900-1930, **$300-400.**

Mellow Rib Pattern Flask, Yellow green, pint, 6-1/4",
20-vertical rib pattern, pontil-scarred base, sheared and tooled
lip, American 1820-1830 . . . . **$800-1,200**

Merry Christmas – And – Happy New Year, Clear, 4", half-pint,
floral design and decoration, smooth base, tooled top, American
1885-1895 . . . . **$100-200**

Mountain Dew (label under glass with pretty woman),
Clear, pint, smooth base, screw top (with cap), American
1910-1930 . . . . **$150-250**

Nailsea Flask, Clear glass with white looping, 6-3/8", polished
pontil, tooled mouth, European 1850-1880 . . . . **$150-250**

**North / American (inside map of North America) / Pan-
American / South / American (inside a map of South
America)**, Clear, 7", smooth base, ground lip, original metal
screw-on cap and screw-on shot glass cover, American 1901
. . . . **$200-300**

Old Rye – Wheeling / VA, Medium blue green, pint, smooth base,
applied mouth, rare, American 1865-1875 . . . . **$600-800**

**Patent – Label reads: Cognac Brandy, George L. Forbush,
Pharmacist, Petersboro, New Hampshire,** Yellow amber,
pint, smooth base, applied double collar mouth, American
1870-1880 . . . . **$100-150**

Pattern Molded Flask, Clear, 7-3/8", 19-oglval pattern, pontil
scarred base, sheared and tooled wide mouth, American
1815-1825. . . . . **$400-700**

Mountain Dew (label under glass with pretty woman), clear, pint, smooth base, screw top with metal cap, American 1910-1930, **$150-250.**

Pike's Peak / Prospector – Eagle, Deep blue aqua, quart, pontil-scarred base, applied mouth, American 1870-1875 .... **$180-200**

Pitkin Flask, Dark amber, 5-3/4", pint, 36 ribs swirled to the left, flattened clockface form, pontil-scarred base, sheared top, American 1800-1830 .... **$500-1,000**

Pitkin Flask, Light green aqua, 5-3/8", 30-broken rib pattern swirled to right, open pontl, sheared and tooled lip, American 1790-1810 .... **$650-800**

Pitkin Flask, Medium yellow olive green, 5-3/4", 36-broken rib pattern swirled to right, open pontil, sheared and tooled lip, American 1790-1810 .... **$800-1,000**

Pitkin Flask with early label (Bourbon Whiskey / Sold by Frank R. Hadley / Druggist & Chemist / New Bedford, Mass, Light olive green, 7", ribbed and swirled to left, 36-ribs, pontil-scarred base, sheared mouth, American 1783-1830, Pitkin Glass Works, Manchester, Connecticut **$1,250-2,500**

Popular – Cocktails – Rheinstron Bros. – Cincinnati USA – (two drinks embossed on reverse side), Clear, half-pint, horseshoe shape, smooth base, screw top with pewter cap and ground and polished lip, American 1905-1915 .... **$75-120**

Return To Joe Gribble – Old Crow Saloon – Douglas, AZ., Clear, 6", half-pint, smooth base, screw top cap with ground lip, very rare, American 1903 .... **$3,300-4,300**

Scroll Flask, Medium to deep amber, pint, red iron pontil, applied mouth, American 1845-1855. . . . . **$700-800**

Scroll Flask, Deep teal blue, pint, pontil-scarred base, sheared and tooled lip, American 1845-1855 . . . . **$4,000-5,000**

Sloop / Star, Aqua, half-pint, open pontil, sheared and tooled lip, American 1825-1835 . . . . **$100-150**

Soldier / Balt. MD – Ballet Dancer / Chapman, Emerald green, pint, open pontil, sheared and tooled lip, rare, American 1850-1865, Chapman's Maryland Glass Works **$200-300**

Spring Garden / Anchor / Glass Works – Cabin, Orange amber, pint, smooth base, applied double collar mouth, American 1860-1870, Spring Garden Glassworks, Baltimore, Maryland **$1,300-1,600**

Spirits Flask (blown), Fiery opalescent milk glass, 4-5/8", multicolored enamel floral and bird decorations, rectangular with beveled corner panes, pontil-scarred base, sheared lip, original pewter mouth band, blown using German half-post method, German 1770-1800 . . . . **$150-250**

Sprits Flask (blown), Deep cobalt blue, 5-3/8", multicolored enamel decorations of a man in colonial dress holding a glass on one side and German script writing on other side, pontil-scarred base, sheared lip, original threaded pewter mouth band, blown using German half-post method, German 1770-1800 . . . . **$800-1,200**

Sprits Flask (blown), Light to medium cobalt blue, 6-7/8", tight broken rib-pattern slightly swirled to right, pontil-scarred base, tooled mouth, blown using German half-post method, European 1770-1800 . . . . **$375-475**

Spirits Flask, Sapphire blue, 6-1/4", white looping conical form tapering from a larger base to smaller neck, pontil-scarred base, applied pewter mouth with screw threads, Southern German 1760-1780 . . . .**$2,000-2,300**

Spirits Flask, Light purple amethyst, 7-5/8", white looping, rectangular form with wide beveled corner panels, pontil-scarred base, applied pewter mouth with screw threads, Southern German 1760-1780 . . . .**$1,200-1,600**

Spirits Flask, Deep cobalt blue, 7-5/8", white looping, rectangular form with wide beveled corner panels, pontil-scarred base, applied pewter mouth with screw threads, Southern German 1760-1780 . . . . **$800-1,000**

Spirits Flask, Purple amethyst, 7-1/2", white herringbone pattern, pontil-scarred base, applied pewter mouth with screw threads, Southern German 1760-1780 . . . . **$800-1,200**

Spirits Flask, Honey amber, 6", white looping, rectangular form with wide beveled corner panels, pontil-scarred base, applied pewter mouth with screw threads, Southern German 1760-1780 . . . . **$800-1,000**

Standing Deer / Good / Game – Willow Tree, Aqua, pint, open pontil, sheared and tooled lip, American 1825-1835, Coffin & Hays Glass Works, Hammonton, New Jersey **$275-375**

Standing Stag – Boar's Head, Horn, Rifle and Sword, Purple amethyst, 5-3/8", pontil-scarred base, inward rolled lip, European 1840-1870 . . . . **$400-600**

Stiegel-Type Spirits Flask, Clear, 4-3/4", multi-colored enamel decoration of a rabbit playing a drum on one side and German script on the other side, scarred base, tooled mouth with original pewter neck ring, blown in Geman half-post method, German 1770-1810 . . . . **$350-450**

Stiegiel-Type Spirits Flask, Deep purple amethyst, 5-3/4", 1-rib pattern swirled to left, pontil-scarred base, tooled lip, blown in German half-post method, German 1780-1810 . . . . **$150-200**

Summer Tree – Winter Tree, Yellow olive, quart, pontil-scarred base, applied double collar mouth, rare, American 1850-1860 . . . . **$1,700-1,900**

Sunburst Flask, Medium olive green, half-pint, pontil-scarred base, tooled mouth, American 1815-1825 . . . . **$600-800**

Sunburst Flask, Medium yellow olive amber, half-pint, pontil-scarred base, tooled mouth, American 1815-1825 . . . **$600-800**

Scroll Flask, Yellow green, quart, iron pontil, sheared lip, American 1840-1850 . . . . **$650-850**

"Union" / Clasped Hands - Eagle With Banner / "E. Wormser & Co / Pittsburg / PA" (GXII-15), teal blue, quart, 1859-1870, **$5,000-6,000**.

"Union" / Clasped Hands – Eagle With Banner (GXII-3), golden yellow olive, (very rare in this color), quart, American 1855-1870, **$550-650.**

The Log Cabin (embossed log cabin) – 167-3rd St. Portland Ore. – Billy Winters Pro, Clear, pint, pumpkinseed form, smooth base, tooled top, American 1885-1895 . . . . . **$325-425**

The Waldorf Cafes – Becker Bros. Inc. – San Francisco – Los Angeles – San Diego – 1915, Clear, pint, smooth base, tooled top, American 1915 . . . . **$100-120**

The Waldorf & Tavern – Reno, Nevada, Clear, 10 oz., smooth base, tooled top, American 1910-1915 . . . . **$200-250**

The – F.G. McCoy Co. Inc – The Wellington Saloon – Prescott, Ariz., Clear, 6", half-pint, smooth base (Design Pat. Aug 9, 1898), tooled top, American 1902-1906 . . . . **$700-900**

Thos. Taylor & Co – Sole Agents P. Vollmer's Old Bourbon Louisville – Virginia, Nev., Clear, pint, coffin flask form, smooth base, tooled top, American 1867-1883 . . **$1,000-2,000**

Traveler's / Star / Companion – Ravenna / Star / Glass Co., Blue aqua, pint, smooth base, applied ringed mouth, American 1855-1870 . . . . **$150-250**

Traveler's / Companion – Star, Deep amber, half-pint, iron pontil, sheared and tooled mouth, American 1850-1860 . . . . **$500-700**

Union / Clasped Hands / FA & CO / Cannon, Amber, pint, smooth base, applied ringed mouth, American 1860-1870, Fahnestock, Albree & Co. Glassworks, Pittsburgh, PA **$80-125**

"Union" / Clasped Hands/ "Old Rye" - Eagle With "A.&D.H.C" Inside Banner / "Pittsburgh" (GX11-9), medium apple green, quart, American 1855-1870, **$3,500-4,500.**

"Union" / Clasped Hands / "WM. Frank & Sons / Pitts" – Cannon (GXII-38) blue aqua with deep olive striations, quart, 1859-1870, **$100-150.**

Union Saloon – John Flack Propr. – San Bernardino, Deep purple, pint, smooth base, tooled top with glass stopper, American 1885-1905 . . . . **$350-450**

Vertical Rib Pattern Flask with Oval Indented Panels, Aqua, pint, 8", pontil-scarred base, sheared and tooled lip, American 1835-1845, Louisville Glass Works, Louisville, Kentucky **$200-275**

W.A. Gaines & Cos. – The Capitol Old Crow Whiskey – Cheyenne Wyo., Clear, pint, smooth base, screw top, American 1900-1920 . . . . **$100-200**

Washington Bar – Coleman & Granger – Tonopah, Nevada, Clear, pint, smooth base, screw top, American 1905-1806 . . . . **$300-500**

Westford Glass / Westford / Conn – Sheaf of Grain, Dark amber, half-pint, smooth base, applied double collar mouth, American 1855-1865 . . . . **$175-225**

Wharton's Whisky – 1850 Chestnut Grove, Medium cobalt blue, 5-1/4", teardrop form, smooth base, applied lip, American 1865-1875 . . . . **$350-550**

Zanesville / City / Glassworks, Yellow amber, pint, smooth base, applied mouth, rare, American 1875-1885, Zanesville Glass Works, Zanesville, Ohio **$500-700**

FOOD AND PICKLE BOTTLES

Food bottles are one of the largest and most diverse categories in the field of collectible bottles. They were made for the commercial sale of a wide variety of food products excluding beverages (except milk). Food bottles are an ideal specialty for the beginning collector, since they are so readily available. Many collectors are attracted to food bottles for their historical value. Nineteenth and early twentieth century magazines and newspapers contained so many illustrated advertisements for food products that many collectors keep scrapbooks of ads as an aid to dating and pricing the bottles.

Before bottling, food could not be transported long distances or kept for long periods of time because of spoilage. Bottling revolutionized the food industry and began a new chapter in American business merchandising and distribution. With the glass bottle, producers were able to save labor, use portion packaging, and sell from long distances.

Suddenly local producers faced competition from great distances, so many interesting bottles were created specifically to distinguish them from others. Green and clear peppersauce bottles, for instance, were made in the shape of Gothic cathedrals with arches and windows (green and clear); mustard jars and chili sauce bottles featured unique embossing; cooking oil bottles were tall and slim; and pickle bottles had large mouths.

The pickle bottle is one of the largest of the food bottles, with a wide mouth and a square or cylindrical shape. While the pickle bottle was often unique in shape and design, its color was almost exclusively aqua, although occasionally you'll find a multi-colored piece. Since there are many variations of designs for these Gothic-looking pickle jars, it's difficult to identify exactly the contents of the bottles and the bottle manufacturer. While the oldest bottles may have used foil labels for identification, paper labels and embossing provide additional identification. When looking through ghost town dumps and digging behind older pioneer homes, you are sure to find these food and pickle bottles in large numbers, since pickles were a common and well-liked food, especially in the mining communities.

Two of the more common food bottles are the Worcestershire sauce bottles distributed by Lea & Perrins and the Heinz sauce bottles. The Worcestershire sauce in the green bottle was in high demand during the 19th century and is quite common.

Henry J. Heinz introduced his sauces in 1869 with bottled horseradish and didn't begin bottling ketchup until 1889.

Acker's – Select Tea – Finley Acker & Co – Tea Specialist – Philadelphia USA (embossed tea leaves and elephant), Medium green, 8", smooth base, ABM top with gold gilded stopper, American 1882-1929 . . . . **$600-800**

Anchor Pickle and Vinegar Works (embossed anchor), Light green, 7-1/2", smooth base (H.N. & Co.), applied top, American 1860-1870 . . . . **$150-170**

Antoine – candy jar with paper label, Clear, 12", smooth base, wide mouth with original lid, American 1900-1930. **$100-150**

Beichs – candy store jar, Clear, 13-1/2", smooth base, wide mouth with original lid, American 1900-1930 . . . . . **$250-350**

Borden's – The Improved – Malted Milk (display jar), Clear, 8", smooth base, wide mouth with original lid, American 1900-1930 . . . . **$450-500**

Buster Brown – Mustard – Steinwender – Stoffregen – Coffee Co. – St. Louis (mustard tin), Red tin with yellow background, 2-1/2", smooth base, American 1900-1930 . . . . **$200-225**

Butter Boy – You'll Like It – Sur-Nuf – Pop Corn – Always Pops (popcorn tin), Red, yellow, and black, 4", smooth base with original lid, American 1900-1930 . . . . **$75-90**

Candy Bros – MF'G – Confectioners – St. Louis, Mo., Clear, 11", smooth base, tooled top with original glass insert (Candy Bros. St. Louis C.R.), American 1890-1910 . . . . **$125-$150**

Cathedral Pickle Jar, Medium emerald green, 7-5/8", open pontil-scarred base, rolled lip, American 1845-1860 . . . . **$250-400**

Cathedral pickle with cross-hatching, light green, 7-1/2", graphite pontil, applied top, American 1860-1870, **$450-550.**

E.C. Flaccus Co., Trade Mark (embossed deer head), medium green, pint, smooth base, milk glass lid, American 1880-1890, **$1,000-1,500.**

Cathedral Pickle Jar, ABA41-229, Medium emerald green, 8-1/2", iron pontil, outward rolled lip, extremely rare, American 1850-1860, Willington Glass Works, Willington, Conn.
. . . . **$3,800-4,300**

This is the smallest of the three sizes of the highly desirable Willington pickle jars., Cathedral Pickle Jar, Medium blue green, 11", diamond patterns on three sides, arched shoulder panels, and a crown on top, smooth base, rolled lip, American 1860-1870 . . . . **$500-700**

Cathedral Pickle Jar, Blue aqua, 11", smooth base, applied ring lip, scarce variant clock face and clamshell on alternating shoulder panels, American 1855-1870 . . . . **$300-400**

Cathedral Pickle Jar, Blue aqua, 11-3/8", smooth base, applied mouth, leafy branches above arch, scarce, American 1860-1870 . . . **$150-175**

Cathedral Pickle Jar, Medium blue green, 11-5/8", smooth base, rolled lip, American 1860-1870 . . . . **$400-600**

Cathedral Pickle Jar, Deep blue aqua, 13-1/8", 6-sided, smooth base, rolled lip, American 1860-1870 . . . . **$180-250**

Cathedral Pickle Jar, Blue aqua, 13-1/4", 6-sided, smooth base, outward rolled lip, American 1855-1870 . . . . **$100-130**

C.L. Stickney – Peppersauce Bottle, Clear, 9", pontil-scarred base, applied top, American 1850-1860 . . . . **$100-150**

Clover Leaf Pickle Jar, Yellow with green tone, 7-3/4", pontil-scarred base, outward rolled mouth, extremely rare, only known example in this color, American 1850-1860, Stoddard Glasshouse, Stoddard, New Hampshire **$1,500-3,000**

Coca Cola – Chewing Gum, Clear, 9", smooth base, ABM wide mouth with glass stopper, counter display Jar, rare, American 1903-1905 . . . . **$700-1,000**

Coca-Cola – Pepsin Gum – Manufactured By Franklin MFG Co, Richmond VA, Clear, 10-1/2", smooth base, original glass lid, rare counter display jar, American 1905-1911 . . . . **$800-1,000**

C.P. Sanborn & Son / Union (inside an American shield) / Boston Pickles, Yellow olive, 5", smooth base, sheared and ground lip, American 1880-1895 . . . . **$75-125**

Diamond Display Jar – Label reads: Mixed Pickles from H.J.Heinz Co. / Trade Mark, H.J. Heinz Co. / Pittsburgh, U.S.A. / Purveyors to the Trade / Try our Sweet Pickles, Preserves, Celery Sauce, Ketchup, Clear glass, 21", smooth base, ground lip with original glass closure, American 1915-1920 **$375-475**

Dodson – Hills – St. Louis – Peppersauce Bottle, Aqua, 8", smooth base, tooled top, American 1892-1915 . . . . . **$350-450**

Draped Shoulder Pickle Jar, Blue aqua, 11-1/4", iron pontil, rolled lip, American 1850-1865 . . . . **$75-100**

E.C. Flaccus Co. – Trade Mark – (embossed deer head), Medium green, pint, smooth base, milk glass lid, American 1880-1890 . . . . **$700-1,500**

EHVB / N.Y. – Pickle Jar, Pale blue green, 12", hexagonal with fancy cathedral arches around the entire mid section, pontil-scarred base, tooled outward rolled mouth, American 1840-1860 . . . . **$800-1,600**

Fancy Embossed Product Jar – Embossed Eagle, Light canary yellow, pint, 4-7/8", smooth base, rough sheared and ground lip, original screw-on metal band, American 1890-1910 . . . **$75-100**

Heinz Evaporated Horse Radish (label), aqua, 6-1/2" / Heinz Grape Jelly (label), aqua 8" / Heinz Evaporated Horse Radish, H.J. Heinz Co. (label), aqua, 6-1/2", American 1930s, **$400-500/set.**

Food Jar – Neck and Front Label Reads: Gordon & Dil_____th, Queen Olives, 563 & 56, Greenwich St., New York, Yellow green, 6-1/4", smooth base, ground lip with original clear glass lid and screw band, American 1885 1910 . . . . **$125-175**

Food Jar, Yellow amber with topaz tone, 8-1/4", cylindrical three-piece mold, smooth base, outward rolled mouth, American 1860-1870, Keene and Stoddard Glass, Stoddard Glasshouse, Stoddard, New Hampshire **$750-1,500**

Heinz sample jugs: Heinz Tomato Chutney, brown and tan, 3" / Prepared Mustard, Heinz, dark and light tan, 3", American 1890-1910, **$200-250/set.**

Four Portrait Pickle Bottle, Clear, 9-1/2", embossed faces of two women, a man, and a Roman soldier, smooth base, flared lip, American 1870-1890 . . . . **$75-125**

Goofus Pickle Jar, Milk glass, 15", embossed rose and basket decoration, smooth base, ground lip, rare, American 1880-1900 . . . . , , , , **$300-400**

Goofus Pickle Jar, Cobalt blue, 15", floral decoration with roses, smooth base, ground mouth, extremely rare color, American 1890-1910 . . . . **$1,000-2,000**

Goofus Pickle Jar, Cornflower blue, 15-1/2", floral decoration with roses, smooth base, ground mouth, American 1880-1910 . . . . . . **$400-800**

Heinz Noble & Co – Pittsburgh PA, Light aqua, 8", smooth base, applied top, rare, "Z" in Heinz and "N" in Noble are backwards, American 1869-1874 . . . . **$175-225**

Hercules (photo of Hercules) – Winslow, Rand and Watson – Pure Coffee (coffee tin), Light orange, 7-1/2", smooth base, original lid, American 1900-1930 . . . . **$400-500**

Horlick's – Malted Milk – Hot or Cold (embossed glass display jar), Clear, 9-1/2", smooth base, wide mouth with original lid, American 1900-1930 . . . . **$200-275**

Huston's – Confectionary – Auburn, Maine – Candy Jar with Label, Clear, 12", smooth base, wide mouth with original lid, American 1900-1930 . . . . **$100-150**

Lowell & Covel – Pure Cream – Caramels – Boston. U.S.A. – Candy Jar, Clear, 10", smooth base, wide mouth with original brass lid, American 1900-1930 . . . . **$250-300**

P.D. Code & Co. – S.F. (Phillip D. Code), Medium green, 11-1/2", smooth base, applied top, American 1867-1898 . . . . **$500-600**

Peppersauce Bottle, Green aqua, 11", 12-sided, open pontil, inward rolled lip, American 1840-1860 . . . . **$120-140**

Perfection – Prepared Cocoanut – Spark Place, NY (jar with label), Aqua, 8", smooth base, threaded top with original lid, American 1900-1920 . . . . **$150-200**

Pickle Jar, Medium blue green, 7-1/2", square form, open pontil, rolled lip, American 1840-1860 . . . . **$150-200**

Pickle Jar, Medium blue green, 11-1/4", five rounded cathedral arched panels, fluted shoulders, and neck, iron pontil, applied mouth, rare, American 1850-1865 . . . . **$800-1,000**

Heinz Pickle Jars: Heinz Keystone Pickles (label), clear, 10" / Mixed Pickles, H.J. Heinz Co., Pittsburg, USA (label) clear, 12", American 1900-1930, **$400-450/set.**

Heinz Grapefruit Marmalade (label), clear, 4-1/2" / Heinz Sweet Mixed Pickles (label), 3" / Heinz Prepared Mustard (label), clear, 2-1/4", American 1900-1930, **$400-450/set.**

Planters – Pennant – 5 Cents Salted – Peanuts – Sold Only in Printed Planters Red Pennant Bags (counter display jar), Clear, 12", smooth base, wide mouth with original lid, American 1900-1920 . . . . **$500-600**

Ribbed Utility Jar, Medium green, 8-1/4", sticky ball pontil, applied lip, American 1850-1860 . . . . **$200-400**

Ribbed Utility Bottle, Aqua, 10", pontil-scarred base, applied top, American 1850-1860 . . . . **$100-125**

Shriver's – Oyster – Ketchup – Baltimore, Medium green, 7-1/2", smooth base, applied top, rare, American 1865-1885 . . . **$800-1,100**

Shriver's – Oyster – Ketchup – Baltimore, Medium green, 9", smooth base, applied top, rare, American 1865-1885 . . . . **$1,500-2,000**

Smokine, (Smokine was used to give meat a smoked flavor), Dark amber, 5", E.G. Booze type cabin, smooth base, tooled top, American 1900-1920 . . . . **$325-425**

T.B. Smith & Co. / Philada – Pickle Jar, Aquamarine, 11-1/2", cylindrical with seven rounded vertical panels (one embossed), fluted shoulder, pontil iron mark, outward rolled collared mouth, extremely rare, American 1845-1860 . . . **$1,000-2,000**

Thompson's – Double Malted Entirely Soluble – Malted Milk, Light brown, 10", porcelain canister, smooth base, original lid, American 1900-1930 . . . . **$200-275**

Thurber & Co – Pure Lemon Fruit Syrup – New York (label), Clear, 10-1/4", smooth base, tooled top, American 1890-1910 . . . . **$75-100**

Wells, Miller & Provost – No. 217 Front St. – New York, Medium olive yellow, 8-3/8", 8-rounded panels, iron pontil, applied double collar mouth, extremely rare color, American 1845-1860 . . . . **$1,000-1,500**

W.M. & P / N.Y. (Wells, Miller and Provost Company) – Peppersauce Bottle, Medium blue green, 9", pontil-scarred base, wide sheared and tooled mouth, rare color, American 1840-1860 . . . . **$100-125**

Walla Walla – Pepsin Gum – Manufactured By Walla Walla Gum Co. – Knoxsville Tenn., Clear, 11", smooth base, ABM mouth with glass lid, American 1890-1910 . . . . **$250-275**

Webster's – High Grade – Coffee (coffee tin), Yellow can with red label, one pound, smooth base, original lid, American 1900-1930 . . . . **$400-450**

Heinz Catsup (label), clear, 9-3/4" / Heinz's Piquant Dressing (label), clear, 7", American 1900-1930, **$150-200/set.**

FRUIT JARS

Unlike food bottles, fruit jars were sold empty for use in home preservation of many different types of food. They were predominant in the 1800s when pre-packaged foods weren't available and home canning was the only option. Although fruit jars carry no advertising, they aren't necessarily common or plain, since the bottle manufacturer's name is usually embossed in large letters along with the patent date. The manufacturer whose advertising campaign gave fruit jars their name was Thomas W. Dyott, who was in the market early, selling fruit jars by 1829.

For the first fifty years, the most common closure was a cork sealed with wax. In 1855, an inverted saucer-like lid was invented that could be inserted into the jar to provide an airtight seal. The Hero Glassworks invented the glass lid in

1856 and improved on it in 1858 with a zinc lid invented by John Landis Mason, who also produced fruit jars. Because the medical profession warned that zinc could be harmful, Hero Glassworks developed a glass lid for the Mason jar in 1868. Mason eventually transferred his patent rights to the Consolidated Fruit Jar Company, which let the patent expire.

In 1880, the Ball brothers began distributing Mason jars, and in 1898, the use of a semi-automatic bottle machine increased the output of the Mason jar until the automatic machine was invented in 1903.

Fruit jars come in a wide variety of sizes and colors, but the most common is aqua and clear. The rarer jars were made in various shades of blue, amber, black, milk glass, green, and purple.

A.B.C., Aqua, quart, smooth base, ground lip, original glass lid embossed (Pat. April 15th, 1884), metal yoke marked "Pat. April 15th 1884," American 1884-1890 . . . . **$375-475**

A. P. Brayton & Co. / San Francisco / Cal, Teal blue, pint, smooth base, ground lip, extremely rare, American 1860-1870 . . . . **$1,500-2,000**

A. Stone & Co., Aqua, quart, smooth base, applied mouth with two internal lugs, original glass closure is embossed (A. Stone & Co. / Philada), American 1860-1875 . . . . **$800-1,000**

Baltimore / Glass Works, Aqua, quart, smooth base, applied wide mouth, American 1855-1860, Baltimore Glass Works, Baltimore, Maryland **$700-900**

BBGMco (monogram), Aqua, midget pint, smooth base, rough sheared and ground lip, embossed on original glass insert (Ball Brother Glass Mfg Co. / Buffalo), zinc screw band, American 1880-1890 . . . . **$600-900**

(Beaver chewing on a log) / Beaver, Light green, midget pint, smooth base, ground lip, Canadian 1890-1900 . . . . **$150-175**

Belle – Pat. Dec. 14th 1869, Aqua, quart, smooth base with three raised feet, ground lip, original domed glass lid with metal and wire enclosure, American 1869-1875 . . . . **$2,000-2,500**

Bennett's / No. 1 (over erased Adams & Co. Manufacturers Pittsburgh, PA), Aqua, quart, smooth base, applied mouth, embossed on original glass stopper (Bennett's Patent / Feb 6th 1866), American 1866-1870 . . . . **$600-800**

Air Tight Fruit Jar, deep blue aqua, quart barrel, iron pontil, rough-sheared mouth with applied groove ring wax seal, American 1850-1860, **$1,000-1,500.**

The / Automatic / Sealer, aqua, half-gallon, (Clayton Bottle / Works / Clayton, N.J.) on smooth base, ground lip, (Patd. Sept 15, 1885) on domed glass lid and wire closure, American 1885-1895, **$250-350.**

F. & J. Bodine / Philada, blue aqua, quart, smooth base, ground lip, American 1850-1865, **$200-250.**

A.P. Brayton & Co / San Francisco / Cal, teal blue, pint, smooth base, ground lip, American 1860-1870, (rare), **$1,500-2,000.**

Bloeser / Jar, Aqua, half-gallon, smooth base, ground lip, embossed lid (Pat Sept 27 1887), wire and metal clamp enclosure, American 1887-1900 .... **$350-450**

Buckeye / 4, Deep blue aqua, quart, smooth base, ground lip, glass lid embossed (Adam's Patd May 20, 1862), metal yoke, American 1862-1870 .... **$180-275**

C. Burnham & Co / Manufacturers / Philada, Aqua, quart, smooth base, ground lip, original iron lid, American 1859-1865 .... **$650-850**

Cadiz / Jar, Aqua, half-gallon, smooth base, ground lip, embossed glass lid (Cadiz Jar Pat. 1883), American 1883-1890 .... **$750-1,000**

C.F. Spencer's / Patd 1868 / Improved Jar, Blue aqua, quart, smooth base, ground lip, original tin lid, American 1868-1875 .... **$1,000-1,500**

C.F. Spencer's / Patent / Rochester / N.Y., Aqua, quart, smooth base, applied mouth, American 1863-1870 .... **$50-75**

C.F. Spencer's / Patent / Rochester / N.Y., Aqua, half-gallon, smooth base, applied mouth, American 1863-1870 ... **$50-75**

Clarke / Fruit Jar Co. / Cleveland, O, Aqua, quart, smooth base (52), ground lip, original glass lid, impressed (Pat. M'ch 17, 1885) metal cam lever closure, American 1885-1895 .... **$300-400**

Cohansey, Aqua, pint, smooth base, ground lip, embossed glass lid (Cohansey Glass Manuf. Co. Philada. Pat. July 16, 1872), wire enclosure, American 1872-1885 .... **$80-120**

Commodore, Aqua, bulbous quart, smooth base, applied mouth, rare, American 1865-1870. . . . . **$1,500-2,500**

Dexter / Improved (around circle of fruits), Aqua, half-gallon, smooth base, ground lip, embossed glass insert (Dexter Improved / Patented Aug 8, 1865) and zinc screw band, American 1865-1875 . . . . **$100-150**

Excelsior / Improved / 5", Aqua, quart, smooth base, ground lip, embossed glass lid (Patd Feby 12, 56, Nov 4, 62 Dec. 6, 64 June 9, 68, Sep. 8, 68) and screw band, American 1875-1885. . . . . **$60-90**

F. & J. Bodine / Philada, Blue aqua, quart, smooth base, ground lip, American 1850-1865 . . . . **$170-250**

Franklin / R.W. King / 90 Jefferson Ave. / Detroit Mich / Fruit Jar, Aqua, quart, smooth base, ground lip, embossed glass lid (Patd Aug. 8th, 1865), American 1865-1875. . . . **$2,000-2,500**

Fridley & Corman's / Patent / Oct. 25th 1859 / Ladies Choice, Blue aqua, quart, smooth base, ground lip, original impress "Fridley & Corman's Patented Oct. 25th 1850," cast iron rim, American 1859-1865 . . . . **$500-700**

GEM – HGW (monogram), Aqua, midget pint, smooth base (Pat Nov 26 76 / Pat Feb 4 73), ground lip, original embossed "HGW" monogram, dated glass insert, original zinc screw band, American 1875-1895 . . . . **$200-300**

Gilberds / (star) / Jar, Aqua, quart, smooth base, ground lip, clear glass lid embossed "Jas Gilberds / Patd / Jan 30 1883 / Jamestown, N.Y.," wire closure, American 1883-1890. . . . . **$200-300**

Eagle, blue aqua, quart, smooth base, applied mouth, American 1875-1885, **$1,000-1,500.**

F. & J. McKee / Pittsburg / PA, clear, half-gallon, pontil-scarred base, flared and finely ground lip, original glass lid with knob, American 1865-1875, **$400-500.**

Fridley & Cornman's / Patent / Oct. 25th, 1859 / Ladies Choice, aqua, quart, smooth base, ground lip, (Fridley & Cornman's Patent Oct. 25th, 1859) on iron rim, American 1859-1865, **$1,000-1,500.**

Gilbreds / (star) / Jar, blue aqua, quart, smooth base, ground lip, (JAS GILBREDS / PATD / JAN 30 1883 / Jamestown, N. Y.) on glass lid with wire closure, American 1883-1890, **$400-500.**

Gilberds / (star) / Jar, Aqua, half-gallon, smooth base, ground lip, original glass lid embossed "Gilberds Improved Jar Cap Jamestown, N.Y. / 3 / Pat / July 31 83," wire closure, American 1883-1890 . . . . **$275-375**

Globe, Yellow with amber tone, half-gallon, smooth base (14), ground lip, original amber glass lid embossed (Patented May 25th 1886), metal closure, American 1886-1890 . . . . **$170-220**

Granger, Aqua, pint, smooth base, ground lip, very rare, American 1875-1890 . . . . **$400-600**

Griffin's Patent Oct. 7 1862 (on lid), Aqua, quart, smooth base, ground lip, embossed glass lid, iron cage clamp, American 1862-1870 . . . . **$100-150**

Hamilton Glass / Works / 1 Quart, Aqua, quart, smooth base, applied mouth, glass lid (Hamilton / Glass Works), American 1875-1885 . . . . **$300-400**

Hoosier Jar, Aqua, quart, smooth base, ground lip, embossed (PATD Sept 12th, 1882, Jan 3D 1883 / Hoosier Jar) on screw-on lid, American 1882-1885 . . . . **$600-800**

Imperial / Trade Mark (hand holding mace), Aqua, quart, smooth base, ground lip, original clear glass lid embossed (Thomas Patent / July 12 1892), metal three-piece clamp closure, Canadian 1892-1900 . . . . **$500-600**

J. D. Willoughby Patented January 4 1850 (on stopper), Aqua, quart, reddish iron pontil, applied mouth, American 1859-1865 . . . . **$300-400**

Mrs. G.E. Haller Patd. FEB. 25. 73 (on stopper), aqua, half-gallon, smooth base, applied mouth, American 1873-1880, **$150-250.**

Improved Standard / Patented / April 17th / 1888, aqua, pint, smooth base, ground lip, American 1888-1895, (rare), **$500-700.**

John M. Moore & Co. / Manufacturers / Fislerville N.J. / Patented Dec. 3rd 1861, Blue aqua, quart, smooth base, applied mouth, embossed glass lid (Patented / Dec. 3D 1861), original rounded iron yoke, American 1861-1875 . . . . **$300-450**

Joshua Wright / Philada, Blue aqua, 10-3/8", half-gallon, barrel form, smooth base, applied mouth, American 1855-1870 . . . . **$700-1,000**

Knowlton Vacuum / (star) / Fruit Jar, Aqua, pint, smooth base, smooth lip, original glass insert, "Knowlton Vacuum Full Glass Top Patented" zinc screw-on lid, American 1903-1905 **$50-75**

Lyon & Bossard's Jar / East Stroudsburg / PA., Aqua, pint, smooth base, ground lip, embossed (Pat. April 15th 1884) glass lid, embossed (Pat Apr 15 84) metal yoke and tightening clamp, rare, American 1884-1890. . . . . **$350-450**

Ludlow's Patent / June 28-1859 / August 6-1861 (on glass lid), Aqua, quart, smooth base, ground lip, glass lid and cast iron cage clamp, American 1861-1870 . . . . **$75-100**

Made In Canada / Perfect / Seal (inside a shield) / Wide Mouth / Adjustable, Medium olive green, pint, smooth base, ABM lip, original glass lid and wire closure, word "Tight" is between the two neck bands, Canadian 1905-1925 . . . . **$75-100**

Mansfield, Pale green aqua, pint, smooth base (Mansfield / Knowlton May 03 / Pat / Glass W'K'S'), original embossed clear glass insert and Impressed screw-on lid American 1903-1908 . . . . **$150-200**

Mason's / Patent / Nov. 30th / 1858 – N.C.L., Blue aqua, midget pint, smooth base (2N), sheared and ground lip, original zinc screw-on lid, scarce, American 1875-1890 . . . . **$150-200**

Mason's / Patent / Nov. 30th / 1858, Medium amber, quart, smooth base (Pat Nov 26 67), ground lip, zinc lid, American 1860-1895 . . . . **$200-250**

Mason's / CJF CO (monogram) / Patent / Nov 30th / 1858, Medium yellow olive, quart, smooth base (FX605), ground lip, zinc screw lid, American 1880-1895 . . . . **$100-150**

Mason's CFJ CO (monogram) patent / Nov 30th / 1858, Medium golden yellow amber, quart, smooth base (79), ground lip, American 1870-1885 . . . . **$400-700**

Mason's / (cross) / Patent / Nov. 30th / 1858, Straw yellow, quart, smooth base (Pat Nov 26 67), ground lip, zinc screw lid, American 1880-1895 . . . . **$200-250**

Moore's / Patent / Dec 3D 1861, Aqua, pint, smooth base, applied mouth, original glass lid, American 1861-1870 . . . . **$200-300**

(Motif of star encircled by fruit), Aqua, quart, smooth base, ground lip, American 1875-1885 . . . . **$250-350**

Mrs. G. E. Haller / Pat'd Feb 25 75 (on stopper), Aqua, quart, smooth base, applied mouth, original clear glass hollow blown stopper, American 1873-1880 . . . . **$100-150**

NE Plus Ultra Air-Tight Fruit Jar / Made By Bodine & Bros' WMS' Town, N.J. / For Their Patent Glass Lid, Blue aqua, 1-1/2 quart size, smooth base, applied mouth, American 1858-1865 . . . . **$600-800**

Manufactured / For / N.O. Fansler / Cleveland / Ohio, aqua, quart, smooth base, applied, (A. Kline / Pat'd / Oct 27 1863 / Use Pin) on original glass stopper, American 1870-1880, **$250-300.**

National / (shield) / Preserve Can – Earle's Patent / (anchor) / Feb 2nd 1864, blue aqua, quart, smooth base, ground lip, American 1864-1870, **$2,500-3,000.**

New / Paragon / 5", Aqua, quart, smooth base, ground lip, embossed (The New Paragon Patented) glass insert and zinc screw band, American 1870-1880 . . . . **$300-400**

Patent / Sept 18, 1860, Blue aqua, quart, smooth base, handpressed wax seal ring, ground lip, American 1860-1870 . . . . **$100-150**

Peerless, Aqua, quart, smooth base, applied mouth, embossed glass lid (Patented Feb 13, 1863), iron yoke clamp, American 1863-1870 . . . . **$200-300**

Pet, Aqua, quart, smooth base, applied mouth, embossed (Patented Aug 31 1869, T. G. Otterson) glass lid and brass wire clamp, American 1869-1875 . . . . **$100-150**

Petal Jar, Deep olive green, half-gallon, red iron pontil, 10-shoulder flutes, thick applied mouth, American 1850-1860. . . . . **$2,000-2,500**

Porcelain / Lined, Aqua, midget pint, smooth base (Pat. Nov. 26 67 / Pat Feb 4 73 / B) ground lip, zinc screw-on lid embossed (Pat'd Sept 3D, Dec. 31 1872), American 1880-1890 . . . . **$150-200**

Protector, Blue aqua, half-gallon, smooth base, ground lip, American 1867-1880 . . . . **$75-100**

Put On Rubber Before Filling / Star & Crescent (motif of moon and star) Self Sealing Jar, Aqua, pint, smooth base (Patented / Dec'r 10th 1896), ground lip, original zinc lid with milk glass insert, American 1896-1900 . . . . **$400-500**

Queensland / (letter "Q" inside a pineapple) / Fruit Jar, Green aqua, quart, smooth base, ground lip, Australian 1890-1900 . . . . **$200-300**

Pansy, medium yellow amber, quart, smooth base, ground lip, Canadian
1880-1890, **$700-1,000.**

S.B. Dewey Jr. / No. 65 / Buffalo St. / Rochester / N.Y., Blue aqua, quart, smooth base, applied mouth, metal stopper (J.D. Willoughby, Patd Apr 4, 1859), American 1860-1870 . . . . **$1,500-1,800**

Spratt's Patent / July 18 1854 / Pat'd April 5 1864 (on lid), Soldered in tin can, original threaded clear glass lid, American 1864-1870 . . . . **$150-200**

Star & Crescent / (motif of moon and star) / Pat. Mar. 11th / 1890, Aqua, quart, smooth base, ground lip, original unmarked flat glass insert and zinc screw band with wire handle, American 1890-1895 . . . . **$400-500**

Sun (inside a radiating sun) / Trade Mark, Aqua, pint, smooth base (J.P. Barstow / 7"), ground lip, embossed glass lid (Monier's Pat- Aprl 90, Mar 12, 95), American 1890-1900 . . . . **$100-150**

The / Alston – Bail Here, Clear glass, quart, smooth base (Pat'd April 1900 Dec 1901), ABM lip, original tin lid, American 1900-1905 . . . . **$500-600**

The / Automatic / Sealer, Aqua, half-gallon, smooth base (Clayton Bottle / Works / Clayton, N.J.), ground lip, original domed glass lid (Patd Sept 15, 1885), wire closure, American 1885-1895 . . . . **$250-450**

The / Best, Clear glass, quart, smooth base (4), ground lip, embossed glass (Patented / August 18th 1868 / The / Best) screw-on closure, American 1868-1875 . . . . **$1,400-1,600**

The / CFJCO (monogram) / Queen, Aqua, midget pint, smooth base, ground lip, American 1870-1880 . . . . **$80-120**

The / Champion / Pat. Aug. 31. 1869, Aqua, quart, smooth base, ground lip, original glass lid and metal yoke clsosure, American 1869-1875 .... **$250-300**

The Chief – K, Aqua, quart, smooth base (Pat. Nov 29 / 1870), ground lip, very rare, American 1870-1880 .... **$375-450**

The Daisy / Jar, Clear glass, half-gallon, smooth base, ground lip, original embossed (Pat Jan 3D 88), glass lid and metal closure, American 1888-1895 .... **$375-475**

The / Doolittle / Self Sealer, Aqua, pint, smooth base (GJCO), ABM lip, embossed glass lid (Patented / January / 1900) with wire and ear enclosure, American 1905-1910 ..... **$200-300**

The / Empire, Aqua, quart, smooth base (Pat. Feb. 13 1866), ground lip, original glass lid, metal clamp, and lever closure, American 1866-1875 .... **$350-450**

The / Leader, Light yellow amber, half-gallon, smooth base (3), ground lip, original glass lid (Patd June 28, 1892), American 1892-1895 .... **$100-150**

The / Leader, Golden yellow amber, half-gallon, smooth base (13), ground lip, original glass lid (Patd June 28, 1892), American 1892-1895 .... **$200-250**

The / Lincoln / Jar, Blue aqua, smooth base, ground lip, very rare, American 1870-1880 .... **$450-600**

The Magic / (star) / Fruit Jar, Aqua, pint, smooth base (?), embossed (Clamp Pat. March 30th 1886) glass lid and metal closure, American 1886-1895 .... **$500-800**

The Model Jar / Patd / Aug. 1867, Aqua, quart, smooth base, ground lip, American 1867-1875 .... **$100-150**

The / Puritan – LSCO (monogram), Aqua, quart, smooth base, ground lip, American 1870-1880 .... **$150-200**

The / Schaffer / Jar / Rochester / N.Y. – JCS (monogram), Aqua, quart, smooth base, ground lip, American 1870-1880 .... **$200-250**

The / Scranton / Jar, Medium yellow green, quart, smooth base (G.H.C. / 2) ground lip, aqua glass lid and spring wire with wooden roller closure, rare, American 1870-1880 .... **$1,500-2,000**

The / Scranton / Jar, Pale aqua, quart, smooth base, applied mouth, glass stopper (A. Kline / Patd Oct 27, 1863, Use Pin), extremely rare, American 1875-1890 .... **$1,800-2,000**

The Valve Jar Co. / Philadelphia, Aqua, quart, smooth base (Pat'd Mar 10 / 1868), ground lip, American 1868-1875 ... **$400-500**

The / Val Vliet / Jar of 1881, Aqua, pint, smooth base, ground lid, original embossed glass lid (Pat May 3D, 1881), iron yoke and wire closure, rare, American 1881-1885 ...... **$2,500-3,500**

Trade Mark / Lightning – HWP (monogram), Aqua, quart, smooth base (Putnam / 2), ground lip, original glass lid with wire closure (Lightning / Patd Apr 25, 92), American 1892-1900 .... **$350-450**

Trade Mark / Lightning, Yellow olive, quart, smooth base (Putnam / 227), ground lip, dated glass lid and lightning-style closure, American 1880-1895 .... **$200-250**

Trade Mark / Lightning, Medium yellow amber, pint, smooth base (Putnam / 109), ground lip, dated glass lid and lightning-style closure, American 1880-1895 .... **$75-120**

Trade Mark / Lightning – Salesman's Sample Fruit Jar, Aqua, 5-1/8", smooth base (Putnam / 359), ground lip, original unmarked glass lid and lightning-style closure, American 1875-1895 .... **$150-250**

Trade Mark / The Dandy, Medium amber, half-gallon, smooth base (Gilberds), ground lip, original glass lid (Pat. Oct. 13th 1885), wire closure, American 1885-1895 .... **$250-350**

Whitemore's / Patent / Rochester / NY, Aqua, quart, smooth base, ground lip, embossed (Patented Jany 14th, 68) double fin lid, original wire bail, American 1868-1875 .... **$200-275**

Winslow Jar, Aqua, half-gallon, smooth base, ground lip, original embossed (Patented Nov. 29th, 1870 / Patented Feb. 25th, 1873) glass lid and iron clamp, American 1870-1880 ..... **$80-140**

WM. L. Haller / Carlisle / PA, Aqua, quart, smooth base, sheared and tooled lip, original stopper (J.D. Willoughby Patented Jan 4 1859), American 1860-1870 .... **$1,000-1,300**

GINGER BEER BOTTLES

The origins of ginger beer can be traced back to England in the mid-1700s. But there was actually an earlier type of ginger beer produced by Mead & Metheglin in the early 1600s in colonial America. Metheglin was more of a natural carbonated, yeast-fermented beverage, often including ginger, cloves, and mace, which proved to be a popular drink in the colonies. The difference was that while ginger beer included the yeast for fermentation, it was also sweetened with honey, cane sugar, or molasses. Additional ingredients included whole Jamaica ginger root and fresh lemons. After brewing, the ginger beer was stored in stoneware bottles and corked to maintain a natural effervescence. When the carbonation process was introduced in 1899, an essence of extract was used to achieve the right taste. But the old English brewmasters observed that naturally fermented ginger beer still produced the best flavor. Until the mid-1800s, a number of ginger beers contained high alcohol content, some with as much as 11 percent.

Ginger beer was eventually introduced to the United States and Canada around 1790, with England shipping large amounts to both countries during the 1800s. England was able to continue this huge export, since its stoneware bottles were of a better quality because of a process developed in 1835 called "Improved Bristol Glaze." After brewing, the bottles were corked and wired to maintain pressure, which kept the alcohol and carbon dioxide in solution, improving preservation and extending shelf life.

The early stoneware bottle was used extensively from 1790 until 1880 to 1890 when industrialization and new manufacturing techniques introduced a new gray stoneware bottle. These new bottles were used from approximately 1885 to 1920 and were stamped with various logos and designs to attract the interest of the buyer.

In the United States, the popularity of ginger beer quickly declined after 1920, when Prohibition was signed into law and never recovered after the repeal of Prohibition in 1933. In England and Canada, the peak occurred around 1935. At one point, there were 300 ginger beer breweries in the United States, 1,000 in Canada, and 3,000 in England. While the breweries have disappeared, today's collector can still enjoy finding many varieties of bottles in green, red, blue, tan, and purple, and displaying unique slogans and logos.

While this chapter presents a good cross section of Canadian ginger beer bottles, I recommend that collectors obtain the following two books authored by Scott Wallace and Phil Culhane, a specialist in the field of Canadian glass and stoneware ginger beers: *Transfer Printed Ginger Beers of Canada* and *Primitive Stoneware Bottles of Canada*. Phil also conducts a number of auctions throughout the year and can be contacted at phil.culhane@rogers.com.

His Web site address is www.cbandsc.com.

ALBERTA

Edmonton Bottling Works Co. Limited – Finest Old Fashion Brewed Scotch – Ginger Beer, Tan top, pint **$350**

McLaughlin's – Ginger Shandy – Made From Pure – Jamaica Ginger Root, Ivory, quart **$120**

Old English – Stone Ginger Beer – Phillips Bros., Medium brown top, pint **$90**

BRITISH COLUMBIA

Country Club – Stone Ginger Beer – Beverage Company – Vancouver, B.C., Tan top, pint **$40**

Chris Morley's – Ginger Beer – Victoria, B.C., Tan top, pint . . **$500**

Crystal Spring Water Supply – Ginger Beer – Victoria, B.C., Tan top, pint **$275**

Fairall Bros. – Victoria West, Tan top, pint **$850**

Kirk & Co. Ltd. – Genuine – Old English – Ginger Beer – Victoria West, Tan top, pint **$90**

Nelson Soda – Stone Ginger Beer – Factory, Tan top, large pint, scarce **$425**

Plain ginger bottle / Chapman Bros. Limited, Rye / Nash & McAllister, Stone, Ginger Beer, Sydney, C.B / Townsend's Extra Quality 1335, Salford / Plain ginger bottle, English & Canadian, **$20-30.**

Old English – Brewed English Beer – Brewed & Bottled By – Union Wholesalers – Victoria, B.C. – Contents 12 oz., Tan top, pint . . **$375**

Regal – Mineral Water Co. – Victoria, B.C., Tan top, pint . . **$45**

MANITOBA

Brandon Brewing Company – Brandon, Tan top, quart . . **$210**

Douglas & King Limited – Kings Old Country – Stone Ginger Beer – Winnipeg, Dark brown top, pint **$45**

Empress Waters – The Empire Brewing Co., Tan top, quart . . **$100**

The Golden Key – Brand – Ginger Beer – E.L. Drewery – Winnipeg, Tan top, quart. **$85**

John's English Brew, Ginger Beer, Jacksonville, Florida / S.H. McKee & Sons, Stone Ginger Beer 1897, 121 King St. Fredericton. N.B. / The N.S.W. Aerated Water & Co. / Excelsior Bottling Estab, Old English Ginger Beer, Calais & St Stephen / Lion Brewing Company Ltd, LB, North Adelaide – U.S. / Canadian / English Ginger Beers, **$30-40 for all.**

NEWFOUNDLAND

Gaden's Aerated Water Works – J.R. Bennett Proprietor – St. John's, N.F. – Stone Ginger Beer, Light tan, pint......**$1,400**

ONTARIO

C. H. Norton – Berlin, Tan top, tall pint, scarce **$650**

Charles Wilson – Ginger Beer – Toronto, Ivory, pint **$325**

Clark Bros. – Toronto, Ivory, pint...................... **$70**

Crescent Bottling Works – Stone Ginger Beer – Niagara Falls, Tan top, small pint **$100**

F.A. Meyer – Seaforth, Dark gray, large quart............ **$80**

G. Kickley (Guelph) – Brewed Ginger Beer, Tan top, pint...**$100**

J. Tune & Son – London, Ont., Tan top, pint **$210**

James Thompson – Ginger Beer – Kingston, Tan top, blue writing, pint..................................... **$70**

London Ginger – Beer Co. – Stone Ginger Beer, Ivory, quart................................... **$150**

Ross Bros – R & B – London – Ont., Dark metallic brown top, large pint.................................**$1,050**

Salisbury – Ginger Beer Of – Toronto – Stone Ginger – Old Country Home Brewed, Tan top, tall pint **$50**

T.H. Hutchinson – St. Thomas, Ont., Tan top, pint **$650**

NEW BRUNSWICK

Dolan Bros. – Stone Ginger Beer – 1896 – 348 Brussels St. – St. John, Cobalt blue top, tall pint, internal threads, correct stopper **$950**

Dolan Bros. – Stone Ginger Beer – 1898 – 348 Brussels St. – St. John, Cobalt blue top, tall quart, internal threads, correct stopper **$185**

Dolan Bros. – Stone Ginger Beer – 1900 – 348 Brussels St. – St. John, Cobalt blue top, tall quart, internal threads, correct stopper **$220**

Dolan Bros. – Stone Ginger Beer – 1913 – 348 Brussels St. – St. John, Cobalt blue top, tall quart, internal threads, correct stopper **$125**

Harlands – Stone – Ginger Beer – 1927 – G.D. Gibbs, Sole Agent – Fredericton, Ivory, pint **$425**

Old – Homestead – International Drug Company – St. Stephen and Calais, Maine – Ginger Beer, Ivory, small quart . . . **$230**

S. H. McKee & Sons – Stone Ginger Beer – 1894 – 121 Kings St. – Fredericton, Ivory, pint . . . . , , , **$75**

S. H. McKee & Sons – Stone Ginger Beer – 1899 – 121 Kings St. – Fredericton, Ivory, pint **$110**

T.A. Hooley – Fairville, Dark brown top, quart **$425**

Terris – Ginger Beer – Saint John, Cobalt blue top, pint, original contents, original stopper **$85**

John Milne Brewed, Ginger Beer, Established 1848, Stonehaven / Sussex Mineral Springs, Sussex New Brunswick / Gurd's Stone Ginger Beer, The Perfect Drink, A Product of Canada, Canadian Ginger Bottles, $40-50 for all

NOVA SCOTIA

Bates – English Ginger Beer – Truro, N.S., Tan top, pint. **$275**

C.B. Mineral – Water Works – Thomas O'Neill – Proprietor – Bridgeport C.B., Tan top, pint **$1,100**

Felix J. Quinn – Ginger Beer Manuf'r – Halifax, Tan top, pint. **$55**

John Dixon – Old Time Ginger Beer – Halifax, Ivory, pint. **$220**

Imperial – Mineral – Water Works – Ginger Beer – Wilson & Sullivan – Halifax, Tan top, pint. **$110**

J. B. Baker – Halifax, Brown glaze over gray, large quart, large donut ring on lip **$600**

Nash & McAllister – Stone Ginger Beer – Sydney C.B., Tan top, quart **$350**

Patrick McAllister – Celebrated Brewed Ginger Beer – PMCA – Sydney, Cobalt blue top, pint **$1,500**

Sydney Mines Bottling Works – A.R. MacDougall, Sydney Mines N.S. – Superior Fermented – Ginger Beer, Ivory, pint. **$900**

W.H. Donovan – Halifax, Ivory, pint, original stopper **$30**

Felix J. Quinn, Ginger Beer Manuf'r, Halifax, N.S, Pollack Bros. of Montreal / G. & C. Moore, Springfield Bottling Stores, Glasgow, Stone Ginger Beer / King's Country Limited, King's Old Country Stone Ginger Beer, Winnipeg, Manitoba / Ye Old Country Stone Ginger Beer, Felix distributors Ltd, Vancouver, B.C., 10 oz, Canadian, **$60-80 for all.**

PRINCE EDWARD ISLAND

Simmons – Charlottetown, Medium tan, pint **$70**

QUEBEC

Allan's – Ginger Beer – Montreal, Ivory, pint **$40**

C. Robillard & Cie – Ginger Beer – Montreal, Tan top, pint **$80**

Elz. – Fortier & Cie – Best Ginger Beer – Quebec, Tan top, pint **$30**

Gurds – Ginger Beer – The Perfect Drink – A Product of Canada, Lime green top, pint, one of only two known lime green top ginger beers........................ **$1,700**

Gurds – Stone Ginger Beer – The Perfect Brew, Blue green top, pint. **$130**

J. Christian & Cie Limitee – Ginger Beer, Medium brown top, pint. **$275**

M. Timmons & Sons – Ginger Beer, Ivory, pint **$425**

P.A. Milloy – Ginger Beer – Montreal, Ivory, pint **$160**

Seth C. Nutter – Sherbrooke – PQ., Tan top, pint **$165**

SASKATCHEWAN

Old English Brew – Crystal Spring Bottling Co. – Moose Jaw, Canada, Tan top, pint **$550**

Regina Aerated – Water Company – Regina, Sask, Tan top, quart **$1,600**

Moerlein's Old Jug - Lager, The Christian Moerlein Brewing Co, Cincinnati, O, two-tone tan glaze, 10-1/2" and 8-1/2", American 1880-1900, **$40-50 for both.**

Reserve Mineral Water Works, McKinlay & Ogilve, Glacier Bay, C.B. / Pink's "None Nicer" Brand Ginger Beer, Guaranteed Brewed, Chichester, English Ginger bottle / Medical, Dublin Stout, Dowson Bros., Gateshead, **$35-40 for all.**

HUTCHINSON BOTTLES

Charles A. Hutchinson developed the Hutchinson bottle in the late 1870s. Interestingly, the stopper, not the bottle itself, differentiated the design from others. The Hutchinson stopper, patented in 1879, was an improvement over cork stoppers, which eventually shrank and allowed air to seep into the bottle.

The new stopper consisted of a rubber disk held between two metal plates attached to a spring stem. The stem was shaped like a figure eight, with the upper loop larger than the lower to prevent the stem from falling into the bottle. The lower loop could pass through the bottle's neck and push down the disk to permit the filling or pouring of it contents. A refilled bottle was sealed by pulling the disc up to the bottle's shoulder, where it

formed a tight seal. When opened, the spring made a popping sound. Thus, the Hutchinson bottle had the honor of originating the phrase "pop bottle" which is how soda came to be known as "pop."

Hutchinson stopped producing bottles in 1912, when warnings about metal poisoning were issued. As collectibles, Hutchinson bottles rank high on the scale of curiosity and value, but pricing varies quite sharply by geographical location, compared to the relatively stable prices of most other bottles.

Hutchinson bottles carry abbreviations of which the following three are the most common.

TBNTBS - This bottle not to be sold

TBMBR - This bottle must be returned

TBINS - This bottle is not sold

A. Harsch – Albuquerque – NM, Aqua, 7", smooth base, tooled blob top, American 1885-1895 . . . . **$500-600**

Albuquerque – Bottling Works – Albuquerque NM, Aqua, 7-1/4", smooth base (CGW), applied blob top, (Backward "S" and "N"), American 1880-1900 . . . . **$600-700**

Biloxi Artesian – Bottling Works – E. Barq Prop., Aqua, 7", smooth base, tooled blob top, American 1885-1895 . . **$95-125**

Brunswick Coca-Cola – Bottling Co. – Brunswick, CA, Clear, 7", smooth base, tooled blob top, American 1885-1900 . . **$1,300-1,500**

C.Andrae / Port Huron / Mich – C. % Co. 2, Medium cobalt blue, 6-5/8", smooth base, applied blob mouth, American 885-1900 . . . . **$120-170**

Central / Bottling Works / Detroit, Mich – This Bottle Is Never Sold / C. Co. Llim No 5, Medium cobalt blue, 7", smooth base (J.J.G.), tooled blob mouth, American 1885-1900 . . . **$75-100**

C.W. Rider / Watertown / N.Y., Deep teal blue, 6-3/4", smooth base, applied blob mouth, rare, American 1890-1900 color . . . **$800-1,000**

Chr Wiegand – Las Vegas – N.M., Medium amethyst, 7", smooth mug base, tooled blob top, American 1880-1895 . . . **$500-600**

Chris Fisher – Central City, Col. – This Bottle To Be Returned to Chris Fischer, Aqua, 6", smooth base, tooled blob top, American 1885-1900 . . . . **$300-400**

Claussen Bottling Works / Charleston / S.C., Medium yellow with amber tone, 6-5/8", smooth base, tooled blob mouth, extremely rare, American 1885-1900 . . . . **$1,800-2,500**

Crystal Spring – Bottling Co. – Barnet, VT (front) – (back) Label reads: Bottled by Crystal Spring Bottling Co, Crab=Apple, Barnet, VT., Clear, 7", smooth base, tooled blob top, American 1890-1910 .... **$200-350**

Birmingham – Coca Cola – Bottling Co., Clear, 7", smooth base, tooled blob top, American 1885-1900 .... **$1,800-2,200**

E. A. Jennings / Hudson / N.Y., Cobalt blue, 6-1/2", smooth base, tooled blob mouth, extremely rare, American 1880-1900...... **$500-1,000**

Elko Bottling – Works – Elko Nev., Aqua, 7-1/2", smooth base, tooled blob top, American 1899-1902 .... **$400-500**

E. Ottenville / Nashville / Tenn – MCC, Medium cobalt blue, 6-5/8", smooth base (25), tooled blob mouth, American 1885-1900 .... **$150-200**

Escambia – Pepsi Cola – Bottling Co. – Pensacola Fla., Aqua, 7", smooth base, tooled blob top, extremely rare, American 1885-1900................................. **$700-900**

G. Layer – Raton – NM, Clear, 7", smooth mug base, tooled blob top, very rare, American 1880-1895 .... **$750-850**

G. Norris & Co. / City / Bottling Works / Detroit, Mich – C & CO LIM, Medium cobalt blue, 6-3/4", smooth base, applied blob mouth, American 1885-1900.................... **$75-125**

Gallup – Bottling Works – Gallup N.M., Aqua, 7", smooth base, tooled blob top, American 1880-1895............ **$450-550**

Geo. Disbro / & Co. / Chicago, Cobalt blue, 7-5/8", smooth base (D), 10-panels on side at base, applied blob mouth, American 1885-1900 .... **$250-350**

Geo. Schmuck's – Ginger Ale – Cleveland, O. – C. & Co. Lim, Yellow amber, 7-3/4", 12-sided, smooth base, tooled blob mouth, American 1885-1900 . . . . **$200-300**

Geo. Schmuck's – Ginger Ale – Cleveland, O., Medium orange amber, 8", 12-sided, smooth base, tooled blob mouth, American 1885-1900 . . . . **$250-350**

Guyette & Company / Registered / Detroit, Mich. – This Bottle Is Never Sold / C. & Co. Lim No. 5, Medium cobalt blue, 6-7/8", smooth base (G), tooled blob mouth, American 1885-1900 . . . . **$95-120**

Hayes Bros / Trade Mark / NB / Registered / Chicago, ILL – MCC, Cobalt blue, 7-3/8", 10-panels on side at base, smooth base, applied blob mouth, American 1885-1900 . . . . **$80-150**

Hendrickson – Bros. – Diamondville – Wyo., Aqua, 7", smooth base, tooled blob top, American 1885-1900 . . . . **$500-600**

Henry Busch – Minnemucca – Nev., (Winnemucca is misspelled Minnemucca. There are no authentic sodas with the correct spelling), Aqua, 7", smooth base, applied blob top, American 1885-1922 . . . . **$650-750**

H.L. Wigert / Burlington / Iowa – This Bottle / To Be Returned, Medium cobalt blue, 6-3/4", smooth base, applied blob mouth, rare color, American 1885-1900 . . . . **$150-200**

Jacob Schmidt / Pottsville, PA, Medium olive green, 6-3/4", smooth base, tooled blob mouth, very rare, American 1890-1900 . . . . **$450-550**

James Dewar – Elko, Nev, Aqua, 7", smooth base, tooled blob top, American 1892-1895 . . . . **$550-650**

James Dewar – Elko, Nev, aqua, 7", smooth base, tooled blob top, American 1892-1895, **$550-650.**

Wagoner – Bottling Works – Wagoner, I.T. (Indian Territory Hutch), aqua, 7", smooth mug base, tooled blob top, American 1880-1890, **$75-100.**

James Dewar – Elko – Nevada, Aqua, 7", smooth base, tooled blob top, American 1892-1895 .... **$1,800-2,000**

James Ray / Savannah / Geo – Ginger Ale, Deep cobalt blue, 7-3/4", smooth base, tooled blob mouth, American 1885-1900... **$300-450**

Jamestown Brewing – Bottling Works N.Y. – Jamestown, Deep aqua, 7", smooth mug base, tooled blob top, American 1885-1900 .... **$75-100**

John Olbert & Co. – Durango – Colo., Medium amethyst, 6", smooth base, tooled blob top, American 1880-1900... **$350-450**

J.F. Deegan / Pottsville / PA – This Bottle / Not To / Be Sold, Deep red amber, 7", mug base, smooth base (Karl Hutter / C / New York), tooled blob mouth, rare, American 1885-1900 .... **$550-650**

J.G. Bolton / Lemont / ILLS – A. & D.H.C., Medium cobalt blue, 6-3/4", smooth base, applied blob mouth, American 1885-1900................................. **$250-375**

J. Weilerbacher – Pittsburgh, PA. – Trade (W inside a sunburst) / Mark / Registered / C.C.C. 149, Yellow amber, 7 5/8", four front panels with a rounded back, smooth base, tooled blob mouth, American 1885-1900................... **$200-300**

Lascheid – Pittsburgh / PA – L (inside a wreath) / Registered / St. Clair / Carbonating / Est., Amber, 8", four front panels and round back, smooth base (ST), tooled blob mouth, American 1885-1900................................. **$100-140**

Lohrborg Bros's / Bed Bud / ILL., Light to medium green, 6-3/4", smooth base, tooled blob mouth, American 1885-1900 .... **$300-400**

Mayfield's – Celery Cola – J.C. Mayfield MFG Co. – Birmingham, **ALA**, Aqua, 7", smooth base, tooled blob top, American 1885-1895 .... **$100-200**

Mill's – Seltzer – Springs, Aqua, 6", smooth base (M), tooled blob top, American 1874-1875 .... **$100-150**

Moxie, Medium green, 7", smooth base, tooled blob top, American 1885-1900.................................... **$150-250**

Norwich Bottling / Works / Norwich / N.Y., Amber, 6-3/8", smooth base, tooled blob mouth, American 1885-1900...... **$225-275**

Mel. Aro (around shoulder) / Eclipse Carbonating Company (inside a horseshoe) / Ecco (monogram) / St. Louis – 2 1/2 Cents Deposit / Required For Return / Of This Bottle, Deep amber, 6-1/2", smooth base (ECCO), tooled blob mouth, American 1885-1900 .... **$100-150**

Moriarty & Carrol / Registered / Waterbury, Conn, Deep amber, 7-3/8", 10-panels on side of base, smooth base, tooled blob mouth, American 1885-1900................... **$350-450**

National – Dope Co. – Birmingham Ala., Aqua, 8", smooth base, tooled blob top, American 1885-1900............ **$150-200**

Pike's Peak – M.W. Co. – Colo. City Colo., Aqua, 7", smooth base, applied blob top, American 1880-1895........... **$300-400**

P.J. Serwazi / Manayunk / PA, Medium olive green, 7-5/8", smooth base (S), tooled blob mouth, original loop with closure, rare, American 1890-1900..................... **$750-950**

Poudre Valley – Fort Collins Colo. – Bottling Works, Clear with amethyst, 7", smooth mug base, tooled blob top, American 1885-1900 . . . . **$550-650**

Registered / C. Norris & Co. / City / Bottling Works / Detroit, Mich. – C &CO. LIM, Medium cobalt blue, 6-3/4", smooth base (CN & CO), tooled blob mouth, American 1885-1900 **$75-100**

Standard / Bottling Works / Minneapolis / Minn. – 8 5 ABC, Deep amber, 6-3/4", smooth base (HR), applied blob mouth, American 1885-1900 . . . . **$100-150**

Standard Bottling – Silverton Colo. – Peter. Orello. Prop (on front) – Paper label on back reads: Birch Beer (large S in circle) – Colored and Flavored – Bottled By Standard Bottling Works – Silverton, Colo, Clear, 7-1/4", smooth base, tooled blob top, American 1885-1900 . . . . **$325-425**

The Boley MFG. Co. / Bottles / & / Demijohns / 414 West 14th St. / N.Y. / Registered, Light to medium yellow-green, 6-7/8", smooth base, tooled blob mouth, American 1885-1900 . . . . **$450-550**

The City / Bottling / Works / Louisville – Seltzer Water, Cobalt blue, 6-5/8", smooth base (MK), applied blob mouth, American 1885-1900 rare color **$800-1200**

The Pioneer Bottling Wks – Victor Colo., Medium amethyst, 7", smooth base, tooled blob top, American 1885-1900. **$200-250**

The Standard Bottling Cripple Creek – Colo., Aqua, 6", smooth base, tooled blob top, American 1880-1895 . . . . **$50-75**

Tonopah – Soda Works – Nev., Aqua, 7", smooth base, tooled blob top, American 1902-1905 .... **$550-650**

Trade Mark / Jal (inside a diamond) / Registered / J.A. Lomax / 14 16 & 18 / Charles Place / Chicago – This Bottle / Must Be Returned, Deep cobalt blue, 6-3/4", smooth base (J.L.), applied blob mouth, American 1885-1900. .... **$75-100**

Union Bottling – Works – Victor Colo., Aqua, 7", smooth base, tooled blob top, American 1885-1900 .... **$100-150**

Wagoner – Bottling Works – Wagoner, I. T. (Indian Territory Hutch), Aqua, 7", smooth mug base, tooled blob top, American 1880-1890 .... **$50-75**

Wiseola – Bottling Co – Birmingham Ala., Clear, 7", smooth base (star embossed on base), tooled blob top, American 1880-1900 .... **$75-100**

INK BOTTLES

Ink bottles are unique because of their centuries-old history, which provides collectors today with a wider variety of designs and shapes than any other group of bottles. People often ask why a product as cheap to produce as ink was sold in such decorative bottles. While other bottles were disposed of or returned after use, ink bottles were usually displayed openly on desks in dens, libraries, and studies. It's safe to assume that even into the late 1880s people who bought ink bottles considered the design of the bottle as well as the quality of its contents.

Prior to the 18th century, most ink was sold in brass or copper containers. The very rich would then refill their gold and silver inkwells from these storage containers. Ink that was sold in glass and pottery bottles in England in the 1700s had no brand name identification, and,

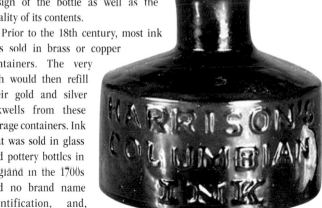

at best, would have a label identifying the ink and/or the manufacturer.

In 1792, the first patent for the commercial production of ink was issued in England, 24 years before the first American patent that was issued in 1816. Molded ink bottles began to appear in America around 1815-1816 and the blown three-mold variety came into use during the late 1840s. The most common shape of ink bottle, the umbrella, is a multi-sided conical that can be found with both pontiled and smooth bases. One of the more collectible ink bottles is the teakettle, identified by the neck, which extends upward at an angle from the base.

As the fountain pen grew in popularity between 1885 and 1890, the ink bottle gradually became less decorative and soon became just another plain bottle.

A.B. Laird's / Ink, Medium blue green, 2-1/8", 8-sided, open pontil, inward rolled lip, American 1840-1860.. **$3,500-4,500**

Albert's / Writing Fluid – Pitts. PA, Blue aqua, 2-1/4", open pontil, rolled lip, extremely rare, American 1840-1860 . . . . **$400-700**

B.A. Fahnestock & Co. / Ink & Ink Stand / Pittsburgh, Blue aqua, 2 3/8", open pontil, rolled lip, extremely rare, American 1840-1860 . . . . **$400-700**

Barrel Ink – Opdyke / Bros / Ink, Blue aqua, 2-1/2", barrel form, smooth base, tooled mouth, American 1875-1890 . . . **$250-350**

Blake & Herring – N-Y, Rich emerald green, 3", 8-sided, open pontil, inward rolled lip, extremely rare, American 1840-1860 . . . .**$2,500-4,500**

Carters – Cloverleaf Ink, Cobalt blue, 2-3/8", 6-sided, smooth base, ABM top, American 1870-1880. . . . . **$100-150**

CA – RT – ER (on side at base) – Label reads: Hill and Kooken, Stationery, 11 Lyman Terrace, Waltham, Mass, Cobalt blue, 8", cathedral arch panels, smooth base (Carters), ABM lip, hard rubber dispenser, American 1920-1930. . . . . **$150-175**

Clark's / Superior / Record / Ink – Boston, Yellow amber, 6", open pontil-scarred base, flared lip, extremely rare, American 1840-1860 . . . . **$500-800**

Cone Ink, Medium olive green, 2-1/4", pontil-scarred base (X and 200), sheared and tooled lip, swirled glass lines, American 1840-1860 . . . . **$600-700**

Barrel ink, Opdyke Bros ink, blue aqua, 2-1/2", smooth base, tooled mouth, American 1875-1890, **$250-300.**

"B-U-T-L-E-R", blue aqua, 2-1/4", 8-sided, reverse '561', open pontil, rolled lip, American 1840-1860, **$200-250.**

Cone Ink, Yellow amber, 2-1/2", open pontil, inward rolled lip, American 1840-1860 . . . . **$400-500**

Cone Ink, Medium cobalt blue, 2-1/2" open pontil, inward rolled lip, American 1840-1860 . . . . **$1,000-1,500**

Cone Ink, Deep blue aqua, 2-3/8", smooth base, tooled mouth, American 1895-1910 . . . . **$120-180**

Cone Ink – Carter Ink (Unlisted), Brilliant emerald green, 2-3/8", tubular pontil scar, outward rolled mouth, American 1840-1860 . . . . **$500-600**

Cone Ink, Carter's Ink, deep blue aqua, 2-3/8", smooth base, tooled mouth, American 1895-1910, **$200-250.**

Harrison's Columbian Ink, medium olive green, 1-3/4", 8-sided, open pontil, inward rolled lip, American 1840-1860, (rare) **$1,800-2,000.**

Cone Ink – R.L. Higgins – Virginia City, Medium green, 2", smooth base, inward rolled mouth, American 1875-1883 . . . **$800-1,000**

Cone Ink – Rogers & Cooper / St. Louis Mo (embossed), Aqua, 3", open pontil, rolled lip, American 1840-1860. . . . **$400-550**

Cone Ink, GWA80-457, Medium cobalt blue, 3-3/4", drape pattern, panel for label, tubular pontil scar, applied double collared mouth, American 1840-1860. . . . . **$4,000-8,000**

Diamond / Ink Co., Medium amber, 3-1/4", square form, smooth base (Diamond Ink Co. / Pat. Appd. For), tooled mouth, American 1885-1900 . . . . **$40-50**

Domed Ink – Bertinguiot, Yellow olive, 2-1/4", pontil-scarred base, sheared mouth, French 1840-1860 . . . . **$200-400**

Domed Ink – A.M. Bertinquiot, Black glass, 2-3/16", pontil-scarred base, sheared mouth, French 1840-1860 . . . **$200-400**

Glass Funnel Inkwell – Simon's – Registered – Birmingham / May 30, 1845 – Clark's Patent (embossed on front), Deep blue green, 3", polished pontil-scarred base, tooled opening, English 1845-1860. . . . . **$500-700**

Farleys – Ink, Yellow olive with amber tone, 3-1/2", 8-sided, open pontil, tooled flared-out lip, American 1840-1860 . . . **$2,000-2,500**

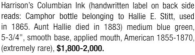

Harrison's Columbian Ink (handwritten label on back side reads: Camphor bottle belonging to Hallie E. Stitt, used in 1865. Aunt Hallie died in 1883) medium blue green, 5-3/4", smooth base, applied mouth, American 1855-1870, (extremely rare), **$1,800-2,000.**

Harrison's Columbian Ink, cobalt blue, 2-1/4", open pontil, rolled lip, American 1840-1860, **$800-1,000.**

Harrison's / Columbian / Ink – Original Label reads: Harrison's Columbian Black Writing Fluid, South 7th Street, Philadelphia, Medium cobalt blue, 2", open pontil, inward rolled lip, American 1840-1860. . . . . **$1,000-1,200**

Harrison's / Columbian / Ink, Medium cobalt blue, 2", open pontil, inward rolled lip, American 1840-1860. . . . . **$600-800**

Harrison's / Columbian / Ink, Deep cobalt blue, 2", open pontil, inward rolled lip, American 1840-1860 . . . . **$800-1,400**

Harrison's / Columbian / Ink – Original label reads: Harrison's Columbian Black Writing Fluid, South 7th Street, Philadelphia, Medium cobalt blue, 4", open pontil, applied mouth, American 1840-1860. . . . . **$800-1,400**

Harrison's / Columbian / Ink, Cobalt blue, 5-3/4", open pontil, applied mouth, American 1840-1860 . . . . **$1,700-1,900**

Hohenthal / Brothers & Co / Indelible / Writing Ink / N.Y., Yellow amber, 7", cylinder, pontil-scarred base, applied mouth with tool crimped pour spout, scarce, American 1840-1860. . . . . **$1,000-1,500**

Hoffman's / Ink – Label reads: Hoffman's Chemical Red Carmine Ink, Bridgeport, Connecticut, Aqua, 2-3/4", smooth base, tooled and ground lip, American 1875-1895. . . . **$40-60**

Hover / Phila, Moss green, 4-1/2", cylindrical form, tubular pontil scar, tool flared mouth, American 1840-1860. . . . . . **$300-600**

Hover / Phila, Sapphire blue, 5", cylindrical form, open pontil, tooled flared-out lip, rare, American 1840-1860. . . **$800-1,200**

Igloo Ink – Label reads: Anti-Corrosive Jet Black Ink, Prepared by John Aannear, 128 Front St., Philadelphia, Aqua, 2", smooth base, sheared and ground lip, American 1865-1875 .... **$150-200**

Inkwell, Clear glass, 2", 14-vertical rib pattern, filler and four-quill opening on top, pontil-scarred base, American 1850-1870 .... **$200-300**

J. & I.E.M. – Label Reads: Moore's Excelsior School Writing Ink, Manfactured by J. & I.E. Moore, Warren, Mass, Aqua, 2-5/8", smooth base, tooled and ground lip, American 1875-1895 .... **$40-60**

J. Raynald, Medium green, 2-1/2", globe form, smooth base, inward rolled mouth, American 1850-1870 .... **$250-350**

J.S. Dunham, St. Louis. M., Brilliant aquamarine, 2-1/4", 12-sided, tubular pontil scar, inward rolled mouth, rare, unknown variant, American 1840-1860 .... **$400-800**

J.S. Mason / Philad.a, Bright blue green, 4-3/8", cylindrical, pontil-scarred base, tooled flared mouth, extremely rare, American 1840-1860 .... **$250-500**

Kosmian / Safety Ink, Brilliant blue green, 7-1/8", square with one indented embossed panel and beveled corners, smooth base, applied square collared mouth, rare, American 1860-1880 .... **$300-600**

Locomotive Ink – Trade Mark – Pat. Oct. 1874, Aqua, 2", locomotive form, smooth base, sheared and ground lip, American 1874-1880, made for Charles L. Lochman, Proprietor of Lochman's Locomotive Ink Company of Carlisle, Penn **$1,000-1,500**

Lyons Ink, Medium cobalt blue, 2-7/8", smooth base, tooled lip, American 1880-1895 . . . . **$175-225**

Master Ink – Carters – Label reads: Carter's – RYTO – Permanent – Blue Black – Ink, Cobalt blue, 7", smooth base, cathedral form, ABM lip, original stopper with screw top cap, American 1920-1930 . . . . **$275-325**

Master Ink – Carter – Label reads: Hill and Kocken Stationery 11 Lyman Terrace, Waltham, Mass. Tel. Waltham 3239-M, Deep cobalt blue, 8", 6-sided, cathedral form, smooth base, ABM lip, original rubber stopper with plastic screw cap, American 1920-1930 . . . . **$275-375**

Master Ink – Carters – Label reads: Carter's – RYTO – Permanent – Blue Black – Ink, Cobalt blue, 9", smooth base, cathedral form, ABM lip, original stopper with screw top cap, American 1920-1930 . . . . **$400-500**

Master Ink – Carters – Label reads: Carter's – RYTO – Permanent – Blue Black – Ink, Cobalt blue, 10", smooth base, cathedral form, ABM lip, original stopper with screw top cap, American 1920-1930 . . . . **$100-150**

Master Ink – Collins Ink Co / Louisville KY, Dark amber, 9-7/8", smooth base, applied mouth with hand tooled pour spout, extremely rare, American 1860-1875 . . . . **$300-400**

Master Ink – Davids & Black – New York (around shoulder), Olive amber, 6-3/8", open pontil, applied sloping collar mouth, rare color, American 1840-1860 . . . . **$450-650**

Master Ink – Gross & Robinson's / American / Writing Fluid, Deep blue aqua, 5-7/8", iron pontil, applied mouth, rare, American 1840-1860 . . . .**$800-1,000**

Master Ink – Hover – Phila, Medium blue green, 7-1/2", open pontil, applied sloping double collar mouth with hand tooled pour spout, scarce, American 1840-1860 . . . . **$300-400**

Master Ink – R.L. Higgins – Virginia, Dark amber, 6", smooth base, applied mouth with pour spout, extremely rare, American 1875-1883 . . . .**$10,000-12,000**

Master Ink – Saltglaze Stoneware – A.W. Harrison / Patent / Columbian Ink / Philadelphia (stamped on side at shoulder), Gray and brown, 10", handled, smooth base, mouth similar to wide applied style, American 1845-1860. . . . . . .**$1,000-1,800**

Master Ink – Stafford's / Ink, Dark puce, 7-3/4", smooth base, applied mouth, hand tooled pour spout, extremely rare color, American 1875-1885 . . . . **$700-800**

Multi-Sided Ink, Blue aqua, 1-3/4", 8-sided, pontil-scarred base, sheared and inward rolled lip, American 1840-1860 . . . **$150-200**

NE Plus Ultra Fluid, Blue aqua, 2", cottage form, smooth base, burst sheared lip, American 1850-1860 . . . . **$275-325**

Patterson's / Excelsior / Ink, Deep blue aqua, 2-3/4", 8-sided, open pontil (reversed 3X), inward rolled lip, rare, American 1840-1860 . . . . **$400-600**

"S. Fine – Blk. ink, aqua, 3-1/8", open pontil, sheared and ground lip, American 1840-1860, **$200-250.**

Rider on Horse (horizontal diamond) – Rider on Horse (horizontal diamond), Dark yellow amber, 1-3/8", open pontil, tooled disk-type lip, blown in a two-piece mold, extremely rare, American 1815-1835,. **$6,500**

S.F. Cal Ink Co, Medium amber, 2", cottage ink, smooth base, inward rolled lip, American 1850-1860 . . . .**$1,800-2,000**

S. Fine / Blk. Ink, Aqua, 3-1/8", open pontil, sheared and ground lip, American 1840-1860 . . . .**$200-300**

S.O. Dunbar / Taunton / Mass, Aqua, 8-5/8", cylinder form, iron pontil, applied mouth, American 1840-1860 ...... **$100-150**

Sheet's – Writing – Fluid – Dayton / O, Blue aqua, 2-5/8", 6-sided, corset-waist form, pontil-scarred base, inward rolled lip, American 1840-1860 .... **$400-700**

Teakettle Ink, Medium cobalt blue, 1-1/2", lobed melon form, smooth base, ground mouth with brass collar and cap, England 1830-1850 .... **$500-1,000**

Teakettle Ink (stoneware) – Compliments Of – The Letort Hotel – James F. Grandone, Prop. – Carlisle. PA, Two-tone light and dark pottery, 2-1/2", smooth base, wide smooth top, American 1880-1910 .... **$125-150**

Teakettle Ink, Jade clambroth, 2-1/2", smooth base, sheared and ground lip, American 1850-1870 .... **$325-425**

Teakettle Ink, Blue clambroth, 2-1/2", smooth base, sheared and ground lip, American 1850-1870 .... **$325-425**

Teakettle Ink – Double Font, Clear glass, 3-1/2", embossed on upper font (D.R.G.M. No. 55922) and lower font (D.R.G.M.), smooth base, sheared lip with original metal neck ring and cap and metal separator ring, rare, double font inkwell provides two different ink colors from the same inkwell, English 1880-1895 ..... **$150-200**

Teakettle Ink – Double Font, Clear glass, 4-1/2", polished pontil base, sheared and ground lip, rare, double font inkwell provides two different ink colors from the same inkwell, American 1880-1895 .... **$500-600**

Teakettle Ink – Miniature Beehive, Aqua, 1-1/8", beehive form, smooth base, sheared and ground lip, American 1880-1895 .... **$200-300**

Teakettle Ink – Beehive, Deep blue aqua, 2", beehive form, smooth base, rough sheared lip, European 1880-1895 ...... **$275-375**

Teakettle Ink – Monroe's / Patent / School / Ink, Aquamarine, 2", 7-sided, two front panels embossed, smooth base, tooled and ground mouth, extremely rare, American 1860-1880 .. **$400-800**

The American Ink Co. / Denver U.S.A., Clear glass, 2-1/2", smooth base (Pat Sept. 4-95), ground lip, original metal screw-on cap, American 1895-1900. .... **$175-220**

The World / J. Raynald (continents of Asia, Europe, North America, South America, Africa), Blue aqua, 2-1/4", smooth base, tooled lip, rare, American 1885-1895. ...... **$750-1,000**

Titcomb's / Ink Cin, Aquamarine, 2-3/4", 12-sided, pontil-scarred base, inward rolled mouth, extremely rare, American 1840-1860 .... **$500-1,000**

Umbrella Ink – Label reads: Adam's Indelible Writing Ink Manufactured by J.C. Moran Bookseller and Stationer, 438 Pa. Av., Washington City, Golden yellow, 2-5/8", 8-sided, open pontil, rolled lip, very rare, American 1840-1860... **$375-500**

Umbrella Ink – Boss' / Patent, Aquamarine, 2-5/8", tubular pontil scar, inward rolled mouth, American 840-1860 .... **$400-800**

Umbrella Ink – J. Gundry / Cincinnati, Aquamarine, 3", 12-sided, tubular pontil scar, inward rolled mouth, American 1840-1860 .... **$400-600**

Umbrella Ink – James S. / Mason & Co., Bright blue green, 2-1/2", octagonal form, tubular pontil scar, inward rolled lip, American 1840-1860 rare **$400-800**

Umbrella Ink – Water's – Ink – Troy N.Y., Light to medium blue-green, 2-3/4", 6-sided, open pontil, inward rolled lip, rare, American 1840-1860 color **$1,000-1,500**

Umbrella Ink – Wide Mouth, Medium pink amethyst, 1-7/8", 8-sided, pontil-scarred base, sheared and tool widened mouth, original cork with material wrap closure, extremely rare, American 1840-1860, found in rubble of the Glassboro N.J. building that was the office of the Whitney Glassworks. **$2,500-3,000**

Umbrella Ink, Dark green, 4-1/2", smooth base, tooled lip, American 1850-1860 . . . . **$250-275**

Zieber & Co – Excelsior – Ink, Deep blue green, 7-1/2", 12-sided, iron pontil, applied mouth, American 1840-1860 . . . . . . **$6,000-8,000**

Zieber is one of the most sought after master inks., Figural Inks, Ink – Log Cabin, Clear glass, 2-1/2", smooth base, tooled flared mouth, American 1880-1890 . . . . **$350-700**

Ink – Two Story Building, Milk glass, 4-3/4", smooth base, tooled squared collared mouth, extremely rare, American 1860-1880. . . . . **$500-1,000**

Teakettle Ink – Turtle, Clear glass, 1-5/8", smooth base, rough sheared lip, English 1880-1895. . . . . **$100-125**

MEDICINE BOTTLES

The medicine bottle group includes all pieces specifically made to hold patented medicines. Bitter and cure bottles, however, are excluded from this category because the healing powers of these mixtures were very questionable.

A patent medicine was one whose formula was registered with the U.S. Patent office, which opened in 1790. Not all medicines were patented, however, because after the passage of the Pure Food and Drug Act of 1907, the ingredients of medicines had to be listed on the bottle. As a result, most of these patent medicine companies went out of business when consumers learned that most medicines consisted of liquor diluted with water and an occasional pinch of opiates, strychnine, and arsenic. I have spent many enjoyable hours reading the labels on

these bottles and wondering how anyone would survive the recommended doses.

One of the oldest and most collectible medicine bottles, the embossed Turlington "Balsam of Life," was manufactured in England from 1723 to 1900. The first embossed U.S. medicine bottle dates from around 1810. When searching for these bottles, always be on the lookout for embossing and original boxes. Embossed "Shaker" or "Indian" medicine bottles are very collectible and valuable. Most embossed medicines made before 1840 are clear and aqua. The embossed greens, ambers, and blues, specifically the darker cobalt blues, are much more collectible and valuable.

ADR / Albany, Medium blue green, 4-3/4", oval form, smooth base, inward rolled lip, American 1840-1860 ...... **$100-125**

A. Leitch & Co / Apothecaries / St. Louis, Deep blue aqua, 6", open pontil, applied mouth, extremely rare, American 1840-1860 .... **$300-400**

Alexanders / Silameau, Sapphire blue, 6-1/4", open pontil, applied mouth, American 1840-1860 .... **$1,200-1,600**

Allan's / Anti Fat – Botanic Medicine Co. – Buffalo, N.Y., Medium cobalt blue, 7-5/8", smooth base, applied mouth, American 1875-1885 .... **$300-400**

American / Oil – Cumberland River – Kentucky, Blue aqua, 6-7/8", pontil-scarred base, wide outward rolled lip, American 1840-1860 .... **$250-300**

American – Medicinal / Oil – Burkesville / KY., Blue aqua, 6-1/2", open pontil, applied mouth, American 1840-1860 .... **$350-450**

B. Denton's – Healing Balsam – Label reads: Denton's Vegetable Healing Balsam, Barton Denton, Madison St. Auburn, N.Y., Aqua, 4-1/8", 8-sided, open pontil, applied sloping collar mouth, American 1840-1860. .... **$150-200**

B. Denton (embossed vine) Auburn, N.Y., Blue aqua, 6-3/8", open pontil, applied mouth, American 1840-1860 ... **$80-120**

Barrell's Indian Liniment – H.C.O. Cary, Aqua, 4-3/4" open pontil, rolled lip, scarce, American 1840-1860 ...... **$75-100**

Bartine's / Lotion, Aqua, 6-1/2", open pontil, applied mouth, American 1840-1860 .... **$140-180**

Bach's – American – Compound – Auburn. N.Y., blue aqua, 7-5/8", open pontil, applied double collar mouth, American 1840-1869, **$100-150.**

Bakers / Vegetable / Blood & Liver / Cure / Look Out Mountain / Medicine Co. / Manufacturers / & / Proprietors / Greenville / Tenn., deep red amber, 9-3/4", smooth base, tooled mouth, American 1880-1890, **$400-500.**

Beekman's – Pulmonic – Syrup – New York, Medium olive green in upper half shading to darker in the lower half, 7-1/4", 8-sided, pontil-scarred base, applied double collar mouth, very rare, American 1840-1860 . . . . **$5,000-7,000**

Bench's / Mixture Of / Cannabis Indica, Aqua Marine, 7-3/4", oval form, open pontil, applied mouth, extremely rare, American 1840-1860 . . . . **$600-800**

Blood Food / Prepared By / G. HandySide, Medium cornflower blue, 6-3/4", smooth base, applied mouth, English 1885-1900 . . . . **$150-200**

Blood Food / Prepared By / G. HandySide, Olive yellow, 7", smooth base, applied mouth, English 1885-1900 . . . **$150-200**

Boston / Lung Institute, Clear, 2-5/8", wide-mouth jar, pontil-scarred base, outward rolled lip, American 1840-1860 . . . . **$200-300**

Butler & Son – London / S.F. Urquhart – Toronto, C.W., Blue aqua, 5-3/4", open pontil, applied mouth, extremely rare, Canadian 1840-1860 . . . . **$450-500**

C. Brinckerhoff – Health Restorative – Price $1.00 – New York, Medium yellow olive green, 7-3/8", pontil-scarred base, applied mouth, American 1840-1860 . . . . **$1,500-2,000**

C.F. Haskell / Coloris / Capilli / Restitutuior, Blue aqua, 7-1/2", oval form, pontil-scarred base, applied mouth, American 1840-1860 . . . . **$250-300**

Carter's – Extract Of / Smart Weed – Erie, Aqua, 5-1/2", open pontil, applied mouth, American 1840-1860 . . . . . . **$200-300**

C. Brinkerhoff's – Health Restorative – Price $1.00 - New York, deep olive green, 7-1/2", pontil-scarred base, applied sloping collar mouth, American 1840-1860, **$1,000-1,300.**

Carter's Spanish Mixture (label reads "Carter's Spanish Mixture, Bennett & Beers, Druggists, General Agents and Proprietors, No. 3 Pearl Street, Richmond, Va"), deep olive green, 8-1/2", iron pontil, applied sloping double collar mouth, American 1840-1860, **$1,000-1,300.**

Carter's / Spanish / Mixture – Label reads: Carter's Spanish Mixture, Bennett & Beers, Druggists, General Agents and Proprietors, No. 3 Pearl Street, Richmond, VA, Deep olive green, 8-1/2", iron pontil, applied sloping double collar mouth, American 1840-1860 . . . . **$800-1,200**

Cattle Liniment – Breinig Fronefield & Co, Pale aqua, 6-1/2", pontil-scarred base, applied mouth, American 1840-1860 . . . . **$250-300**

Cerisiaux – Rheumatic / Antidote – Or Electric – Liniment – New York, Aqua, 5-1/4", open pontil, applied mouth, very rare, American 1840-1860. . . . . **$200-250**

Chloride / Calcium – St. Catharines – Canada, Blue aqua, 5-3/4", open pontil, applied mouth, Canadian 1840-1860 . . . .**$250-350**

Clark's / Syrup, Medium blue green, 9-3/4", smooth base, applied double collar mouth, American 1855-1865 . . . . **$400-600**

Clement's – Genuine Osceola / Liniment – Prepared By – J. Cochran / Lowell / Mass, Aqua, 6-7/8", open pontil, applied double collar mouth, extremely rare, American 1840-1860. . . . . **$500-700**

Cloud's Cordial – Cloud's Cordial, Straw yellow with olive tone, 10-1/2", tapered form, American 1870-1880. . . . . . . **$400-600**

Cordial Balm – Of Health – Prepared By – Dr Braddee, Medium yellow olive, 4-1/4", open pontil rolled lip, extremely rare, currently the only known example, American 1830-1840. . . . . **$2,500-4,500**

Connell's Brahminical / Moonplant / East Indian / Remedies (embossed feet inside a circle of stars — label reads "Aperient"), medium yellow amber, 8-1/4", smooth base, applied double collar mouth, American 1870-1880, **$500-600.**

Dr. Craig's / New Discovery / Rochester, N.Y., blue aqua, 9-1/2", smooth base, applied mouth, American 1865-1875, **$200-300.**

Curtis & Trall / New York, Blue aqua, 9-1/4", iron pontil, applied mouth, American 1840-1860 . . . . **$300-400**

Davis & / Miller / Druggists / Baltimore (in a slug plate), Medium sapphire blue, 8-1/2", iron pontil, applied mouth, American 1840-1860 . . . . **$300-400**

Davis' – Vegetable – Pain Killer, Aqua, 4-7/8", open pontil, applied double collar mouth, American 1840-1860 . . . . **$300-400**

Doctor – Geo. W. Blocksom – Druggist – Zanesville, Light sapphire blue, 8-1/4", 12-sided, iron pontil, applied squared collar mouth, extremely rare, American 1840-1860 . . . .**$1,000-1,500**

Doctor Oreste / Sinanide's / Medicinal / Preparation / Orestorin, Deep cobalt blue, 4-5/8", smooth base, tooled lip, American 1890-1910 . . . . **$200-300**

D.P. Brown – Buffalo, N.Y., Yellow olive amber, 1-1/4", 12-sided salve jar, smooth base, rough sheared lip, American 1855-1870 . . . . **$300-400**

Dr. Bruce's – Indian Vegetable / Panacea – New Castle, KY, Blue aqua, 9", smooth base, applied mouth, American 1855-1865 . . . .**$1,800-2,200**

Dr. Cooper's – Ethereal / Oil – For / Deafness, Aqua, 2-3/4", open pontil, flared lip, rare, American 1840-1860 . . . . . . **$250-300**

Dr. D. Fahrney & Son – Preparation For / Cleansing The Blood / Boonsboro, M.D., Medium copper topaz, 9-5/8", smooth base, applied mouth, very rare, American 1865-1875 . . . . **$700-900**

Dr. D. Jayne's / Ague Mixture – Philadelphia, Aqua, 7-7/8", open pontil, applied tapered mouth, American 1840-1860 . . . **$400-500**

Dr. Duncan's – Expectorant / Remedy, Deep blue aqua, 6-3/8", open pontil, rolled lip, American 1840-1860 . . . . . . **$200-250**

Dr. Edwards' – Tar Wild Cherry / & Naptha – Cough Syrup, Blue aqua, 5-1/8", open pontil, tooled top, American 1840-1860 . . . . **$75-100**

Dr / E.J. Coxe – New Orleans – Southern / Cough Syrup, Medium green, 7-3/8", cylinder form, open pontil, applied mouth, extremely rare Southern colored pontil, American 1840-1860 . . . . **$3,500-4,500**

Dr. Friend's – Cough Balsam – Morristown, N.J., Blue aqua, 6-1/8", pontil-scarred base, applied sloping collar mouth, rare, American 1840-1860 . . . . **$300-400**

Dr. Forsha's – Alternative / Balm, Green aqua, 5-1/2", open pontil, applied double collar mouth, rare color, American 1840-1860 . . . . **$400-600**

Dr. John Bull's / King Of Pain / Louisville KY, Aqua, 6-7/8", oval form, pontil-scarred base, applied sloping collar mouth, American 1840-1860 . . . . **$180-250**

Dr. H. Anders – Iodine Water (face on sun) – Hauriexhag / Fontevitale – 1855, Aqua, 8-1/8", smooth base, applied mouth, rare, American 1855-1865 . . . . **$250-350**

DRS. Ivans / & Hart / New York, Aquamarine, 7-3/8", 8-sided, open pontil, applied mouth, extremely rare, American 1840-1860 . . . . **$700-900**

Dr. Browder's / Compound Syrup / Of Indian Turnip – Label reads: Dr. Browder's Compound Syrup / Of / Indian Turnip / For The Cure Of / Consumption, Coughs, Colds, Spillage, Blood, and All Other Complications of the Chest, Aqua, 7", open pontil, applied mouth, American 1840-1860 . . . . **$700-900**

Dr. Foord's – Pectoral / Syrup – New York, Aqua, 5-3/8", open pontil, applied mouth, American 1840-1860 . . . . . . **$120-160**

Dr. Hamilton's – Indian / Liniment, Aqua, 5-3/8", oval form, open pontil, rolled lip, American 1840-1860 . . . . . . **$350-450**

Dr. Hershey's / Worm Syrup, Aqua, 5-1/2", open pontil, inward rolled lip, rare, American 1840-1860 . . . . **$200-275**

Dr. Hoofland / Balsamic Cordial – C.M. Jackson / Philadelphia, Aqua, 7", open pontil, applied double collar mouth, American 1840-1860 . . . . **$90-125**

Dr. Kellinger's – Magic Fluid – New York, Aqua, 3-3/4", open pontil, rolled lip, scarce, American 1840-1860 . . . . . . **$80-100**

Dr. Kelling's / Pure Herb / Medicines, Aqua, 6-3/8", cylinder form, open pontil, applied mouth, American 1840-1860 . . . . **$75-100**

Dr. Kennedy's – Medical / Discovery – Roxury, Mass, Blue aqua, 8-5/8", open pontil, applied mouth, American 1840-1860 . . . . **$100-150**

Dr. Meeker's Casca Rilla Tonic, The Meeker Medicine Co., Established 1854, Chicago, ILL, Olive green, 5-7/8", pontil-scarred base, applied double collar mouth, American 1855-1860 . . . . **$350-450**

Dr. H. Swayne's – Vermifuge – Philada, Aqua, 4-5/8", square form, open pontil, thin flared-out lip, American 1840-1860 . . . . **$100-150**

Dr. S.A. Weaver's / Canker & / Salt Rheum / Syrup, Aqua, 9-1/2", oval form, iron pontil, applied mouth, American 1840-1860 . . . . **$150-250**

Dr. S.C. Marsh / Druggist / Newark N.J., Blue aqua, 6-1/4", open pontil, tooled lip, American 1840-1860 . . . . **$75-100**

Dr. S.S. Fitch – 707 B. Way, N,Y – Dr. Fitch's Tonic Wash, Deep blue aqua, 2-7/8", open pontil, flared lip, American 1840-1860 . . . . **$100-150**

Dr. S.S. Fitch – 707 B. Way, N,Y – Dr. Fitch's Tonic Wash, Deep blue aqua, 4-1/2", open pontil, flared lip, American 1840-1860 . . . . **$100-150**

Dr. W.J. Haas's – Expectorant – Schuylkill Haven – PA, Aqua, 5-3/8", open pontil, thin flared-out lip, extremely rare, American 1840-1860 . . . . **$300-400**

Dr. W.N. Handy / Easton, N.Y., Deep olive green, 8-3/4", 12-sided, smooth base, applied mouth, extremely rare, American 1855-1860, blown at Mt. Pleasant Glass Works, New York. **$800-1,200**

Dr. White / Cini. Ohio, Medium sapphire blue, 4", pontil base, rolled lip, very rare, American 1850-1865 . . . . **$200-225**

Dr. White's / Magic / Liniment, Medium sapphire blue, 4", smooth base, rolled lip, very rare, American 1850-1860 . . . . . **$200-225**

Dr. Wistar's – Balsam Of – Wild Cherry – Philada, Aqua, 8-sided, open pontil, applied mouth, American 1840-1860 . . **$300-400**

Durno's / The / Mountain / Indian / Liniment, Blue aqua, 6", cylinder form, open pontil, inward rolled lip, very rare Indian medicine bottle, American 1840-1860. . . . . **$500-700**

E.A. Buckhout's / Dutch / Liniment / (standing man) – Prepared At / Mechanicville Saratoga, Co. N.Y., Blue aqua, 4-3/4", open pontil, rolled lip, American 1840-1860 . . . . **$400-500**

E.C. Allen / Concentrated / Electric Paste – OR / Arabian Pain / Extractor – Lancaster / Pa, Medium emerald green, 3-1/8", open pontil, inward rolled lip, American 1840-1860 . . . . . **$900-1,200**

EDW. Wilder's / Compound Extract / Of Wild Cherry – Patented / (motif of five-story building) – EDW. Wilder & Co / Wholesale Druggists / Louisville Ky, Clear, 8-1/2", semi-cabin form, smooth base, tooled mouth, American 1885-1895 . . . . **$275-375**

EDW. Wilder's / Compound Extract / Of Wild Cherry – Patented / (motif of five-story building) – EDW. Wilder & Co / Wholesale Druggists / Louisville Ky, Clear, 7-1/4", semi-cabin form, smooth base, tooled mouth, American 1885-1895 . . . . **$275-375**

Flagg's Good – Samaritan's – Immediate – Relief – Cincinnati, O, Aqua, 3-3/4", 5-sided, open pontil, outward rolled lip, American 1840-1860 . . . . **$300-400**

For Colds / Coughs Croup & C / Immediate Relief / & / Speedy Cure, Amber, 4-7/8 , pumpkinseed flask, smooth base, applied mouth, extremely rare form, American 1875-1885 . . . . **$800-1,000**

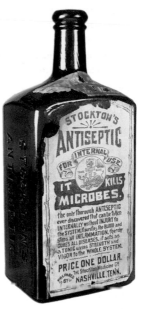

Gargling Oil – Lockport. N.Y., yellow amber, 5-1/2", smooth base, tooled mouth, American 1880-1890, **$250-300.**

Stockton's / Antiseptic – Stockton Medicine Co. / Nashville, Tenn, label reads: Stockton's Antiseptic For Internal Use, It Kills Microbes, Price One Dollar, Prepared by the Stockton Medicine Co., Nashville, Tenn, medium amber, 10", American 1885-1895, **$200-300.**

Follansbee's – Elixir – Of Health, Deep blue aqua, 8-3/4", iron pontil, applied mouth, extremely rare, American 1840-1860 . . . . **$1,000-1,300**

Forshas – Balm / Liniment, Medium green, 4-1/4", smooth base, thin flared-out lip, rare color, American 1840-1860 . . . . **$250-350**

French's / Freckle Remover, Opaque milk glass, 5-1/8", smooth base, tooled mouth, American 1885-1895 . . . . **$140-180**

Gargling Oil / Lockport. N.Y., Medium emerald green, 7-3/8", smooth base, applied sloping collar mouth, rare in this large size, American 1865-1875 . . . . **$140-180**

Genuine – Swaim's / Panacea – Philadelphia, Aqua, 7-7/8", open pontil, applied mouth, American 1840-1855 . . . . **$600-700**

Germ Bacteria Or / Fungus Destroyer / WM. Radam's / Microbe Killer / (man clubbing a skeleton) / Registered Trade Mark Dec. 13, 1887 / Cures / All / Diseases, Yellow amber, 10-1/2", smooth base, sheared and tooled lip, American 1890-1900 . . . . **$300-400**

G.W. Merchant / Chemist / Lockport / N.Y., Blue green, 7", smooth base, applied tapered collar mouth, American 1860-1870 . . . . **$200-250**

G.W. Simonds' Vegetable Pain Curer – An Internal and External Remedy, Prepared by G.W. Simonds, Fitzwilliam, N.H., Price 25 Cents (label only), Medium olive amber, 7-3/8", pontil-scarred base, applied sloping collar mouth, blown in a three-piece mold, American 1840-1860 . . . . **$375-475**

(Front and Back) Gargling Oil – Lockport. N.Y., deep cobalt blue, 5-7/8", smooth base, ABM mouth, American 1910-1920, **$100-150.**

Gibb's / Bone Liniment, Medium olive green, 6-3/8", 6-sided, open pontil, applied tapered collar mouth, American 1840-1860 . . . .**$1,400-1,800**

Girolamo – Pagliano, Medium lime green, 4-1/4", open pontil, inward rolled lip, rare, American 1840-1860 . . . . . . **$100-150**

Gregory's Elixir of Opium – Prepared by W.L. Gregory, Pharmaceutical Chemist, 931 Main Street, Buffalo, N.Y. (label), Yellow olive amber, 7-1/4", cylinder form, pontil-scarred base, applied double collar mouth, American 1830-1845 . . . . **$275-375**

Hamptons / V. Tincture / Mortimer / & Mowbray / Balto, Deep copper puce, 6-1/4", oval form, smooth base, applied square collar mouth, American 1855-1865 . . . . **$180-225**

Hamptons / V. Tincture / Mortimer / & Mowbray / Balto, Medium yellow topaz, 6-3/8", smooth base, applied mouth, American 1855-1865 . . . . **$275-325**

Holme & Kidd, Deep blue aqua, 7-5/8", iron pontil, outward rolled lip, American 1840-1860 . . . . **$140-180**

Honduras / Tonic / W.E. Twiss & Co / MFR, Medium golden yellow amber, 8-7/8", oval form, smooth base, tooled mouth, American 1880-1900 . . . . **$100-150**

Hubbell, Medium sapphire blue, 5-5/8", open pontil, applied mouth, very rare, American 1840-1860 . . . . **$500-600**

I. Covert's – Balm Of Life, Medium yellow olive green, 6", open pontil, applied mouth, American 1840-1860. . . . . **$1,200-1,400**

Germ, Bacteria, Or / Fungus Destroyer / WM Radam's / Microbe Killer (motif of man clubbing a skeleton) Registered Trade Mark Dec. 13 1887 (inside shield) / Cures / All / Diseases, medium amber, 6-5/8", smooth base, tooled mouth, American 1887-1910, **$200-300.**

Constitutional / Beverage / W. Olmstead & Co. – New York, medium amber, 10-1/4", American 1865-1875, **$275-375**.

I.L. St. John's – Carminative – Balsam, Aqua, 4-5/8", pontil-scarred base, rolled lip, very rare, American 1840-1860 ...... **$250-350**

Indian / Clemens (standing Indian) Tonic / Prepared By / Geo. W. House, Blue aqua, 5-1/2", open pontil, outward rolled lip, American 1840-1860 .... **$800-900**

Indian / Liniment, Blue aqua, 4-1/2", oval form, open pontil, rolled lip, American 1840-1860 .... **$140-180**

Indian – Vegetable – Balsam, Aqua, 4-1/2", open pontil, thin flared-out lip, American 1840-1860 .... **$200-250**

J.B. Wheatly's / Compound Syrup / Dallasburgh, KY – Label reads: Wheatley's Compound Syrup Cure of Chills & Fever, Prepared by J.B. Wheatley, Dallasburg, Ky, Blue aqua, 6", cylinder form, pontil-scarred base, applied double collar mouth, American 1840-1860 .... **$250-375**

J.B. Wilde & Co / Louisville, Blue aqua, 6-3/4", open pontil, applied mouth, American 1840-1960 .... **$75-100**

J.D. Thompsons – Rheumatic & Neuralgic / Liniment – Pitts PA, Blue aqua, 4-3/4", open pontil, rolled lip, American 1840-1860 .... **$375-475**

J. Folely's – Indian / Botanic – Balsam, Aqua, 6-3/4", open pontil, applied mouth, extremely rare, American 1850-1860 .. **$600-800**

John Fabers / Elixir Of / Oryza / N.Y., Deep blue aqua, 8", rectangular wedge form, open pontil-scarred base, applied sloping double collar mouth, extremely rare in this form, American, 1840-1860 .... **$350-450**

John Gilbert & Co / Druggist / 177 North 3D. St. / Philada, Aqua, 12-1/4", 1-gallon, smooth base, applied mouth, American 1855-1865 . . . . **$275-325**

John Hart & Co. – John Hart, Deep amber, 7-1/8", heart form, smooth base, applied double collar mouth, American 1865-1875 . . . . **$450-550**

John / Youngson – Extract Of / American Oil, Aqua, 4", open pontil, rolled lip, American 1840-1860 . . . . **$90-125**

Judson's – Cherry / & / Lungwort – Extract, Blue aqua, 8-1/4", open pontil, applied mouth, extremely rare, American 1840-1860 . . . . **$600-800**

L.P. Dodge – Rheumatic / Liniment / Newburg, Medium yellow amber, 6-1/8", open pontil, applied mouth, rare Newburg, New York colored pontil, American 1840-1860. . . . . . **$1,800-2,000**

Lindsey's – Blood / Searcher – Pittsburgh, PA, Deep blue aqua, 8-3/4", red iron pontil, applied double collar mouth, American 1840-1860 . . . . **$1,000-1,500**

Lindsey's – Blood / Searcher – Hollidaysburg, Medium blue green, 9", smooth base, applied double collar mouth, rare in this color with Hollidaysburg embossing, American 1860-1870 . . . . **$2,000-3,000**

Log Cabin – Extract – Rochester, N.Y., Amber, 7", smooth base (Pat. Sept 6th / 1887), tooled mouth, American 1887-1895 . . **$375-450**

Log Cabin – Extract – Rochester, N.Y., Amber, 8-5/8", smooth base (Pat. Sept 6th / 1887), tooled mouth, American 1887-1895 . . . . **$375-450**

London – W.B. No 6, Deep green aqua, 5-1/2", pontil-scarred base, outward rolled lip, rare embossed variant, English 1830-1850 . . . . **$140-180**

Masury's / Sarsaparilla / Cathartic, Blue aqua, 9", smooth base, applied double collar mouth, American 1855-1870 . . . . **$200-300**

Mathewson's – Horse – Remedy – Price 50 CTS, Aqua, 6-3/4", pontil-scarred base, applied double collar mouth, scarce, American 1840-1860 . . . . **$200-300**

McCombie's / Compound / Restorative, Aqua, 6-7/8", open pontil, applied mouth, rare, American 1840-1860 . . . **$90-125**

Morse's / Celebrate Syrup / Prov. R.I., Deep blue green, 9-1/2", oval form, open pontil, applied mouth, American 1840-1860 . . . . **$2,500-3,000**

Mystic Cure – For / Rheumatism / And / Neuralgia – Mystic Cure – Label reads: Detchon's Mystic Cure for Rheumatism and Neuralgia, I.A. Detchon, M.D. Crawfordsville, Indiana, Price 75 Cents, Pale aqua, 6-1/2", smooth base, tooled lip, American 1890-1900 . . . . **$150-200**

Mrs. Dr. Secor / Boston, Mass, Deep cobalt blue, 9-1/2", smooth base, tooled lip, American 1885-1895 . . . . **$100-150**

Mrs. E. Kidder / Dysentery / Cordial / Boston, Aqua, 7-3/4", open pontil, applied sloping collar mouth, American 1840-1860 . . . . **$100-150**

Mrs. M. Cox's / Indian Vegetable / Decoction / Balto, Aqua, 8-3/8", cylinder form, open pontil, applied mouth, American 1850-1860 . . . . **$400-700**

From The – Laboratory – G. W. Merchant – Chemist - Lockport – N.Y., medium blue green, 5-5/8", iron pontil, applied sloping collar mouth, American 1840-1860, (rare variant with the blocked out letters "LO" in Lockport), **$450-550.**

Mexican – Mustang – Liniment, deep blue aqua, 7-1/2", iron pontil, applied sloping collar mouth, American 1840-1860, **$75-100.**

Mrs. M. N. Gardners – Indian Balsam / Of Liverwort, Aqua, 5-1/8", cylinder form, open pontil, thin flared lip, American 1840-1860 . . . . **$75-100**

New York / C.F. Haskell / Coloris / Capilli / Restitutor, Aqua, 7-1/2", oval form, open pontil, applied mouth, rare, American 1840-1860 . . . . **$100-150**

N.Y. Medical – University – (embossed measure) – Label reads: Compound Fluid Extract of Cancer-Plant, Directions for Taking, and Prepared by the New York Medical University, Nos 6 7 8 University Place, New York City, Deep cobalt blue, 7-3/8", smooth base, tooled lip, scarce bottle made rare by the addition of the original label, American 1885-1900 . . . . **$500-600**

No 1 / Shaker Syrup – Canterbury, N.Y., Blue aqua, 7-3/8", open pontil, applied mouth, American 1840-1860 . . . . . . **$200-275**

Ober & McConkey's – Specific – For – Fever & Aqua – Balt MD, Aqua, 6-5/8", 6-sided, open pontil, applied mouth, rare, American 1840-1860 . . . . **$300-400**

O'Rourke & Hurley / Prescription Chemists / Little Falls, N.Y., Emerald green, 5-1/2", smooth base (C.L.C. Co.), tooled lip, American 1890-1900 . . . . **$80-140**

Pelletier's – Extract Of / Sarsaparilla – Hartford Conn, Blue aqua, 10-3/4", open pontil, applied double collar mouth, American 1840-1860 . . . . **$600-800**

Peruvian Syrup, Medium teal blue, 9-3/4", cylinder form, iron pontil, applied sloping collar mouth, rare color, American 1845-1860 . . . . **$1,845-1,860**

Prepared By – Dr. Easterly – St. Louis, MO, Blue aqua, 6", iron pontil, applied mouth, American 1840-1860 . . . . . . **$150-200**

Procter & Gamble / Glycerine, Clear, 7-7/8", wedge shape, smooth base, applied mouth, American 1850-1860 . . . . **$400-500**

Pure – Family – Nectar, Clear, 8-7/8", open pontil, applied mouth, American 1840-1860 . . . . **$200-250**

Radway's – Sarsaparillian / Resolvent – R.R.R. – Entd. Acord / To Act Of / Congress, Medium lime green, 7-3/8", smooth base, applied double collar mouth, American 1870-1880 . . . . **$250-300**

R.E. Sellers & Co. – Pittsburgh, Blue aqua, 6-7/8", iron pontil, applied double collar mouth, rare, American 1840-1860 . . . . **$150-200**

Rev. T. Hill's / Vegetable Remedy, Aqua, 5", oval form, open pontil, applied mouth, American 1840-1860 . . . . **$90-150**

Rev. T. Hill's / Vegetable Remedy, Aqua, 6", oval form, open pontil, applied mouth, American 1840-1860 . . . . **$90-150**

Roswell Van Bushkirk / Druggist / Newark N.J., Blue aqua, 6", open pontil, applied square collar mouth, American 1840-1860 . . . . **$275-400**

R.R.R. / Radway's Ready Relief / One Dollar / New York – Entd Accord To – Act Of Congress, Blue aqua, 8", open pontil, applied mouth, American 1840-1860 . . . . **$250-350**

Russian – Hair Rye – No. 1, Blue aqua, 3-3/8", open pontil, tool flared-out lip, American 1840-1860 . . . . **$140-160**

S & M – Label reads: Fluid Extract of Valerian, Prepared Only by Smith & Melvin, Chemist, 825 Washington Street, Boston, Pale aqua, 4-1/4", 12-sided, open pontil, tool flared-out lip, American 1840-1860 . . . . **$200-300**

Shakers' / Aromatic Elixir Of Malt / Pleasant Hill, / KY, Blue aqua, 8-3/4", smooth base, applied square collar mouth, American 1870 1880 . . . . **$150-200**

Shaker Syrup / No. 1 – Canterbury, N. H. – Label reads: Corbett's Shaker, Compound Concentrated Syrup of Sarsaparilla, Prepared at Shaker Village, Merrimack Co., N.H.**, Aqua, 7-1/2", open pontil, applied mouth, American 1840-1860 . . . . **$500-600**

Shaker Syrup – D. Miller & Co, Blue aqua, 7-1/4", open pontil, applied sloping collar mouth, American 1840-1860. . . . **$400-500**

Sheperd's – Vermifuge, Aqua, 4-7/8", open pontil, rolled lip, American 1840-1860 . . . . **$90-125**

Smith's – Green Mountain – Renovator – East Georgia, VT, Yellow amber, 7", rectangular with wide beveled corner panels, iron pontil, applied double collar mouth, American 1840-1860 . . . . **$1,200-1,600**

S.M. Kier – Petroleum – Pittsburgh, PA, Blue aqua, 6-5/8", open pontil, applied collar mouth, American 1840-1860 . . . **$50-60**

Sparks / Kidney & Liver / Cure / Trade Mark / (upper torso of a man) / Perfect Health / Camden, N.J., Medium yellow amber, 9-1/2", smooth base, tooled mouth, very rare, American 1880-1900 . . . . **$800-1,200**

Swaim's Panacea Philada, deep olive amber, 7-7/8", pontil-scarred base, applied sloping double collar mouth, American 1840-1860, **$350-400.**

Dr. Hoofland's / Balsamic Cordial, C.M. Jackson / Philadelphia, aqua, 7", American 1840-1860, $140-180. **$275-375**.

Sweet's Bl'K Oil – Rochester. N.Y., Blue green, 6", open pontil, applied sloping collar mouth, rare, American 1840-1860 . . . . **$1,800-2,700**

Taylor's – Indian – Ointment, Aqua, 3", 6-sided, open pontil, rolled lip, extremely rare, American 1840-1860 . . . . **$350-450**

U.S.A. / Hosp. Dept, Yellow amber olive, 9-1/4", smooth base (SDS), applied double collar, American 1863-1870 . . . .**$900-1,200**

U.S.A. / Hosp. Dept, Blue aqua, 9-1/4", smooth base (X), applied mouth, American 1863-1870 . . . . **$400-500**

U.S.A. / Hosp. Dept, Yellow olive green, 9-3/8", smooth base (six-pointed star), applied double collar mouth, American 1863-1870 . . . . **$1,700-2,000**

Wakelee's / Camelline, Pale ice blue, 3-1/4", smooth base, tooled lip, American 1890-1900 . . . . **$100-150**

Winant's / Indian / Liniment, Aqua, 4-7/8", open pontil, rolled lip, rare, American 1840-1860 . . . . **$300-400**

Worner's / Rattler Oil / Phoenix, ARZ, Clear, 3-1/2", smooth base, tooled lip, rare, American 1890-1900 . . . . **$100-150**

MILK BOTTLES

The first patent date for a milk bottle was issued to the "Jefferson Co. Milk Assn." in January 1875. The bottle featured a tin top with a spring clamping device. The first known standard-shaped milk bottle (pre-1930) was patented in March 1880 and was manufactured by the Warren Glass Works of Cumberland, Maryland.

In 1884, A.V. Whiteman patented a jar with a dome-type tin cap to be used with the patented Thatcher and Barnhart fastening device for a glass lid. No trace exists of a patent for

the bottle itself, however. Among collectors today, the Thatcher milk bottle is one of the most prized. There are several variations on the original. Very early bottles were embossed with a picture of a Quaker farmer milking his cow while seated on a stool. "Absolutely Pure Milk" is stamped into the glass on the bottle's shoulder.

An important development in the design of the milk bottle was the patent issued to H.P. and S.L. Barnhart in September 17, 1889, for their methods of capping and sealing. They developed a bottle mouth that received and retained a wafer disc or cap. It was eventually termed the milk bottle cap and revolutionized the milk bottling industry.

Between 1900 and 1920, not many new bottles were designed or had patents issued. With the introduction of the Owens semi-automatic and automatic bottle machines, milk bottles became mass produced. Between 1921 and 1945, the greatest number of milk bottles were manufactured and used. After 1945, square milk bottles and paper cartons became common.

Recently, there has been a renewed interest in collecting milk bottles. Two types of milk bottles are especially collectible. The first is the "Baby Top" bottle, which featured an embossed baby's face on the upper part of the bottle's neck. The second is the "Cop-the-Cream," which displays a policeman's head and cap embossed into the neck. The "Baby Top" design was invented in 1936 by Mike Pecora, Sr., of Pecora's Dairy in Drums, PA. Pecora's Dairy used quart, pint, and half-pint round bottles with pryo printing. Fifteen years after the original baby face was introduced, a "twin face" Baby Top was made with two faces, back to back, on opposite sides of the bottle. The Baby Top and Cop-the-Cream, as well as Tin Tops, are very rare and valuable.

The color mentioned in the following bottle descriptions is the color of the lettering on the bottle.

BABY TOPS

Associated Dairies, Los Angeles, CA, Red and blue **$125**

Bomgardner Dairy, Orange **$75**

Coweset Farm, Black **$75**

Dickson Dairy, Dickson, PA, Red **$75**

Fairyland Farms, Red **$75**

Associated Dairies, Los Angeles, CA, red and green, **$250.**

Edgewood Dairy – Beloit, WI, orange and black, **$100.**

Julius Anderson, Rockland, ME, Red **$75**

Orchard Farm Dairy, Schenectady, NY, Orange **$75**

Riviera Dairy, Santa Barbara, CA, Orange and green **$100**

Reservoir Farm, Moonsocket, RI, Orange **$125**

Strathbar Farms, Frankfort, NY, Red and blue **$125**

Sunbury Dairy, Orange **$100**

Sunshine Dairy, Red **$35**

Webb Brook Farm, Red **$50**

COP THE CREAM

Bentley's Dairy, Fall River, MA, Orange **$100**

Crestall Dairy, Carlstadt, NJ, Red **$125**

Eberhart & Rhodes Dairy, Puxsutawney, Pa, Red . . . **$125**

Glenside Dairy, Deep Water, NJ, Brown **$100**

Harpers Dairy, Wominister, MA, Orange **$125**

Losten Dairy, Chesapeake, Md, Red **$125**

Manor Dairy, Madison, WI, Red **$150**

Old Homestead Dairy, Windsor, VT, Red **$125**

Roe Dairy, Blue **$150**

Watkins Dairy – Westminster, VT, red, **$150.**

CREAM TOPS

Bitter Root Parlor Dairy, Stevenson, MT, Brown and red .. **$75**

Bordens Dairy Delivery Co., Red. **$75**

Gateway Pure Milk, Red and blue **$200**

Graduate Milk Bottles, Red **$50**

Hanson Dairy, Watervliet, MI, Black and tan. **$40**

Indiana Dairy Co., Indiana, PA, Black. **$45**

Mayflower Dairy – Vancouver, WA, red, **$50.**   Round Top Farm – Dammariscota, ME, green, **$50.**

Locust Grove Stock Farm, Rehoboth, MA, Red and blue . . . **$75**

Maine Dairy, Portland, ME, Red **$45**

Miller Dairy, Connersville, IN, Red and blue. **$50**

Modern Top Dairy, Red and tan **$75**

Mountain Meadow Dairy, Bisbee, AZ, Brown and red **$75**

Netherland, Red **$30**

Sanitary Dairy, Fort Dodge, IA, Red **$35**

Star Dairy, New London, CT, Red. **$25**

Sunshine Dairies, Utica, NY, Red and blue **$45**

QUARTER PINTS

Benty & Sons, Fairbanks, AK (semi-rare), Red **$50**

Bill Bros., Cortland, N.Y., Red. **$20**

C.A. Dorr Dairy, Watertown, N.Y., Orange **$20**

Casey Dairy, Cortland, N.Y., Red **$20**

Cramers Dairy, Fairbanks, AK (semi-rare), Red and black. . . . **$50**

Gillette & Sons Dairy, Red. **$10**

H.J. Whitmore, Clayton, N.Y., Red **$20**

J.R. McNulty, Watertown, N.Y., Orange. **$30**

Rico's Dairy, Lihue, HI (semi-rare), Red **$50**

Rock Castle Heavy Whipping Cream, Lynchburg, VA, Green . . . **$30**

Bay City – San Leandro, CAL, red, **$30** (USQP01); Dairy Products Laboratory, blue, **$50** (USQP01a); Elkhorn Farm, Watsonville, CA, orange, **$20.**

Rutland Hills Farm, Watertown, NY, Orange **$20**

Women's Missionary Conference of the M.E. Church, Clarksburg, WV, Red **$50**

Wildwood Dairy, Santa Rosa, CA, black, **$30.**

GALLONS

Bergman's Dairy, Derry, PA, Red **$50**

Carson County Creamery, Rawlins, WY, Orange **$50**

Indiana Dairy, Indiana, PA, Black **$50**

Keystone Dairy, New Kensington, PA, Red **$50**

Linger Light Dairy, New Castle, PA, Orange **$50**

Model Dairy, Corry, PA, Orange **$50**

North Hills Dairy, Pittsburgh, PA, Red **$50**

Page's Milk, Pittsburgh, PA, Orange **$50**

P.S. McGee Dairy, Blair County, PA, Red **$50**

R.W. Cramer & Sons, PA, Red **$50**

Harmony Dairy, Pittsburg, PA, red, **$50**.

Page's Pittsburgh Milk Co, Pittsburg, PA, red, **$50**.

Magic Milk, green, **$10**; Monence, Monence, IL, purple, **$10**; Crane Dairy, orange, **$10**; J & J Dairy, Atlantic City, NJ, red, **$10**; Sunflower, red, **$20**.

SQUARE QUARTS

Bechtel's Dairy, PA, Green	**$10**
Brook Hill Farm, Acidophilus Milk, Red	**$20**
Central Dairy, Central Bridge, N.Y., Red	**$25**
Crane Dairy Co., Orange	**$10**
Guard Your Health, Orange	**$10**
Mauer's Dairy, PA, Orange	**$10**
Merry's Dairy, Ben Avon, PA, Red and green	**$30**
Meyer's Milk, 57th Anniversary, Purple	**$30**
Monence Dairy, Monence, Il, Black	**$10**
Woodlawn Dairy, Red	**$30**

Meyer's Milk - 57th Anniversary, purple, **$30**.

COFFEE CREAMERS

All Star Dairies, Red. **$20**

Blanding Dairy, St. Johns, MI, Red **$20**

Cattlemen's Café, Oklahoma City, OK, Black. **$50**

Indiana Dairy, Indiana, PA, Black. **$40**

Kenmore Lanes, Kenmore, N.Y., Black. **$50**

Kennersley Farm, MD, Red **$30**

Link's, Randolph, N.Y., Red. **$40**

Marion Center Creamery, Indiana, PA, Red **$20**

Meadow Gold Milk, Red **$20**

New London Mohegan Dairy, CT, Brown **$20**

Mountain Dairy, Sunbury, PA, red, **$20**.

Strickler's – It's Better – Cream, Huntingdon, PA, orange, **$20**.

Picket's Pasteurized Products, Sheridan, IN, orange, **$40**.

Norman's Kill, Albany, N.Y., Orange. **$30**

Potomac Farms, MD, Orange. **$20**

Rehoboth Dairy, Rehoboth, DE (semi-rare), Red **$50**

R.J. Murphy & Sons Dairy, Orange **$30**

Royale Dairy, Keyser, W.V., Red **$30**

Tin-Top Milks, Benedict Bros. – Milk & Cream – 548 Castro St., Clear, half-pint cream **$100**

Ewells XL Dairy – Bottled Milk – Depot 21st & Folsom Streets – Trade Mark – This Bottle To Be Washed And Returned, Clear, half-pint cream **$100**

Fairmont 42 – Randall Dairy, Clear, pint, American 1885-1905 . . **$100**

Jersey Creamery M.Y.S. 1413 Park St., Alameda – This Bottle Must Be Returned, Clear, pint, includes tin-top, American 1885-1905 . . . . **$160**

Jersey Creamery M.Y.S. 1413 Park St., Alameda – This Bottle Must Be Returned, Clear, half-pint, includes tin-top, American 1885-1905 . . . . **$50**

Jersey Farm – 83/Howard St. This Bottle To Be Washed and Returned, Clear, half-pint cream **$100**

Merced Dairy – Solomon Bros. – 1507 Broderick St., Clear, pint, includes tin-top, American 1885-1905 . . . . **$100**

Milbrae California Milk Co. – Folsom & 21st Sts. – S.F. Cal, Clear, pint, includes tin-top, American 1885-1905 . . . . . . **$120**

People's Creamery Hatch and Orth 3776-24th St. – S.F., Clear, quart, American 1885-1905. . . . . **$100**

MISCELLANEOUS

Alta Crest Farms – Spencer Mass (embossed with cow's head), Medium lime green, quart, smooth base, ABM top, American 1950. . . . . **$1,000-1,100**

A. Rosa & Co. – Between 5th & 6th – 20 Oak Grove Ave., Clear, pint, smooth base **$100**

Big Elm – Dairy – Company – One Quart – Liquid – Registered, Green, quart, 9-1/4", smooth base (B-34), ABM lip with cap seat, American 1920-1930 . . . . **$150-200**

Bordens, Ruby red, quart, U.S. Pat. No. 2,177,396 60 – Royal Ruby – Anchor Glass (around base), American 1950, manufactured by Anchor Hocking for experimental purposes for the Borden Milk Company, fewer than twelve were made. . . **$1,800-2,000**

Dairy Delivery Co. – San Francisco – Wash and Return, Clear, pint, smooth base, American 1900-1910. . . . . **$100-125**

E.F. Mayer – Phone – Glen D3887R – 289 Hollenbeck Street, Medium amber, quart, smooth base (34 & M), ABM top, American 1940-1950 . . . . **$100-125**

Merced Dairy – Salomon Bros. – 1507 Broderick St., Clear, pint, smooth base, American 1940-1950 . . . . **$100**

One Quart / Liquid / Carrigan's / Niagara / Dairy Co. / Reed, Bright green, quart, 9-3/8", smooth base, ABM lip with cap seat, American 1920-1930 . . . . **$375-450**

People's Dairy – 24th & Church Strs., Clear, pint, American 1885-1905 . . . . **$50-75**

Absolutely / Pure Milk (motif of man milking cow) / The Milk Protector – To Be Used Only As Designated / Milk / & Cream / Jar – Thatcher MF'F. CO. / Potsdam N.Y., clear glass quart, 1886-1895, **$700-1,000.**

Absolutely / Pure Milk (motif of man milking cow) / The Milk Protector – To Be Used Only As Designated / Milk / & Cream / Jar, clear glass pint, 1886-1895, **$500-700.**

San Mateo County Dairy – Trade Mark – Phone Mission 227. 1818-1822 Howard St., Clear, pint, American 1885-1905.....**$100-125**

San Pedro & X.L. Dairy Co. – S.F. 1515 California St., Clear, pint, smooth base, American 1990-1920 ....**$75-100**

Sorge's – Selected Milk / Manitowog – Dairy Co. / 1 Quart Sealed – Pat'd Sept 22 1925 – On Applied Token: Sorges Brand, Clear, quart, smooth base, ABM lip, rare, American 1925-1935 ....**$100-150**

To Be Washed – And Returned – Not To Be Bought or Sold (in circular slug plate), Medium amber, 9-5/8", smooth base, applied double collar mouth, American 1900-1915......................**$180-120**

Weckerle / Reg –Weckerle / 1 QT, Bright green, quart 9-1/4", smooth base (W), ABM with cap seat, American 1920-1930 ....**$275-375**

To Be Washed / And Returned / Not To Be Bought Or Sold (circular slug plate), medium amber half-gallon, 1900-1915, **$180-220.**

MINERAL WATER BOTTLES

Mineral water, also known as spring water, was a very popular beverage for a full century, with peak consumption between 1860 and 1900. Consequently, most collectible bottles were produced during these years. While the earliest bottles are pontilled, the majority are smooth based. The water came from various springs that were high in carbonates (alkaline), sulfurous compounds, various salts, and were often naturally carbonated. The waters were also thought to possess medical and therapeutic qualities and benefits.

Although the shapes and sizes of mineral bottles are not very creative, the lettering and design, both embossed and paper, are bold and interesting. The bottles were produced in a variety of colors and range from 7 inches to 14 inches high. Most were cork-stopped and embossed with the name of the glasshouse manufacturer. In order to withstand the the high-pressure bottling process and the gaseous pressure of the contents, the bottles were manufactured with thick, heavy glass. Their durability made them suitable to be refilled many times.

A. D. Schnackenberg & Co. / Mineral Water / Brooklyn, N.Y., Deep amber, pint, smooth base, applied mouth, very rare, American 1870-1880 . . . . **$300-400**

Aletic China Water / Discovered By / (coat of arms) / Prof. Lavender, Yellow olive green, half-pint, smooth base, applied mouth, American 1870-1880. . . . . **$180-275**

Andrew Lawrence / York, PA, Medium emerald green, 7-3/8", iron pontil, applied blob mouth, extremely rare, one of only two known examples, American 1840-1860 . . . . **$500-700**

A. Schroth / Sch.ll Haven – Superior / Mineral Water / Union Glass Works, Medium cobalt blue, 7-3/8", mug base, iron pontil, applied mouth, scarce, American 1840-1860 . . . . . **$700-1,000**

Avery Lord, Medium cobalt blue, 7-1/4", smooth base, applied mouth, American 1855-1870. . . . . **$100-150**

Avery N. Lord – Utica N.Y., Aqua, 7-1/4", smooth base, applied mouth, American 1855-1870. . . . . **$100-150**

A.W. Rapp's / Improved / Patent Mineral Water – Soda Water / R / New York, Emerald green, 6-7/8", iron pontil, applied mouth, American 1835-1845. . . . . **$300-400**

B. Bick & Co – Mineral Water – Cincinnati – B, Cobalt blue, 7-1/2", 10-sided with embossed tear drop in each panel around shoulder, iron pontil, applied blob mouth, rare, American 1840-1860 . . . . **$200-300**

Buffum & Co / Pittsburgh – Sarsaparilla / And / Mineral Water, Deep cobalt blue, 8", smooth base, applied mouth, American 1855-1865 . . . . **$400-500**

Adirondack Spring / Westport, N.Y., deep blue green, quart, smooth base, applied collar mouth, American 1865-1875, **$400-500.**

European Mineral Water / After / Dr. Struve's Method / Manufactured / By / Schnackenberg & G_____Z / Brooklyn, L.I., deep yellow olive green, 3/4 quart, smooth base, applied sloping double collar mouth, American 1870-1880, **$200-250.**

Carter & / Wilson / Manuf's / Boston – Soda & / Mineral / Water, Deep blue green, 6-7/8", iron pontil, applied sloping collar mouth, American 1840-1860. . . . . **$400-600**

Carter & / Wilson / Manuf's / Boston – Soda & / Mineral / Water, Deep blue green, 6-3/4", iron pontil, applied sloping collar mouth, American 1840-1860. . . . . **$400-600**

Champion Spouting Spring / Saratoga Mineral / Springs / (CSS monogram) / Limited / Saratoga N.Y. – Champion / Water, Blue aqua, pint, smooth base, applied mouth, American 1865-1875 . . . . **$75-100**

Clark & White / C / New York / NII, Deep olive green, pint, smooth base, applied mouth, rare, American 1860-1865 . . . **$180-220**

Clark & White / C / New York, Deep olive green, pint, smooth base, wide mouth with rolled lip, early widemouth salt jar, extremely rare, American 1855-1865 . . . . **$7,000-9,000**

Congress & Empire Spring Co / Hotchkiss' Sons / C / W / New York / Saratoga, N.Y., Olive green, half-pint, smooth base, applied mouth, American 1865-1875 . . . . **$250-350**

Congress & Empire Spring Co / Columbian Water / Saratoga, N.Y., Medium blue green, pint, slope shoulder, smooth base, applied mouth, American 1865-1875 . . . . **$2,000-3,000**

Covert / Morristown / N.J. – Superior / Mineral / Water, Medium cobalt blue, 6-7/8", iron pontil, applied mouth, American 1840-1860 . . . . **$3,000-4,000**

Crystal Spring Water / C.R. Brown / Saratoga Springs / N.Y., Deep emerald green, quart, smooth base, applied mouth, rare, American 1865-1875 . . . . **$1,200-1,600**

Darling & Cobb's / Improved / Mineral Water – Boston / C, Light blue green, 6-7/8", iron pontil, applied sloping collar mouth, American 1840-1860 . . . . **$150-275**

Demott's / Celebrated / Soda or Mineral / Waters – Hudson County / N.J., Cobalt blue, 7-3/8", iron pontil, applied sloping collar mouth, American 1840-1860 . . . . **$100-200**

Excelsior / Spring / Saratoga, N.Y., Medium blue green, quart, smooth base, applied mouth, American 1865-1875 . **$200-300**

Exelsior / Spring / Saratoga, N.Y., Yellow olive green, pint, smooth base, tooled mouth, American 1865-1875 . . **$200-275**

Francis / Schellenberg (in a slug plate), Blue green, 6-7/8", squat form, iron pontil, applied mouth, American 1840-1860 . . . . **$150-200**

Geo. Upp, Jr. / York, PA – Mineral / Water, Medium cobalt blue, 7-3/4", iron pontil, applied blob mouth, very rare, American 1840-1860 . . . . **$700-900**

Geyser Spring / Saratoga Springs / State / Of / New York – The Saratoga / Spouting Springs, Deep blue green, pint, smooth base, applied mouth, very rare color, American 1865-1875 . . . . **$3,500-4,500**

Geyser Spring / Saratoga Springs / New York – Avery N. Lord / 66 Broad St. / Utica, N.Y., Blue aqua, quart, smooth base (A & HDC), applied mouth, rare, American 1865-1875 . . . . **$550-750**

Gettysburg – Water, Deep olive green, tall magnum quart, smooth base, applied mouth, extremely rare, American 1865-1875 . . . . **$2,500-3,500**

Guilford Mineral / GMSW (monogram) / Guilford / VT. / Spring Water, Olive yellow, quart, smooth base, applied mouth, scarce color, American 1865-1875 . . . . **$250-350**

G.W. Weston & Co / Saratoga / N.Y., Deep olive amber, quart, pontil-scarred base, applied mouth, American 1848-1855 . . **$400-500**

H. Borgman / Mineral Water / Manufacturer / Cumberland, MD, Blue green, 8-3/8", iron pontil, applied blob mouth, extremely rare, American 1850-1860 . . . . **$2,000-2,500**

Hand & Murtha / Mineral Waters – H & M, Aqua, 7-1/4", iron pontil, applied mouth, extremely rare, American 1845-1860 . . . . **$500-600**

Harris's / Albany / Mineral Water, Medium blue green, 7-1/4", iron pontil, applied mouth, very rare, American 1840-1860 . . . . **$200-300**

Highrock Congress Springs / (motif of rock) / C & W / Saratoga, N.Y., Teal blue, pint, smooth base, applied mouth, American 1865-1875 . . . . **$400-600**

Highrock Congress Spring / (motif of rock) / C & W / Saratoga, N.Y., Yellow amber, pint, smooth base, applied mouth, American 1865-1875 . . . . **$200-300**

I.C. / Vreeland / Newark / N.J. – Superior Water / Union Glass Works / Phila, Teal blue, 7-1/2", iron pontil, applied blob mouth, American 1840-1860, , , , , , . . **$150 200**

J.B. Edward – Mineral Water / Columbia / PA, Deep blue, 7-5/8", iron pontil, American 1840-1860 . . **$500-700**

Highrock Spring / (motif of rock) / Saratoga, N.Y., dark olive amber (black), pint, smooth base, applied sloping double collar mouth, American 1865-1875, (rare), **$1,000-1,500.**

John H. Gardner & Son / Sharon Springs / N.Y. – Sharon / Sulphur / Water, medium blue green, pint, smooth base, applied sloping double collar mouth, American 1865-1875, **$400-600.**

J. Dowall (in a slug plate) – Union Glass Works Phila – / Superior / Mineral Water, Deep cobalt blue, 7-1/2", mug base, iron pontil, applied blob-type mouth, American 1840-1860 ....**$2,500-3,000**

J. Lake / Schenectady , N.Y., Deep cobalt blue, 8-1/8", iron pontil, applied mouth, American 1840-1860 ....**$1,000-1,600**

John Boardman – New York – Mineral Waters, Cobalt blue, 7-1/4", 8-sided, iron pontil, applied blob mouth, American 1840-1860 ....**$400-600**

Knickerbocker / Mineral Water / Bottles Registered / According To Law – Boughton & Chase / Rochester, Medium cobalt blue, 7-1/2", iron pontil, applied blob-type mouth, American 1840-1860 ....**$500-800**

Lynch & Clarke / New York, Deep olive green, quart, pontil-scarred base, applied mouth, American 1825-1830 .....**$1,200-1,600**

Lynch & Clarke / New York, Yellow olive amber, pint, pontil-scarred base, applied mouth, American 1825-1835.........**$700-900**

Keys – Burlington / N.J., Medium blue green, 7-1/8", iron pontil, applied blob mouth, American 1840-1860 ....**$200-300**

Keys – Burlington (in an arch) / N.J., Medium emerald green, 7-1/4", iron pontil, applied mouth, American 1840-1860 ....**$125-175**

Massena Spring / (monogram) / water, Medium teal blue, quart, smooth base, applied mouth, American 1865-1875..........................**$150-200**

Middletown Healing Springs / Grays & Clark / Middletown VT, medium yellow amber, quart, smooth base, applied sloping double collar mouth, American 1865-1875, **$500-700.**

Lithia Mineral Spring Co. / Gloversville, aqua, pint, smooth base, applied mouth, American 1865-1875, (rare), **$600-800.**

Middletown / Healing / Springs / Grays & Clark / Middletown VT, Deep emerald green, quart, smooth base, applied mouth, rare color, American 1865-1875 . . . . **$400-500**

Middletown / Healing Springs / Grays & Clark / Middletown VT, Deep yellow amber, quart, smooth base, applied mouth, American 1865-1875 . . . . **$900-1,200**

Missisquoi / A / Springs – (Indian woman with papoose), Yellow olive, quart, smooth base, applied mouth, American 1865-1875 . . . . **$250-300**

Oak Orchard / Acid Springs – H.W. Bostwick / Agt. No 574 / Broadway, New York, Dark amber, quart, smooth base (Glass From F. Hitchings Factory / Lockport, N.Y.), applied mouth, American 1865-1875 . . . . **$200-275**

Oak Orchard / Acid Springs – Alabama / Genesee Co. N.Y., Medium blue-green, quart, smooth base, applied mouth, American 1865-1875 . . . . **$250-350**

Powell's – Mineral Water – Burlington – N.J., Medium sapphire blue, 7-5/8", 8-sided, iron pontil, rare Powell bottle, American 1840-1860 . . . . **$2,500-3,500**

Powell & – Dr. Burr's Mineral Water – Burlington – N.J., Medium cobalt blue, 7-3/4", 8-sided, iron pontil, applied mouth, American 1840-1860 . . . . **$1,500-2,500**

Rockbridge / VA / Alum Water Yellow olive green, 6-7/8", squat form, pint, iron pontil, applied mouth, American 1845-1860 . . . . **$10,000-14,000**

Mineral water bottle and stand: Eureka Spring Co. – Saratoga N.Y., deep emerald green, torpedo pint, smooth base, applied sloping double collar mouth, silver stand is plated and engraved with "Gould's Hotel" on top, and base is stamped "Gorman Co.", American 1865-1875, **$700-1,000.**

Pavilion & United States Spring / P / Saratoga / N.Y. – Pavilion / Water, medium blue green, pint, smooth base, applied sloping double collar mouth, American 1865-1875, **$300-400.**

Rockbridge / Alum / Water – Alum Springs / Virginia, Deep emerald green, 13-1/4", smooth base, applied mouth, extremely rare, American 1855-1865 .... **$10,000-15,000**

S. Keys / Burlington / N.J. – Union Glass Works / Superior / Mineral Water, Medium cobalt blue, 7-3/4", paneled mug base, iron pontil, applied mouth, American 1840-1860.... **$450-650**

Saratoga High Rock Spring / (motif of rock) / Saratoga, N.Y., Emerald green, pint, smooth base, applied mouth, American 1865-1875 .... **$1,000-1,300**

Saratoga / (star) / Spring, Olive green, quart, smooth base, applied mouth, scarce color, American 1865-1875 .... **$275-375**

Saratoga Seltzer Water, Medium green, pint, smooth base, applied mouth, American 1870-1885 .... **$200-300**

Saratoga Vichy Spouting Spring / V / Saratoga / N.Y., Aqua, three-quarter pint, smooth base, applied mouth, rarely seen in this size, American 1765-1875.................. **$250-350**

Saratoga Vichy Spouting Spring / V / Saratoga / N.Y., Aqua, half-pint, smooth base, tooled mouth, American 1865-1875 .... **$180-222**

St. Catherines / Mineral Water / G.L. Mather Agent / Astor House / New York, Medium yellow amber, 11-3/8", cylinder form, smooth base, applied sloping collar mouth, American 1865-1875 .... **$1,100-1,300**

St. Regis / Water / Massena Springs, Black olive amber, quart, smooth base, applied mouth, American 1865-1875 .... **$375-450**

St. Regis / Water / Massena Springs, deep emerald green, quart, smooth base, applied sloping double collar mouth, American 1865 1875, **$250-300.**

Hathorn Spring / Saratoga NY, dark amber, pint, smooth base, applied sloping double collar mouth, American 1865-1875, **$200-300.**

Star Spring co / (star) / Saratoga, N.Y., Deep amber, pint, smooth base, applied mouth, American 1865-1875 . . . . **$200-250**

Teller's / Mineral Water / Detroit – The Bottle / Must Be / Returned, Deep cobalt blue, 8-3/8", smooth base, applied mouth, American 1855-1865. . . . . **$300-400**

Vermont Spring / Saxe & Co. / Shelton, VT., Yellow olive, quart, smooth base, applied mouth, scarce color, American 1865-1875 . . . . **$120-150**

Vermont Spring / Saxe & Co. / Sheldon, VT., Yellow amber, quart, smooth base, applied mouth, American 1865-1875. . . . . **$600-800**

Washington Spring Co (bust of Washington) / Ballston Spa / N.Y. – C, Deep blue green, pint, smooth base, applied mouth, American 1865-1875 . . . . **$400-500**

W. Heiss, Jr's / Mineral Water / No. 213 N. 2nd. St. / Phila – Improved / H / Patent, Medium blue green, 7", tubular pen pontil, applied mouth, American 1835-1845 . . . . . . **$350-400**

WM. P. Davis & Co – Excelsior – Mineral Water – Brooklyn, Cobalt blue, 7-3/8", 8-sided, iron pontil, applied blob mouth, American 1840-1860 . . . . **$900-1,200**

POISON BOTTLES

By the very nature of their contents, poison bottles form a unique category for collecting. While most people assume that poison bottles are plain, most are very decorative, making them easy to identify their toxic contents. In 1853, the American Pharmaceutical Association recommended that laws be passed requiring identification of all poison bottles. In 1872, the American Medical Association recommended that poison bottles be identified with a rough surface on one side and the word poison on the other. But as so often happened during that era,

passing of these laws was very difficult and the manufacturers were left to do whatever they wanted. Because a standard wasn't established, a varied group of bottle shapes, sizes, and patterns were manufactured including skull and crossbones, or skulls, leg bones, and coffins.

The bottles were manufactured with quilted or ribbed surfaces and diamond/lattice-type patterns for identification by touch. Colorless bottles are very rare, since most poison bottles were produced in dark shades of blues and browns, another identification aid. When collecting these bottles, caution must be exercised, since it is not uncommon to find a poison bottle with its original contents. If the bottle has the original glass stopper, the value and demand for the bottle will greatly increase.

Friedgen (irregular hexagon poison), Yellow green, 6-7/8", smooth base (C.L.G. CO. /Patent Applied For), tooled lip, extremely rare, no other example in the 12 oz. size is known to exist, American 1890-1910 . . . . **$4,500-5,500**

Gift / Flache (skull and crossbones), Olive green, 6-1/4", smooth base, tooled lip, German 1890-1930 . . . . **$90-150**

Gift / Flasche (skull and crossbones), Golden yellow amber, 9-3/8", 6-sided, smooth base, ABM lip, German 1920-1930 . . . . . . **$50-75**

Not To Be Taken, Cobalt blue, 5", 4-sided, smooth base, tooled top, American 1890-1910 . . . . **$75-100**

Not To Be Taken – Label reads: What Home Without a Clean Bed, Mexican Brand Insect Fluid Compound, (woman in bedroom using the product), Mexican Roach Food Co, Buffalo, N.Y., Under the Insecticide Act of 1910, Serial No. 269, Cobalt blue, 5-1/2", hexagonal form, smooth base (4), tooled lip, Canadian 1900-1915 . . . . **$140-180**

Not To Be Taken, Brilliant green, 7", ribbing and cross design around entire bottle, smooth base, tooled top, American 1900-1915 . . . . **$250-275**

Figural skull poison (embossed skull in relief), clear glass cylinder with skull face, 4-1/8", "Pat / June 8 1875" on smooth base, tooled mouth, American 1880-1910, (extremely rare, less than five known examples), **$5,500-6,500.**

Gray & Pearse / Apothecaries / Poison / Take Care / Cheyenne / Wyo., deep cobalt blue, 3-5/8", "W.T. & Co." on smooth base, tooled mouth, American 1890-1910, (very rare), **$1,400-1,600.**

Not To Be Taken / Patent – Caution, lime green, 3-1/2", triangular form with finger grip corners, "1 OZ" on smooth base, tooled lip, English 1899-1910, (J. Wilson Patent Poison of 1890), **$150-200.**

J.W. McBeath / Kimberly / Poison, medium cobalt blue, 5-3/8", "W.T. & Co. / U.S.A. / Pat. Dec. 11. 1894" on smooth base, tooled mouth, Australian, 1890-1910, **$150-200.**

Poison - Lewis Bear Drug Co / Pensacola, Fla., clear glass, 4-1/8", four-sided diamond form with sawtooth edges, smooth base, tooled mouth, American 1890-1910, **$1,000-1,200.**

Poison (label reads "Strychnine Sulphate"), cobalt blue, 3-1/8", "E.R.S. & S" on smooth base, tooled mouth, sawtooth glass stopper embossed with "E.R.S. & S", American 1890-1910, **$100-150.**

Poison – F.A. Thompson & Co. – Detroit – Poison, medium amber, 3-1/4", American 1890-1910, **$600-900**.

Poison – Poison (original label for "Mercuric Chloride"), medium cobalt blue, 7-3/4", coffin shape, "Norwich /16A" on smooth base, tooled mouth, American 1890-1910, **$850-950.**

(Front and Back) Poison – Poison (original label for "Bardoxy Mercury OXYcyanide, C.R. Bard Ind. New York"), medium amber, 4-7/8", "Norwich / 48" on smooth base, tooled mouth, American 1890-1910, **$550-650.**

Not To Be Taken, Dark cobalt blue, 8-1/2", 4-sided, smooth base, tooled top, American 1900-1915 . . . . **$150-300**

Poison, Cobalt blue, 2-1/2", star shaped, smooth base, screw top, American 1900-1930 . . . . **$50-60**

Poison, Medium cobalt blue, 3", coffin form, smooth base, tooled top, American 1890-1915 . . . . **$90-125**

Poison, Medium amber, 3", 3-sided, smooth base (JTM), tooled top, American 1900-1915 . . . . **$35-40**

Poison, Cobalt blue, 3-1/4", triangular form, smooth base (U.D. CO.), ABM top, American 1890-1910 . . . . **$50-70**

Poison, Cobalt blue, 3-3/4", smooth base, tooled top, American 1890-1910 . . . . **$100-200**

Poison, Cobalt blue, 4", quilted around entire bottle, smooth base, tooled top, original glass stopper embossed "Poison," American 1890-1910 . . . . **$75-100**

Poison – Use With Caution, Cobalt blue, 4", irregular hexagon, smooth base, ABM top, American 1890-1910 . . . . **$50-60**

Poison – Star / Skull / Crossbones – Poison, Yellow with amber tone, 4-3/4", oval form, smooth base (S&D / 231), tooled lip, American 1890-1910 . . . . **$700-1,000**

Poison, Medium amber, 4-7/8", smooth base (S & D), tooled mouth American 1890-1910 . . . . **$150-200**

Poison, Medium amber, 5", triangular form, smooth base, tooled top, American 1900-1920 . . . . **$650-750**

Poison, cobalt blue, 3-1/2", coffin shape, smooth base, tooled mouth, American, 1890-1910, **$150-200** / Poison, amber, 3-1/2", coffin shape, smooth base, tooled mouth, American, 1890-1910, **$150-200.** (Both have label reading "Mercuric Chloride The Norwich Pharmacal Co., Norwich, New York".)

Poison – (stars above and below skull and crossbones) / Poison, yellow with amber tone, 4-5/8", "S & D" on smooth base, tooled mouth, American 1890-1910, **$460-550.**

Poison (skull and crossbones) DP CO – Poison – Written on faded label: R, 3 cents a piece, Cobalt blue, 5", coffin form, smooth base, tooled mouth, rare middle size, American 1890-1910 ....**$5,000-10,000**

Poison, Green aqua, 5-5/8", rectangular form, smooth base, tooled mouth, American 1890-1910 ....**$750-950**

Poison, Cobalt blue, 5", quilted around entire bottle, smooth base, tooled top, original glass stopper embossed "Poison," American 1890-1910 ....**$75-100**

Poison, deep cobalt blue, 3-1/8", oval shape, "Davis & Geck Inc / DG (monogram inside diamond) / Brooklyn, N.Y. U.S.A." on smooth base, tooled mouth, American 1890-1910, **$250-300.**

Poison, Cobalt blue, 6", quilted around entire bottle, smooth base, tooled top, original glass stopper embossed "Poison," American 1890-1910 . . . . **$75-100**

Poison, Violet blue, 8", quilted around entire bottle, round form, smooth base (HB CO), glass stopper, tooled top, American 1900-1915 . . . . **$100-130**

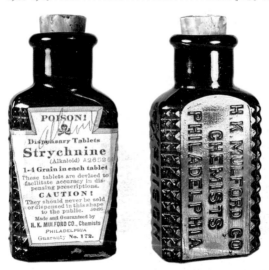

(Front and Back) (Skull and crossbones) Poison - H.K. Mulford Co. / Chemists / Philadelphia - (skull and crossbones) (original label reads "Strychnine"; label cork reads "M"), deep cobalt blue, 3-1/4", smooth base, tooled mouth, American 1890-1910, **$175-225.**

Poison, Medium amber, 8", diamond cornered design, smooth base, tooled top, American 1890-1915 . . . . **$300-350**

Poison, Cobalt blue, 8", triangular form, smooth base, tooled top, American 1890-1915 . . . . **$2,500-3,000**

Poison, Violet blue, 9-1/4", quilted around entire bottle, round form, smooth base, glass stopper that reads "Poison" on thee sides, tooled top, American 1900-1915 . . . . **$175-200**

Poison, Violet blue, 12", quilted around entire bottle, round form, smooth base, glass stopper, tooled top, American 1900-1915 . . . . **$550-650**

Poison – Bowman's / Drug Stores – Poison – Label reads: Denatured Alcohol, Poison, Bowman Drug Co., Oakland, Cobalt blue, 7", irregular hexagon form, smooth base (G.L.G. & Co. / Patent Appl'd For), tooled lip, American 1890-1910 . . . . **$1,000-1,500**

Poison – Carbolic Acid – Use With Caution, Cobalt blue, 8-3/4", smooth base, tooled top, American 1890-1915 . . . . **$70-80**

Poison – The Owl Drug Co. (motif of owl on mortar and pestle), Cobalt blue, 4", smooth base, ABM top, American 1900-1915 . . . . **$50-60**

Poison – The Owl Drug Co. (motif of owl on mortar and pestle), Medium amber, 4-1/2", smooth base, ABM top, American 1900-1915 . . . . **$100-125**

Poison – The Owl Drug Co. (motif of owl on mortar and pestle) – Label reads: Solution of Formaldehyde, Cobalt blue, 7-3/4", smooth base, tooled mouth, rare with label, American 1890-1915 . . . . **$375-475**

(Skull and crossbones) Poison – H.K. Mulford Co. / Chemists / Philadelphia – (skull and crossbones) Poison (neck label reads "Arsenous Acid"; cork reads "M") Poison, yellow amber, 3-1/4", smooth base, tooled mouth, American 1890-1910, **$350-400.**

Poison – The Owl Drug Co. (motif of owl on mortar and pestle), Cobalt blue, 9-5/8", triangular form, smooth base, tooled top, American 1890-1915 .... $800 **1,100**

Poison (skull and crossbones) / H.K. Mulford Co. – Chemist – Philadelphia, Cobalt blue, 3-1/4", smooth base, tooled top, American 1900-1915 .... **$175-200**

(Front and Back) Poison (original label reads "Poison-Toxitabellae Hydrargyri Chloride Corrosivi–R. Squibb & Sons") cobalt blue, 5-1/4", "T.C.W. Co. / U.S.A". on smooth base, tooled mouth, sawtooth glass stopper embossed "E.R.S. & S", American 1890-1910, **$400-600.**

(Front and Back) Poison - Poison (label reads "Mercury Bichloride"), clear glass, 5-1/8" triangular form, smooth base, tooled mouth, American 1890-1910, $300-400.

Poison (skull and crossbones) / Gift (skull and crossbones) / Veleno, Olive green, 8-1/4", smooth base, ABM lip, German 1890-1930 .... **$90-150**

Poison, Amber, 8-3/8", hexagonal form, smooth base (E.B. & CO. LO/5000), tooled lip, English 1900-1920 .... **$200-300**

Poison, Cobalt blue, 5-3/8", smooth base (U.S.P.H.S.), tooled lip with a wide mouth, American 1890-1910......... **$150-250**

Poison, Cobalt blue, 5-5/8", smooth base (H.B. CO.), tooled lip, original stopper embossed with "Poison," scarce, American 1890-1910 .... **$75-125**

Super / Pittsburg, sapphire blue, 3-3/8", vertical ribbed body with indented label panel, smooth base, tooled flared lip, American 1890-1910, (a rare bottle from Super Pharmacies of Pittsburg), **$100-125.**

Poison, Medium amber, 5", coffin form, smooth base (Norwich 16A), tooled round collared mouth, American 1890-1900 .... **$500-700**

Poison, Medium amber, 7-1/2", coffin form, smooth base (Norwich 16A), tooled round collared mouth, extremely rare, American 1890-1900 ....**$7,000-14,000**

Poison, Cobalt blue, 14-3/4", cylindrical with tall wide flutes around the circumference of the midsection, smooth base, tooled collared mouth, American 1880-1900 ...... **$300-600**

(Skull and crossbones) Poison / Tinct / Iodine, cobalt blue, 3-1/8", American 1890-1910, **$100-150** / (Skull and crossbones) Poison / Tinct / Iodine, cobalt blue, 2-1/8", American 1890-1910, **$100-150.**

Poison - Poison, medium amber, 2-5/8",
"WRW & Co" on smooth base, tooled mouth,
American 1890-1910, **$150-200.**

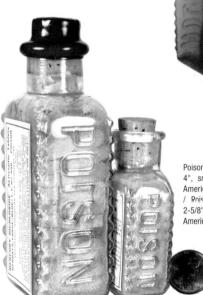

Poison - Poison, clear glass,
4", smooth base, tooled mouth,
American 1890-1910, **$90-115**
/ Poison - Poison, clear glass,
2-5/8", smooth base, tooled mouth
American 1890-1910, **$90-115.**

Poison - Poison ("Lilly" inscribed on cork), amber, 10-1/2", smooth base, tooled mouth, American 1890-1910, **$150-200.**

Poison, medium yellow amber, 4-7/8", "S & D" on smooth base, tooled mouth, American 1890-1910, **$100-125.**

Poison – Poison, Medium amber, 3", coffin shape, smooth base, tooled lip, extremely rare, one of only two known examples, American 1890-1910 . . . . **$3,500-4,500**

Poison – Poison, Medium green, 5", irregular hexagon, smooth base, tooled top, American 1890-1915 . . . . **$100-150**

Poison – Poison, Light cobalt blue, 5", irregular hexagon, smooth base, tooled top, American 1890-1915 . . . . **$50-70**

Poison – Poison, Dark cobalt blue, 5", irregular hexagon, smooth base, tooled top, American 1890-1915 . . . . **$500-600**

Poison – Poison, Medium green, 5-1/2", smooth base (C.L.G. CO. / Patent Applied For), tooled mouth, rare color, American 1890-1910 . . . . **$150-250**

Poison – Poison (on reverse), Cobalt blue, 7-1/4", coffin form, smooth base (Norwich 16 A), tooled top, American 1890-1910 . . . . **$800-1,100**

Skull and Crossbones (embossed on bottle), Yellow amber, 2-1/2", smooth base (P.D. & CO.), tooled lip, American 1890-1910 . . . . **$60-80**

Strychnia / 1/8 oz. / Poison Rosengarten & Sons / Manufacturing Chemists / Philadelphia (label), Clear, 2-1/2", smooth base, tooled lip with original cork, American 1900-1920 . . . . **$100-150**

Vorsicht / (skull and crossbones) / Gift! – Attention! / (skull and crossbones) Poison – Attenzione! / (skull and crossbones) / Veleno, Yellow green, 9", square form with embossing on three panels in three languages, smooth base, ABM lip, European 1915-1935 . . . . **$125-150**

SODA BOTTLES

After years of selling, buying, and trading, I have come to believe that soda bottles support one of the largest collector groups in the United States. Even collectors who don't normally search for soda bottles always seem to have a few on their table (or under the table) for sale.

Soda is basically artificially flavored or unflavored carbonated water. In 1772, an Englishman named Joseph Priestley succeeded in defining the process of carbonation. Small quantities of unflavored soda were sold by Professor Benjamin Silliman in 1806. By 1810, New York druggists were selling homemade seltzer as cure-all for stomach problems, with flavors being added to the solution in the mid-1830s. By 1881, flavoring was a standard additive in these seltzers.

Because of pressure caused by carbonation, bottle manufacturers had to use a much stronger type of bottle, which eventually led to the heavy-walled blob-type soda bottle. Some of these more common closures were the Hutchinson-type wire toppers, lightning stoppers, and Codd stoppers.

Soda bottles generally aren't unique in design, since the manufacturers had to produce them as cheaply as possible to keep up with demand. The only way to distinguish among bottles is by the lettering, logos, embossing, or labels (not very common).

A. Allen / Lumberton / N.J. – Milford Glass Works, Blue green, 6-3/4", squat form, iron pontil, applied mouth, American 1840-1860 . . . . **$400-600**

A. R. Cox / Norristown, Deep blue green, 7-1/4", iron pontil, applied mouth, American 1840-1860 . . . . **$400-500**

A. W. Cudworth / & Co / San Francisco / Cal (in a slug plate), Emerald green, 7-1/2", iron pontil, applied blob mouth, American 1850-1860 . . . . **$250-375**

A. Wood / Pittsg / PA, Medium blue green, 7-3/8", tubular open pontil, applied sloping collar mouth, very rare, American 1840-1860 . . . . **$1,000-1,500**

Blanchard & Defreest / Troy, N.Y. – Superior / B & D / Soda Water, Sapphire blue, 7-3/4", iron pontil, applied blob mouth, American 1840-1860 . . . . **$700-900**

Block & / Brandon / FRL – Levenworth / City / K.T., Blue aqua, 7-1/2", pontil-scarred base, applied top mouth, rare, Kansas Territory, American 1858-1860 . . . . **$2,000-3,000**

Boughton & Chase, Medium cobalt blue, 7", graphite pontil base, 10-sided, applied top, American 1865-1875 . . . . **$2,500-3,000**

Brownell / & Wheaton / New Bedford – This Bottle / Never Sold, Deep sapphire blue, 7-3/8", smooth base, applied blob type mouth, American 1855-1865. . . . . **$180-275**

Carbutt & Hamilton / Manufacturers / Cincinnati, Blue aqua, 7-7/8", smooth base, applied mouth, American 1855-1870. . . . . **$375-450**

A.W. Cudworth / & CO / San Francisco / CAL (in a slug plate), emerald green 7 1/2", iron pontil, applied blob-top mouth, American 1850-1860, **$275-375.**

C. Garforth / Wheeling – G, blue aqua, 7 1/2", iron pontil, applied reverse sloping collar mouth, American 1840-1860, **$400-500.**

Carpenter – & Cobb – Knickerbocker – Soda Water – Saratoga – Springs, Blue green, 7-1/2", 10-sided, iron pontil, applied blob mouth, rare, American 1840-1860 . . . . **$700-900**

Cassin's English Aerated Waters, Emerald green, 10", rounded smooth bottom, applied top, Western soda, American 1875-1885 . . . . **$325-425**

C.B. Hale & Co – Camden / N.J. (in an oval), Medium emerald green, 7", iron pontil, applied sloping double collar mouth, very rare, one of only three or four known to exist, American 1840-1860 . . . . **$200-300**

C.C. Haley / & Co / Celebrated / California / POP Beer – Patented / Oct. 29th 1872 / This Bottle / Is Never Sold, Deep amber, 11-1/8", smooth base, applied mouth, scarce, American 1872-1875 . . . . **$250-350**

C. Garforth / Wheeling – G, Blue aqua, 7-1/2", iron pontil, applied reverse sloping collar mouth, American 1840-1860 . . . . **$350-450**

Chas. Grove / Cola. PA (in a slug plate) – Brown / Stout, Blue aqua, 6-1/2", squat form, iron pontil, applied mouth, rare, American 1840-1860 . . . . **$100-150**

Cha's Grove / Columbia, PA (in a slug plate), Medium blue green, 6-7/8", iron pontil, applied mouth, rare, American 1840-1860 . . . . **$750-850**

C. M. Walter / M. Holly / N.J. (in a slug plate), Deep green aqua, 7", squat form, smooth base, applied mouth, American 1855 -1865. . . . . **$400-600**

Crystal Palace / Premium / Soda Water / W. Eagle / New York (motif of Crystal Palace) / Union Glass Works / Phila, teal blue, 7-3/8", iron pontil, applied blob-type mouth, American 1845-1860, (scarce), **$1,000-1,200.**

H. Ferneding / Dayton. O (on shoulder), deep olive amber, quart, pontil-scarred base, applied sloping double collar mouth, three-piece mold, American 1851-1852, **$200-300.**

Cream / Ale – A. Templeton / Louisville (around mug base), Deep red amber, quart, smooth base (L & W), applied sloping double collar mouth, American 1870-1880 . . . . . . **$450-550**

C. Whittemore / New York, Light blue green, 7-1/2", iron pontil, applied "top hat" mouth, American 1840-1860 . . . . **$100-150**

Davenport & Cos. / Mineral & Soda / Water – D.G. & K / Patent, Deep blue green, 6-7/8", pontil-scarred base, applied mouth, American 1830-1840 . . . . **$450-650**

D. Harkins / Richmond / PA (in a slug plate), Deep blue green, 7-1/4", iron pontil, applied mouth, extremely rare, found in the Port Richmond, Pennsylvania area, where many early glass houses were located in Kensington and Union, American 1840-1860 . . . . **$600-800**

D.L. Ormsby, Cobalt blue, 7-1/8", iron pontil, applied blob mouth, American 1840-1860 . . . . **$375-450**

E. Bigelow / & Co / Springfield / Mass – Soda / Water, Deep emerald green, 7-1/8", iron pontil, applied mouth, scarce color, American 1840-1860 . . . . **$350-450**

Elias Barth / Burlington / N.J., Blue green, 7", smooth base (B), applied blob mouth, American 1855-1865 . . . . **$100-150**

F. Gleason / Rochester. N.Y., Medium blue green, 7", iron pontil, applied inverted cone sloping collar mouth, American 1840-1860 . . . . **$400-600**

F. Gleason / Rochester / N.Y., Medium sapphire blue, 7-1/2", backward "N" in Gleason and "NY", iron pontil, applied blob type mouth, American 1840-1860 . . . . **$250-350**

G. – S., Emerald green, 7-1/4", 8-sided, pontil-scarred base, applied blob mouth, very rare, American 1840-1860. . . . . **$600-800**

G.A. Cook & Bro / Philipsburg / N.J. (in a slug plate) – Dyottville Glass Works / Philada, Medium blue green, 6-1/2", iron pontil, applied sloping double collar mouth, extremely rare, one of only three known examples, American 1840-1860 . . . . **$500-800**

Geo. Eagle, Deep blue green, 7", rib body pattern, iron pontil, applied mouth, American 1840-1860 . . . . **$800-1,200**

Golden Gate, Dark green, 7", smooth base, applied top, San Francisco soda, American 1865-1875 . . . . **$250-350**

H. Ferneding / Dayton. O. (on shoulder), Deep olive amber, quart, pontil-scarred base, applied sloping double collar mouth, three-piece mold, American 1851-1852 . . . . **$180-275**

H. Nash & Co / Root Beer / Cincinnati, Deep cobalt blue, 8-1/2", 12-sided, iron pontil, applied blob mouth, American 1840-1860 . . . . **$500-700**

H. Sproatt, Medium cobalt blue, 10", 15-sided , smooth base, applied top American, 1865-1875 . . . . **$1,500-1,700**

H. & V.B. / Newton / N.J., Emerald green, 7", smooth base, applied mouth, American 1860-1870. . . . . **$180-275**

Hausmann & Co. / Belvidere, N.J., Medium blue green, 7-1/4", smooth base, applied mouth, extremely rare, American 1855-1865 . . . . **$150-250**

Henke & Maack, Emerald green, 9", smooth base, round bottom, applied mouth, extremely rare Washington D.C. soda bottle, American 1855-1865 . . . .**$5,500-6,500**

H. Daub / Wheeling VA, deep blue aqua, 7-3/8", smooth base, applied blob-type mouth, American 1865-1875, **$200-300.**

H Maw & Co. Eureka Nevada, aqua, smooth base, applied top, 7", American 1881-1888, (only known specimen with a "W" instead of "U"), **$1,500-2,000.**

H Mau & Company, Eureka Nevada, aqua, smooth base, 7", American 1881-1888, **$150-200.**

J & A Dearborn / & Co / New York - Soda Water, deep cobalt blue, 7-1/8", iron pontil, applied blob-type mouth, American 1840-1860, **$300-400.**

Hogan & Thompson / San Francisco / Cal. (in a slug plate) – Union Glass Works / Philada, Deep cobalt blue, 7-1/2", pontil-scarred base, applied blob top, rare, American 1853-1856 .... **$400-600**

Howell & Smith / Buffalo, Medium sapphire blue, 7-3/8", iron pontil, applied "top hat" type mouth, American 1840-1860 ...**$200-250**

IRA Harvey – H, Emerald green, 6-3/4", squat form, iron pontil, applied mouth, American 1840-1860 .... **$200-300**

J.B. Edwards / Columbia / PA (in a slug plate) – Brown / Stout, Emerald green, 6-1/4", squat form, iron pontil, applied mouth, very rare, American 1840-1860................ **$900-1,100**

J. Foy / Burlington / N.J. (in a slug plate) – Brown Stout, Medium blue-green, 7-1/8", squat form, iron pontil, applied mouth, very rare, one of only two known examples, American 1840-1860 .... **$1,500-1,700**

J. & H. Casper / Lancaster / PA – Cold Cream / Soda, Aqua, 6", smooth base, applied mouth, American 1870-1880 .. **$150-200**

J. Lake / Schenectady, N.Y., Sapphire blue, 7-7/8", iron pontil, applied mouth, rare color, American 1840-1860 **$1,000-1,500**

J. Lukens / Wheeling, Brilliant cobalt blue, 7-3/8", iron pontil, applied sloping collar mouth, American 1840-1860 ...... **$1,200-1,600**

J. Marbacher / Easton / PA – Improved / M / Patent, Medium green, 7-3/8", iron pontil, applied mouth, American 1840-1860 .... **$220-275**

John R. Owens / Parkesburg, Emerald green, 7", squat form, iron pontil, applied mouth, scarce, American 1840-1860....**$275-375**

J. & JM. Ensinger / Wheeling, VA, light apple green, 7-1/4", smooth base, applied blob-type mouth, American 1865-1875, **$250-350.**

J. Lukens / Wheeling, cobalt blue, 7-3/8", iron pontil, applied sloping collar mouth, American 1840-1860, **$1,400-1,600.**

John R. Owens / Parkesburg, emerald green, 7", squat shape, iron pontil, applied mouth, American 1840-1860, **$275-375.**

L. Snider / Wheeling, emerald green, 7-1/2", iron pontil, applied blob-type mouth, American 1840-1869, (rare), **$1,000-1,500.**

L.L. Belland / Newark / N.J. (in a slug plate), Deep green aqua, 6-3/4", iron pontil, applied mouth, American 1840-1860. . . . . **$150-200**

L. Schmitt / Columbia (in a slug plate), Medium sapphire blue, 7", iron pontil, applied mouth, very rare, Pennsylvania soda, American 1840-1860 . . . . **$400-600**

L. Snider / Wheeling, Deep emerald green, 7-1/2", iron pontil, applied blob type mouth, very rare, American 1840-1860. . . . **$800-1,400**

J. Wismann / Dayton / Ohio, Deep blue aqua, 7-5/8", 12-sided, red iron pontil, applied blob mouth, American 1840-1860. . . . . **$350-450**

(Star) / Morton / 1851 / Newark, N.J. (in a slug plate), Light blue green, 6-3/4", squat form, iron pontil, applied mouth, American 1840-1860 . . . . **$250-350**

Nash & Co / Root Beer / Cincinnati, Deep cobalt blue, 8-3/8", 12-sided, iron pontil, applied blob mouth, American 1840-1860. . . . .**$800-1,200**

O.G.M. / Gaines / Columbia / PA (in a slug plate) – Brown Stout, Blue green, 6-3/8", squat form, iron pontil, applied mouth, American 1840-1860 . . . . **$350-450**

P. Kellett / Newark / N.J., Medium blue, 7-3/8", iron pontil, applied blob type mouth, American 1840-1860 . . . . . **$75-125**

Polk & Co / Barnums / Building – Cor Fayette / & St. Pauls St / Baltimore, MD, Medium cobalt blue, 8", smooth base, applied tapered collar mouth, extremely rare, American 1850-1860. . . . . **$500-800**

Pacific Congress Springs, aqua, 7", smooth base, applied top, American 1880-1900, **$750-1,000.**

S. Smith Auburn N.Y, 1856 KR.S Water, cobalt blue, 7", iron pontil, 8-sided blob top, American 1856, **$200-300.**

Polk & Co. / Barnums / Building / Balto, Medium cobalt blue, 8-3/4", smooth base, rounded bottom, applied mouth, rare, American 1850-1860 . . . . **$2,500-3,500**

Pomroy & Hall, Medium emerald green, 7-1/4", mug base, iron pontil, applied blob mouth, original neck ring is stamped "Allenders Patent July 24, 18_ Mauf'd by S.A. Bailey, New London, Ct," rare, American 1840-1860 . . . . **$500-800**

Robinson, Wilson & Legallee / 102 / Sudbury St. / Boston, Medium emerald green, 6-5/8", iron pontil, applied sloping double collar mouth, American 1840-1860 . . . . **$100-150**

San Francisco / Glass Works, Deep blue aqua, 7-1/8", smooth base, applied mouth, American 1870-1876. . . . . **$75-125**

S & C / Elkton / M.D. (in a slug plate), Deep blue green, 6-7/8", iron pontil, applied sloping collar, rare, Maryland soda, American 1840-1860 . . . . **$650-850**

Shaw & Co / Cape May (in a slug plate), Medium blue green, 7-1/8", smooth base, applied mouth, American 1855 1865 . . . . **$200-300**

Southwick – & – Tupper – New York, Medium blue green, 7-5/8", 10-sided, iron pontil, applied blob mouth, American 1840-1860 . . . . **$550-750**

Smedley & Brandt (in a slug plate), Emerald green, 7-1/4", iron pontil, applied mouth, rare, American 1840-1860 . . . **$250-350**

S.W. Bell / 1861 / New Brunswick – B, Light blue green, 7-1/4", smooth base, applied blob, mouth, American 1860-1870 . . . . **$75-125**

Taylor's – Best, Deep cobalt blue, 8-1/4", 6-sided, cucumber form, iron pontil, applied mouth, extremely rare, only one of two examples known, American 1848 . . . . **$700-900**

This soda bottle was produced to coincide with Whig Parties nomination of Zachary Taylor for President at the Philadelphia Convention in June 1848., T.H. Paul / Glassboro / N.J., Medium blue green, 7-1/2", squat form, iron pontil, applied double collar mouth, extremely rare, American 1840-1860 . . . . **$400-600**

Tiffany & Allen / Washington Market / Cor / Fair & Washington / St. / Patterson / N.J. Spruce Beer – Please / Return Bottle / Soon As / Empty, Cobalt blue, 7-5/8" pint, cylinder form, smooth base, applied mouth, American 1865-1875 . . . . . . **$1,400-1,600**

T.M. Richardson / Burlington / N. J., Medium blue-green, 7-1/4", squat form, iron pontil, applied mouth, American 1840-1860 . . . . **$150-250**

Toram's / Brown Stout – 65 / South St. / Phila, Medium green, 7-1/4", iron pontil, applied mouth, American 1840-1860 . . . . **$200-300**

T & R Morton / 1851 / Newark, N.J. – M, Light blue green, 7-5/8", iron pontil, applied mouth, American 1840-1860 . . . . **$140-180**

Tweddle's / Soda Water / New York – Patent, Emerald green, 6-5/8", pontil-scarred base, applied mouth, American 1830-1840 . . . . **$450-550**

U & I.D. Clinton / Woodbridge / Conn. – Premium / Soda Water, Medium blue green, 7-3/8", iron pontil, applied blob mouth, American 1840-1860 . . . . **$150-250**

Union Lava Works / Conshohocken / Patented 1852 (blank slug plate on reverse side of bottle), Deep cobalt blue, 7-1/8", iron pontil, applied blob mouth, very rare, American 1852-1860 .... **$450-550**

Valentine / & Vreeland / Newark / N.J. – Supr. Soda Water / Union Glass Works / Phila, Cobalt blue, 7-1/2", iron pontil, applied blob mouth, American 1840-1860 .... **$200-300**

W. Eagle / Canal St. NY – Philadelphia / Porter / 1860, Blue green, 7", smooth base, applied mouth, rare, American 1855-1865 .... **$180-220**

W. Ryer – R / Union Glass Works / Philada, Deep cobalt blue, 7-1/8", iron pontil, applied blob mouth, American 1840-1860 .... **$400-600**

Willis & Ripley / Portsmouth – W & R, Sapphire blue, 7-3/8", iron pontil, applied mouth, American 1840-1860 .... **$375-400**

W.M. & DT Cox / Port Jervis / N. Y., Medium blue green, 7-1/8", iron pontil, applied sloping collar mouth, rare, American 1840-1860 .... **$500-700**

WM. H. Weaver / Belvidere (in a slug plate) – Mineral / Water, Medium emerald green, 7", iron pontil, applied blob top, American 1840-1860 .... **$450-650**

WM. H. Weaver / Hackettstown (in slug plate) – This Bottle Is Never / Sold, Blue green, 7", squat form, iron pontil, applied mouth, American 1840-1860 .... **$400-600**

SODA FOUNTAIN SYRUP DISPENSERS

When was the last time anyone remembers hanging out at the local corner drugstore, or sitting down at the soda fountain counter and ordering an ice cream soda or a rootbeer float, where the syrup was squirted into the glass from a decorative ceramic dispenser? Sounds good, doesn't it? Unless you entered that drugstore 75, or maybe even 100 years ago, you didn't have the fun of enjoying that experience.

U.S. pharmacists first began selling all types of fountain drinks for a number of various physical ailments from the common cold to lung diseases during the 1850s. In fact, the majority of these early drink mixes consisted of various drugs such as codeine, alcohol, and cocaine mixed with water. The pharmacists soon realized that by mixing different fruit extracts, along with sugar and carbonated water, they could produce a drink that everyone would buy.

Following the early successes of Coca-Cola and Pepsi with their flavored drinks in the late 1880s and 1890s, other new soft-drink companies began to produce additional soda flavors and sold their syrup bases to drugstores. As the competition heated up and soda syrup began to be mass-produced, it didn't take long for the pharmacists to figure out that having a soda fountain in their drugstore might make more money than selling drugs.

As a gimmick to sell the syrups, the companies gave the dispensers away as free advertising to drugstore owners who continued to purchase large amounts of soda syrup. This wasn't difficult, since the use of soda fountains became extremely popular during the 1920s with the help of Prohibition. The active use of a small number of drugstore soda fountains, with their unique and ornate dispensers, continued into the 1950s. But, with the arrival of modern technology and the onslaught of fast food chains, drugstore soda fountains became a thing of the past. It should be noted that while all the dispensers are decorative and valuable, the ceramic dispenser demands the highest prices at auctions.

Always Drink – Fowler's – Cherry (picture of red drink cup with 5 cents in middle of green leaf) – Smash – Our Nation's Beverage, Tan, red and green label, 14", pump at top of dispenser, American 1900-1930. . . . . **$2,000-2,200**

Always Drink – Fowler's Cherry (picture of cherries in middle of green leaf) Our Nation's Beverage, Tan, red and green label, 16", pump at top of dispenser, American 1900-1930 . . . **$2,000-2,500**

Always Drink – Fowler's Cherry (picture of cherries in middle of green leaf) Our Nation's Beverage, Dark tan, orange and green label, 16", pump at top of dispenser, American 1900-1930 . . . . **$2,000-2,500**

Armours – Vigoral (decoration of red carnations), White, 19", porcelain, copper reservoir, spigot at base of dispenser, five matching cups, lid, American 1910-1935 . . . . **$600-700**

Buckeye – Label reads: Cleveland Fruit Juice Co. – Root Beer (Buckeye Root Beer embossed), Light brown glaze, 14", pump at top of dispenser, American 1900-1925 . . . . . . **$2,000-3,000**

Buckeye – Root – Beer (painted on front) – Label reads: Cleveland Fruit Juice Co., Tan, 15", pump at top of dispenser, American 1900-1925 . . . . **$2,000-3,000**

Buckeye – Root Beer, Dark brown in tree stump shape, 14", pump at top of dispenser, American 1910-1930 . . . . **$500-600**

Buckeye – Root Beer, Black in heart type shape, 14", pump at top of dispenser, American 1910-1930 . . . . **$1,000-1,200**

Cherri Bon, Red with green base with cherry leaves, cherry shape, 14", original pump at top of dispenser, American 1900-1925 . . . **$23,750**

Buckeye Root Beer, 5 Cent, cream, 7-1/2", decorated with baby satyrs around bottom perimeter, American 1900-1930, **$1,400-1,600.**

Christo – Ginger Ale – Christo Manufacturing Co. – Richmond, VA, White, 16", barrel form, pump at top of dispenser, American 1900-1920 . . . .**$4,250**

Drink – California – Iron Port – 5 cents (picture of man holding world on shoulders) 5 cents – You'll Like It, White with red color on the label, pump at top of dispenser, American 1900-1910 . . . . **$10,000-11,000**

Drink – Clayton's – Smack – Trade Mark Reg. U.S. Pat. OFE – Artificial Flavor and Color – Ice Cold, White with blue label, 16", ceramic, pump at top of dispenser, American 1890-1920 . . **$17,250**

Drink – Crawford's – Cherry-Fizz – It's Jake-A-Loo, White, 16", pump at top of dispenser, American 1910-1930 . . . .**$8,750**

Drink – Dr. Swett's – Root Beer – On The Market Seventy Five Years, White with yellow, 14", pump at top of dispenser, American 1900-1920 . . . .**$5,600**

Drink – Dixie-Flip – The Wonder Drink (encircled with wreath of grapes), White, 16", ceramic, horseshoe-style pump at top of dispenser, American 1900-1915. . . . . **$34,750**

Drink – Dr. Pepper – The Year Round – An Ideal Beverage – 5 cents, White, 17", ceramic, spigot center of dispenser, American 1900-1920 . . . . **$25,250**

Drink – Fan-Faz – "Drink of the Fans" – A Pennant Winner, White, ceramic, 16", baseball shape original pump at top of dispenser marked "Fan-Taz," American 1900-1920 . . **$25,700**

Drink – Grapefruitola – 5 cents, Light yellow, green leaves around dispenser top, white base, 15", ceramic, plunger cap insert at top of dispenser, American 1913. . . . . **$31,750**

Fowler's Cherry Smash, Your Nation's Beverage, cream, 9-1/2", American 1900-1930, **$1,800-1,900**.

Drink – Grape – Julep, Purple with white base, 16", pump at top of dispenser, American 1905-1925 . . . . **$1,800-2,000**

Drink – Hires – It Is Pure, Tan, 14", hourglass shape, pump at top of dispenser, American 1905-1925 . . . . **$300-400**

Drink Hires Rootbeer – Drink Hires 5 cents – Hires Rootbeer – Is Luscious and Pure (picture of Hires "ugly" boy in blue dress and pink bib), Brown trim and light cream, ceramic, spigot center of dispenser, Germany 1880-1930, Villeroy and Boch, Mettlach, Germany **$61,000**

Drink – Howel's – Original – Orange – Julep – 5 cents, Red with white base, 16", pump at top of dispenser, American 1905-1930 . . . . **$5,500-6,000**

Drink – Orange – Julep, Orange with white base, 16", pump at top of dispenser, American 1905-1925 . . . . **$1,800-2,000**

Drink – Rosary – Root Beer – Try It, White, 16", barrel shape, pump at top of dispenser, American 1910-1930 . . . . **$3,400**

Dr. Swett's – Root Beer, White, 16", barrel shape, pump at top of dispenser, American 1910-1930. . . . . **$6,500**

Drink – Stein's – Famous – Root Beer, White, 16", original style pump at top of dispenser, American 1910-1930 . . . . . . **$7,000**

Getz Blend – Root Beer, White, 16", pump at top of dispenser, American 1900-1930 . . . . **$3,900**

Green's – Muscadine – Punch, Light brown, 16", barrel shape, pump at top of dispenser, extremely rare, American 1900-1910 . . . . **$3,000-4,000**

Grape Crush, amethyst glass, early pump, 15", American 1900-1920, **$1,000-1,200.**

Indian Rock – Ginger Ale, White, 16", original pump with Indian Rock Ginger Ale on ball, American 1905-1930 . . . . . . **$11,000**

Jersey – Crème – Perfect – Trade Mark (monogram with JC in middle), White, 15-1/2", original pump at top of dispenser, American 1905-1930 . . . . **$900-1,000**

Jim Dandy – Root Beer – Delicious and Refreshing, White, 15", ceramic, pump at top of dispenser, American 1900-1930 . . . . **$40,750**

Liberty – Root Beer – Big Stein – 5 cents, Dark brown, 14", barrel shape, pump at middle of dispenser, American 1900-1920 . . . . **$1,000-2,000**

Magnus – Concordia Punch, Cream color porcelain over metal, 14", pump at top of dispenser, American 1910-1930 . . . **$1,000**

Mission Orangeade – Ice Cold, Orange art deco design depicting slices of oranges, 15-1/2", spigot on back side of dispenser, American 1930 . . . . **$1,000-1,100**

Mission Rickey – Lime – Ice Cold, Lime green Art Deco design depicting slices of limes, 15-1/2", spigot on back side of dispenser, American 1930 . . . . **$900-1,000**

Murray's – Old Fashion – Root Beer, Tan and dark brown, 12", barrel sitting on tree stump, dispenser in the middle of barrel, American 1910-1935 . . . . **$550**

Pepsi – Cola, Strengthening – Refreshing – Satisfying – Invigorating, Blue and green with forest background, ceramic, 19", American 1902, Avon Works, Wheeling, WV **$31,750**

Wards Lemon Crush, light and dark green, ceramic, contemporary pump, 13-1/2", American 1900-1930, **$1,000-1,200.**

Philadelphia Soda Fountain Co – Patented # 1128 (very ornate engraving on entire dispenser), Silver plated, 26" h. x 19" w., two fancy dispensers, one on each side, American 1880 . . **$2,000-2,500**

Richardson's – Liberty – Root Beer, Tan and dark brown, 13", barrel sitting on tree stump, dispenser in the middle of barrel, American 1910-1935 . . . . **$700**

Schuster's – Root Beer, Light and dark brown, 15", barrel shape, pump is not correct and incomplete, American 1901-1925 . . **$500**

So. Cas. Co. – Orange Ale – Artificially Colored – Mixed Citric Acid, Orange, 16", ceramic, original pump at top of dispenser, American 1900-1925 . . . . **$25,750**

Texberry, White with metal bands, 16", barrel shape, pump at top of dispenser, American 1910-1925 . . . . **$900**

Ward's – Lemon – Crush, Yellow with green base, 13", lemon shape, original pump at top of dispenser, American 1900-1930 . . . . **$2,800-3,000**

Ward's – Lime – Crush – Color Added, Lemon, 14", lime shape, pump at top of dispenser, American 1900-1930 . . **$5,000-6,000**

Ward's – Orange – Crush – Color Added, Orange, 15", orange shape, pump at top of dispenser, American 1900-1930 . . . . **$900-1,000**

Zipp's – 5 cents – Cherri-o, White, 15", barrel shape, pump at top of dispenser, American 1905-1925 . . . . **$3,800**

Zipps's – Root Beer, White, 15", barrel shape, pump at top of dispenser, American 1905-1925 . . . . **$2,100**

Wards Lime Crush, light and dark green, ceramic, contemporary pump, 13-1/2", American 1900-1930, **$3,500-3,500.**

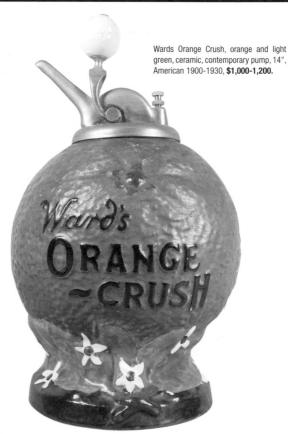

Wards Orange Crush, orange and light green, ceramic, contemporary pump, 14", American 1900-1930, **$1,000-1,200.**

TARGET BALLS

Target balls, round bottles the size of a baseball, were filled with confetti, ribbon, and other items. Used for target practice from the 1850s to early 1900s, they gained considerable popularity during the 1860s and 1870s in exhibitions and Wild West shows with Buffalo Bill Cody and Annie Oakley. During one summer, the Bohemian Glass Works manufactured target balls at the rate of 1,250,000 over a six-month period. Others such as Bogardus and Ira Paine had their target balls manufactured by various glassmakers throughout the country, as well as Europe, especially England.

Some of the most popular colors were amber, various shades of light blue, purple (amethyst), and green. Around 1900, clay pigeons began to be used in place of target balls. Because they were made to be broken, they are, unfortunately, extremely difficult to find, and have become very rare, collectible, and valuable.

Bogardus Glass Ball – Pat'd April 10 1877, Brilliant emerald green, amethyst striation in lower half of ball and overall diamond pattern above and below the center band, 2-3/4" dia., rough sheared mouth, embossed "8" inside one of the diamonds above the "A" in Aprl, American 1877-1900 ....**$2,500-3,000**

Bogardus Glass Ball – Pad'd April 10 1877, Yellow amber with light olive tone, 2-3/4" dia., overall diamond pattern above and below center band, rough sheared mouth, American 1877-1900 .... **$500-700**

Bogardus Glass Ball – Pat'd Apr. 10 1877, Medium sapphire blue, 2-5/8" dia., diamond pattern above and below center band, smooth base, rough sheared lip, English 1877-1900 **$700-900**

C. Bogardus / Patd / Apr 10th / 1877 / Glass Ball (on base), Yellow amber with olive tone, 2-5/8" dia., overall diamond pattern, rough sheared lip, rarest and most sought after of the Bogardus grouping, American 1877-1900 ..... **$4,000-5,000**

E. Jones Gunmaker – Lancaster Blackburn, Cobalt blue, 2-1/2" dia., lattice embossed ball with cross on base, rough sheared lip, English 1880-1900.......................... **$500-800**

For Hockey's Patent Trap, Pale olive yellow, 2-3/8" dia., rough sheared lip, English 1880-1900.............. **$1,000-1,500**

Glasshutten Dr. A. Frank – Charlottenburg, Yellow olive, 2-3/4" dia., overall diamond pattern, rough sheared lip, German 1880-1900 .... **$275-375**

Target ball, "Bogardus" glass ball, PATD APRL 10 1877, emerald green, 2-3/4", overall diamond pattern, embossed "8" inside of the diamond, rough-sheared mouth, blown in three-piece mold, American 1877-1900, **$2,500-3,000.**

Target ball, Maurītz Widorūs, yellow with amber tone, 2-5/8", rough-sheared lip, blown in two-piece mold, Swedish 1880-1900, (rare), **$800-900.**

Ira Paine's Filled – Ball Pat. Oct 23 1877, Yellow amber, 2-1/2" dia., smooth base, rough sheared mouth, blown in three-piece mold, American 1877-1900 . . . . **$300-400**

Ira Paine's Filled – Ball Pat. Oct 23, 1877, Light yellow with olive tone, 2-5/8" dia., smooth base, rough sheared lip, blown in a three-part mold, American 1877-1900 . . . . **$350-450**

Mauritz – Widfors, Yellow with amber tone, 2-5/8" dia., blown in two-piece mold, rough sheared lip, extremely rare, possibly only one of two known examples, Swedish 1880-1900 . . **$700-900**

N.B. Glass works Perth – N.B. Glass Works Perth, Green aqua, 2-5/8" dia., diamond pattern above and below center band, smooth base, rough sheared lip, English 1880-1900 **$150-200**

N.B. Glass Works Perth – N.B. Glass Works Perth, Deep cobalt blue, 2-5/8" dia., upside down "P" and backward "S", diamond pattern above and below center band, rough sheared mouth, English 1880-1900. . . . . **$150-200**

Range Ball (five pointed stars on both sides), Medium cobalt blue, 2-1/8" dia., rough sheared long neck, English 1880-1910 . . . . **$120-160**

Range Ball (embossed star on either side), Medium sapphire blue, 2-1/8" dia., rough sheared mouth, long neck, English 1880-1900 . . . . **$100-150**

Range Ball, Deep purple amethyst, 2-1/2" dia., smooth base, rough sheared lip, blown in a two-piece mold, American 1880-1900 . . . . **$140-180**

Target ball, clear glass with a diamond pattern and a man shooting in two opposite side circular panels, 2-5/8", English 1880-1900, **$200-250.**

Target ball, deep amber, 2-5/8", rough-sheared mouth, blown in three-piece mold, G3 (on base), American 1880-1900, **$150-200.**

Target Ball, Olive yellow, 2-5/8" dia., smooth base, rough sheared lip, blown in three-piece mold, scarce, American 1880-1900 .... **$150-200**

Target Ball "II" (on shoulder), Light sapphire blue, 2-5/8" dia., smooth base (G2 embossed), sheared mouth, blown in three-piece mold, scarce, American 1880-1900 .... **$100-150**

Target Ball – Stars Ball, Yellow amber center shading to a deep color amber in the upper and lower areas, 2-5/8" dia., sheared lip, blown in a three-part mold, a number of rows of four pointed stars covering the entire ball, rare, American 1880-1900 .... **$3,500-5,000**

Target Ball – Stars and Bars, Yellow with amber and olive tones, 2-5/8" dia., rough sheared lip, intricate pattern of a series of horizontal lines along both mold seams with closely patterned dots on both sides and base, American 1880-1900 .... **$2,500-3,700**

Target Ball (man pointing a shotgun in two opposite side circles), Light to medium emerald green, 2-5/8" dia., smooth base, rough sheared lip, English 1880-1900 ...... **$400-800**

Target Ball, Cobalt blue, 2-5/8" dia., smooth base, rough sheared lip, French 1880-1900 .... **$40-60**

Target Ball, Medium sapphire blue, 2-5/8" dia., square pattern above and below blank center band, rough sheared mouth, English 1880-1900 .... **$200-300**

Target Ball, Medium golden yellow amber, 2-5/8" dia., embossed with line across center of bases, rough sheared mouth, blown in three-piece mold, American 1880-1900 .... **$120-160**

Target ball, cobalt blue, 2-5/8", rough-sheared mouth, blown in five-piece mold, American 1880-1900, **$150-200.**

Target ball, tobacco amber, 7 vertical embossed bands, 2-5/8", rough-sheared mouth, blown in a three-piece mold, American 1880-1900, **$250-300.**

Target ball, medium copper puce, overall diamond pattern, 2-3/4", ground mouth, German 1880-1900, **$200-250.**

Target Ball, Bright yellow green, 2-5/8" dia., overall diamond pattern, long neck, rough sheared, Czechoslovakian 1885-1900 .... **$200-300**

Target Ball, Dark amber, 2-1/2" dia., 7 horizontal rings around the entire ball, smooth base, rough sheared lip, American 1880-1900 .... **$600-800**

Target Ball – "K" embossed on the side, Amber, 2-1/2" dia., smooth base, rough sheared lip, American 1880-1900 .... **$300-600**

Target Ball, Medium cobalt blue, 2-1/2" dia., smooth base (G.8), three raised dots on shoulder, rough sheared lip, blown in three-part mold, rare, American 1880-1900 .... **$200-300**

Target Ball, Medium amber, 2-1/2" dia., smooth base, rough sheared mouth, blown in three-piece mold, large diamond on base, American 1880-1900 .... **$120-150**

Target Ball, Deep Prussian blue, 2-1/2" dia., rough sheared lip, overall diamond pattern, European 1880-1900 .... **$180-275**

Target Ball – Patd Sept 25th 1877 (around shoulder), Deep sapphire blue, 2-1/2" dia., overall sand grain finish (the sand grain texture was applied so the shot would not slide off when hitting the ball, giving a better chance of breakage. Only a few of these types exist), rough sheared lip, blown in three-piece mold, extremely rare, Corning Glass Co., American 1877-1900 .... **$4,000-6,000**

Target Ball, Cobalt blue, 2-1/2" dia., large square pattern above and below an unembossed center band, smooth base, rough sheared lip, French 1880-1900 . . . . **$150-250**

Target Ball – Wide Mouth, Clear glass with medium turquoise blue, 2-3/4" dia., overall mottled pattern and sand grain finish, sheared and ground 1" mouth, English 1890-1910 . . . . **$550-750**

Van Cutsem – A St Quentin, Cobalt blue, 2-1/2" dia., diamond pattern above and below the embossed center band, smooth base, rough sheared lip, French 1880-1900 . . . . **$100-150**

W.W. Greener – St. Marys Works – Birmm & 68 Haymarket London, Medium amethyst, 2-5/8" dia., diamond pattern above and below center band, smooth base, rough sheared lip, English 1880-1900 . . . . **$400-600**

W.W. Greener – St. Marys Works – Birmm & 68 Haymarket London, Smoky olive green, 2-5/8" dia., diamond pattern above and below center band, smooth base, rough sheared lip, rare color, English 1880-1900. . . . . **$1,700-2,000**

W.W. Greener – St. Marys Works – Birmm & 68 Haymarket London, Cobalt blue, 2-5/8" dia., diamond pattern above and below center band, smooth base, rough sheared lip, English 1880-1900 . . . . **$180-275**

WHISKEY BOTTLES

Whiskeys, sometimes referred to as spirits, come in an array of sizes, designs, shapes, and colors. The whiskey bottle dates back to the 19th century and provides the avid collector with numerous examples of rare and valuable pieces.

In 1860, E.G. Booz manufactured a whiskey bottle in the design of a cabin embossed with year 1840 and the words "Old Cabin Whiskey." According to one theory, the word booze was derived from his name to describe hard liquor. The Booz bottle is also given the credit of being the first to emboss the name on whiskey bottles.

After the repeal of Prohibition in 1933, the only inscription that could be found on any liquor bottles was "Federal Law Forbids Sale or Re-use of This Bottle," which was continued through 1964.

A.M. Bininger & Co. / 19 Broad St. / N.Y., Yellow amber,12-1/4", cannon barrel form, smooth base, rough ground mouth, American 1860-1880 . . . . **$500-1,000**

B.F. & Co. / N.Y. – Seal Whiskey Jug, Golden amber, 9", pattern-molded conical form, 26 vertical rib-pattern, applied handle with seal applied to the rigaree of the handle, applied double collar mouth with pour spout, rare, American 1840-1860 . . **$500-1,000**

Bininger's / Knickerbocker / A.M. Bininger & Co. / No. 19 Broad St. N.Y., 79-348, Medium yellow amber, 6-1/2", open pontil, applied sloping collar mouth, handle second hardest to obtain of the four handled Bininger bottles, American 1855-1875 . . . .**$750-950**

Buchanans / Absolutely Pure / Malt / Whiskey, Medium orange amber, 8-7/8", cannon shape, smooth base, tooled mouth, American 1875-1885 . . . . **$350-450**

Callahan's / Old Cabin / Whiskey, Yellow amber, 9", rectangular tall log cabin form with cathedral arched windows and doors, smooth base, applied sloping collared mouth, American 1865-1880, this very bottle was used for the 33 cent American Glass postage stamp developed by Richard Sheaf. On display at the Corning Museum of Glass. **$8,000-16,000**

Chestnut Grove / (crown) / Whiskey / C.W. – label reads: Diploma Awarded by the Pennsylvania State Agricultural Society, to Chas. Wharton, Jr. for Chestnut Grove Whiskey at the Exhibition of 1859, Chas Wharton, Jr Wholesale Agent, No 116 Walnut St., Philada, Yellow amber, 9-1/8", open pontil, applied ringed mouth, handle, American 1859-1870 . . . . . . **$500-700**

Bininger's / Travelers / Guide / A.M. Bininger & Co. No. 19 Broad St NY, medium golden amber, tear drop flask, 6-7/8", smooth base, applied double collar mouth, American 1860-1875, **$700-1,000.**

Distilled in 1848 / Old Kentucky / Bourbon / 1849 / Reserve / A.M. Bininger & Go. 388 Broadway, N.Y., deep amber, barrel, 8", pontil-scarred base, applied double collar mouth, American 1855-1865, **$400-500.**

Cognac / W & Co. – On Applied Seal, Medium amber, 6", globular form, pontil-scarred base, applied ring mouth, handle, American 1860-1875 . . . . **$400-500**

Crane & Brigham / San Francisco (inside a leaf), Medium yellow amber, 10-1/4", smooth base, applied ringed mouth, American 1880-1890 . . . . **$650-850**

Dr. Girard's / Ginger Brandy / London, Medium amber, 10", pontil-scarred base, applied double collar top, applied handle, American 1855-1875 . . . . **$650-750**

E.G. Booz's / Old Cabin / Whiskey – 1840 – 120 Walnut St. / Philadelphia – E.G. Booz's / Old Cabin / Whiskey, Medium amber, 7-5/8", cabin form, smooth base, applied mouth, rare, few peaked corner bottles exist, American 1860-1875, Whitney Glassworks, Glassboro, N.J. **$3,500-4,500**

E.G. Booz's / Old Cabin / Whiskey – 1840 – 120 Walnut St. / Philadelphia – E.G. Booz's / Old Cabin / Whiskey, Dark amber, 7-7/8", cabin form, smooth base, applied sloping collar mouth, rare, few peaked corner bottles exist, American 1860-1875, Whitney Glassworks, Glassboro, N.J. **$6,000-7,000**

E.I.J. – Seal Whiskey Bottle, Yellow olive, quart, applied shoulder seal, large iron pontil mark, applied sloping collared mouth with ring, extremely rare, only known example, American 1845-1860 . . . . **$1,000-2,000**

Fine Old Bourbon Whiskey, The Travellers, Sol. Age (label), Deep strawberry puce, 8-1/4", open pontil, applied mouth, applied handle, American 1860-1875 . . . . **$250-350**

Forest / Lawn / J.V.H., Yellow olive green, 7-1/2", bulbous form, pontil-scarred base, applied mouth, American 1865-1875 . . . . **$750-950**

Golden Eagle / (motif of embossed eagle) / Distilleries Co. / San Francisco Cal., Dark amber, 11", smooth base, tooled top, American 1902-1910 . . . . **$300-600**

Golden Treasure, Blue aqua, 4 3/4", barrel form, smooth base, applied square collar mouth, American 1855-1865 . . . . **$175-225**

I.R.T. & Co. / Philad, Medium amber, 7", pontil-scarred base, applied double collar top, applied handle, American 1855-1875 . . . . **$500-600**

Embossed Star / IXL Valley Whiskey / E & B Bevan / Pittston Pa / Embossed Star, Dark amber, 8", pontil-scarred base, applied double collar top, American 1855-1875 . . . . **$2,500-2,800**

Flora Temple / Standing Horse / Harness Trot 2.19 – Label on reverse reads: Established 1839 / S.T. Suits / Kentucky / Salt River Bourbon / Whiskey / Distilleries / Jefferson, Co. Ky., Deep strawberry puce, 8-1/2", smooth base, applied ring mouth and handle, American 1859-1869, Whitney Glass Works, Glassboro, N.J. **$1,300-1,600**

Fort Trumbull Glass Co., Yellow amber, quart, three-piece mold, smooth base, applied sloping collared mouth with ring, extremely rare Fort Trumbull Glass Works, New London, Connecticut, American 1865-1868 . . . . **$750-1,500**

Greeley's / Bourbon Whiskey / Bitters, Deep plum purple, 9-3/8", barrel form, smooth base, applied square collared mouth, American 1860-1880. . . . . **$1,000-2,000**

Greeting / Theodore Netter / 1232 Market St / Philadelphia, Medium cobalt blue, 6", barrel form, smooth base, tooled mouth, American 1885-1895. . . . . **$200-300**

G.W. Huntington – On Applied Seal, Medium teal, 11-3/4", large iron pontil, applied mouth, extremely rare, American 1845-1865. . . . .**$2,000-2,500**

Heidelberg / Branntwein – A.M. Bininger & Co., Olive green, 9-5/8", smooth base, applied sloping collar mouth, rare, American 1865-1875 . . . . **$850-950**

HF & B / NY (embossed lettering in embossed shield), Yellow with a green tone, 9", melon form, smooth base, applied sloping collared mouth with ring, rare, American 1860-1870
. . . . **$500-1,000**

HF & B / NY (embossed lettering in embossed shield), Apricot puce, 9-1/8", melon form, smooth base, applied sloping collared mouth with ring, rare, American 1860-1870 . . . . **$500-1,000**

Hopatkong / Whiskey / J.C. Hess & Co. Phila, Deep cobalt blue, 10-1/4", 12-fluted panels in lower half, smooth base, applied ring mouth, extremely rare, American 1865-1875 . . . . **$3,000-4,000**

I. Nelson's / Old Bourbon / Maysville, KY, Yellow amber, 7-3/8", barrel form, smooth base, applied mouth, rare, American 1860-1870. . . . .**$3,500-4,000**

Jacob A. Wolford – Chicago (around shoulder) / Wolford / Z – Whiskey, Yellow amber, 8-5/8", smooth base (A & D.H. Chambers Pittsburgh, PA / Pat Aug 6th 72), applied mouth with internal screw threads, original threaded stopper is embossed "Pat. Aug. 6th 72, American 1875-1880 . . . . **$500-800**

J.F.T. & Co. / Philad, Amber, 7-1/8", jug, molded vertical rib pattern, open pontil, applied double collar mouth, handle, American 1860-1875 . . . . **$500-900**

JH Cutter / Old / Bourbon / A.P. Hotling & Co. / Sole Agents – "A No 1" on reverse, Medium amber, 12", smooth base, applied top, American 1877-1880 . . . . **$150-175**

J.T. Gayen / Altona, Red amber, 13-5/8", cannon form, smooth base, applied blob mouth, American 1865-1875 **$1,500-2,000**

J. Moore / (antlers) / Old Bourbon / Trade Mark, Dark amber, 11-1/4", smooth base, applied top, American 1875-1888 . . . . **$300-600**

Jockey Club / Whiskey / GW Chesley & Co. / SF, Golden amber, 11-7/8", smooth base, applied top, extremely rare, American 1873-1878 . . . . **$5,000-8,000**

John Coyne / Cor Fayette & Seneca STS / Utica, N.Y., Medium yellow green, strap-side pint, smooth base, applied double collar mouth, American 1875-1885 . . . . **$300-400**

Label Under Glass – Rum Punch – Label: picture of lady with orange and green background, Clear glass, 12", smooth base, applied top, American 1875-1895 . . . . **$1,800-2,000**

Label Under Glass – Cherry – Label: picture of lady with orange and green background, Clear glass, 12", smooth base, applied top, American 1875-1895 . . . . **$1,500-1,700**

Label Under Glass – Gin – Label: picture of lady with peach and gold background, Clear glass, 12", smooth base, applied top, American 1875-1895 . . . . **$2,000-2,200**

Label Under Glass – Kummel – Label: picture of lady with orange and green background, Clear glass, 11", fluted shape, smooth base, applied top, American 1875-1895 . . . . **$1,300-1,500**

Label Under Glass – Encased Whiskey Bottle – Multicolored label with a pretty woman – Label reads: Benj. F. Stratton, Pottstown, PA, Wicker basket, 11-3/4", tooled mouth, metal and cork stopper on chain, extremely rare, American 1880-1895 . . . . **$500-700**

Label Under Glass – Label reads: Our Private Stock / (motif of whiskey barrels) / Bourbon / McLeod Hatje Proprietors / San Francisco, Clear glass, 12", smooth base, applied top, American 1875-1895 . . . .**$1,800-2,000**

Lancaster / Glass Works / Lancaster N.Y. (embossed on base), Yellow amber, 9-1/4 ", barrel form, smooth base, applied square collared mouth, American 1860-1870. . . . . **$500-1,000**

Lancaster / Glass Works / Lancaster N.Y. (embossed on base), Brilliant yellow amber with topaz tone, 9-1/2", smooth base, applied double collared mouth, American 1860-1870 . . . . **$500-1,000**

Lilienthal & Co. / (motif of embossed monogram and crown) / San Francisco, Light yellow with green tone, 11-1/2", smooth base, applied top, American 1885-1895 . . . . **$500-1,200**

M. Gruenberg & Co. / Old Judge KY / San Francisco (light embossing), Medium amber, 11-3/8", four-piece mold, smooth base, applied top, American 1879-1881 . . . . **$700-1,500**

M. Gruenberg & Co. / Old Judge KY / San Francisco (strong embossing), Dark amber, 11-3/8", four-piece mold, smooth base, applied top, American 1879-1881 . . . . **$700-1,500**

M. Schwartzkoff / Liquors / 301 / Penn Ave. / Scranton, PA, Brilliant yellow olive, 9-3/4", strap sided quart, smooth base, applied double collar mouth, American 1880-1890 . . . . **$900-1,100**

May & Fairall / Grocers / Baltimore, Yellow amber, 11-3/8", smooth base, applied mouth, American 1870-1880 . **$500-600**

McKennas / Nelson County / Extra / Kentucky Bourbon / Whiskey / W & K Sole Agents, Medium amber, 12", smooth base, applied top, American 1874-1878 . . . . . . **$1,500-1,700**

Milton J. Hardy / Old / Bourbon / Trade Mark (eagle) / Wellington A. Hardy / Manufacturer / Louisville / K.Y., Yellow amber with faint olive tone, 11-3/4", smooth base, applied mouth, American 1878-1880. . . . . **$5,000-8,000**

Neal's Ambrosia / Philada / Whiskey – On Applied Seal, Cobalt blue, 9-1/4", smooth base, applied collar mouth, American 1865-1875 . . . . **$3,500-4,500**

Old / Fashion / Hand / Made / Sour / Mash / Belle / Of / Anderson, Milk glass, 6-7/8", smooth base, tooled lip, American 1885-1900 . . . . **$100-150**

Old / Fashion / Hand / Made / Sour / Mash / Belle / Of / Anderson, Milk glass, 8-1/8", smooth base, tooled lip, American 1885-1900 . . . . **$100-150**

Neal's Ambrosia / Philada Whiskey (on applied seal), 9-1/4", American 1865-1875, **$3,500-4,500.**

Old Monogahela / B / Rye Whiskey (on applied seal), 9-3/8", American 1870-1875, **$250-350.**

Old Monogahela / B (sheath of grain) / Rye Whiskey – On Applied Seal, Deep olive amber, 9-3/8", smooth base, applied sloping double collar mouth, American 1870-1875 . **$250-350**

Old Monogahela / C (sheath of grain) H / Rye Whiskey – On Applied Seal, Dark amber, 9-1/2", smooth base, applied sloping double collar mouth, American 1870-1875 . . . . **$250-350**

Old Wheat / 1835 / Whiskey, Golden amber, 12-1/4", iron pontil, tooled mouth with ring, American 1845-1860 . . . **$500-1,000**

P.F. Goddard & Co / 223 / Dock / St. / Phila – On Applied Seal, Lime green, 11-1/4", smooth base (Whitney Glass Works), "Patent" on shoulder, applied collar mouth, American 1870-1880 . . . . **$600-800**

P & V – Seal Whiskey Bottle, Aquamarine, 11-1/4", smooth base, three-piece mold, applied sloping collared mouth with ring, extremely rare, only known example, American 1860-1870 . . . .**$1,000-2,000**

Pure Cognac – On Applied Seal, Medium amber, 9", cone form, pontil-scarred base, applied double collar mouth, handle, American 1865-1875 . . . . **$700-900**

Redington & Co / R & Co (monogram) / San Francisco, Medium yellow amber, 10-1/4", smooth base, applied ring mouth, scarce, American 1880-1890 . . . . **$200-300**

Reed's / Old Lexington Club, Medium amber, 11-3/4", smooth base, applied top, very rare, American 1887-1895, Whitney Glass Works, Glassboro, New Jersey **$2,000-3,000**

P.F. Goddard & Co / 233 Dock St. / Phila 11-1/4", American 1870-1880, **$600-800.**

Russ's / Aromatic – Schnapps – New York, olive green, 9-7/8", smooth base, applied sloping double collar mouth, American 1865-1875, **$150-200.**

Renault & Co. / Cognac / 1805 / W.H.Y. – Seal Whiskey Bottle, Yellow olive, 11", smooth base (Dyottville Glass Works Phila) applied sloping collared mouth with ring, three-piece mold, American 1860-1870, Dyottville Glass Works, Philadelphia, Pennsylvania **$1,500-3,000**

Russ's / Aromatic – Schnapps – New York, Olive green, 9-7/8", smooth base, applied sloping double collar mouth, American 1865-1875 . . . . **$200-250**

Schreiber Bros. Co. / (motif of two deer with SB emblem) The Largest Jewish Liquor House Of The West / Chicago, ILL, Clear, 9-1/4", smooth base, ABM lip with wooden handle, American 1900-1920 . . . . **$250-350**

SOP / S.M. & Co – On Applied Seal, Medium orange amber, 7-1/2", cone form, pontil-scarred base, applied ring mouth, handle, American 1860-1875 . . . . **$500-700**

T. Goddard & Co / 233 Dock / St. / Philada – Seal Whiskey Bottle, Bright yellow green, 11", embossed seal applied upside down, smooth base, applied sloping collared mouth with ring, extremely rare, seal is upside down, American 1860-1870 . . . . **$750-1,500**

Tabec / De / A. Delpit / Nouvelle / Orleans – On Applied Seal, Deep olive amber, smooth base, applied collar mouth, blown in three-piece mold, American 1860-1870 . . . . **$350-450**

The Duffy Malt / (monogram) / Whiskey Co. – Sample Bottle, Medium amber, 4", smooth base, tooled top, American 1885-1900 . . . . **$100-175**

W.B. Bordman Old Bourbon, 9-1/4",
American 1860-1870, **$200-275.**

Wicker-encased label-under-glass whiskey, clear glass with
multicolored label under glass showing a pretty woman and
reading "Benj. F. Stratton, Pottstown, Pa", smooth base, tooled
mouth, 11-3/4", American 1880-1895, **$500-700.**

The / Old Mill / Whitlock & Co. – On Applied Seal, Yellow amber, 8-1/4", cone form, pontil-scarred base, applied double collar mouth, large seal with neck chain and handle, American 1860-1875 . . . .**$1,200-1,500**

Trade Mark / Gold Dust / (motif of embossed horse) Kentucky Bourbon / N. Van Bergen & Co. / Sole Proprietors, Blue aqua, 11-3/4 ", smooth base, applied drippy top, American 1877-1883 . . . . **$700-1,400**

Trade Mark / Gold Dust / (motif of embossed horse) Kentucky Bourbon / N. Van Bergen & Co. / Sole Proprietors, Medium amethyst, 11-7/8", smooth base, tooled top, extremely rare variant, one of only five known examples, American 1880-1882 . . . . **$500-1,000**

Turner Brothers / New York, Orange amber, 9-3/4", barrel form, smooth base, applied square collared mouth, American 1860-1880 . . . . **$500-1,000**

Van Beil & Co. / Phila / 1861 – On Applied Seal, Yellow olive, 12-1/8", smooth base (Whitney Glass Works Glassboro, NJ), applied mouth with internal screw threads, embossed on correct screw-in stopper (Pat. Jan 1861), three-piece mold, American 1865-1875 . . . . **$400-700**

Weeks & Potter – Boston (on shoulder), Medium golden amber, 11-1/2", smooth base, applied sloping double collar mouth with internal threads, original glass screw stopper embossed "PAT," blown in three-piece mold, American 1875-1885 . . . **$150-225**

W.F. & B / N.Y., Dark amethyst, 11", 6-sided, smooth base, applied mouth, rare, American 1865-1875 . . . . **$400-500**

Star Whiskey / New York / W.B. Crowell Jr.,
8-1/2", American 1860-1875, **$500-800.**

W.B. Bordman/ Old Bourbon, Yellow amber, 9-1/4", case gin form, smooth base, applied double collar mouth, very rare, American 1860-1870 . . . . **$200-275**

Wharton's / Whiskey / 1850 / Chestnut Grove, Orange amber, Jug, smooth base (Whitney Glass Works / Glassboro, N.J.), applied handle, sheared and tooled lip with pour spout, American 1860-1875 . . . . **$550-650**

Whitlock & Co. / New York – BM & EA, Medium grass green, 9-3/8", smooth base, applied mouth, rare, American 1865-1875 . . . . **$700-900**

BACK BAR BOTTLES AND DECANTERS

Bar Bottle – Pattern Molded, Medium teal green, 10", 16 vertical rib-pattern, open pontil, applied top, American 1780-1840 . . . . **$800-1,000**

Bar Bottle, Fiery opalescent cranberry, 11", red with white swirl pattern, smooth base, tooled mouth, American 1885-1910 . . . . **$750-950**

Bar Bottle, Cobalt blue, 11-3/8", cylinder, smooth base, applied ringed mouth, raised oval panel on front, blown in three-piece mold, American 1870-1880 . . . . **$200-300**

Crystal Spring (white lettering), Clear, 11-1/4", swirled glass, smooth base, applied top, American 1885-1900   **$250-400**

Whitlock & Co. / New York – BM & EA, 9-3/8", American 1865-1875, **$700-900.**

Thos Jacobs & Co (on seal), large iron pontil, 1850-1860, 11-3/4", **$150-250**

Decanter – Buffalo Club (picture of buffalo in brown enamel), Clear, 9-1/4", corset waist form, cut shoulder and panel, polished pontil, tooled lip, original glass stopper, American 1890-1910 . . . .**$1,000-1,200**

Guckenheimer / Rye Whiskey / Nothing Better (white lettering), Clear, 11-1/4", swirled glass, smooth base, applied top, American 1885-1900 . . . . **$250-400**

Label Under Glass – Portrait of beautiful Victorian woman wth red, gold, blue, black, and white background, Clear, 10", smooth base (W.N. Walton Pat. Sept. 23/62), tooled flared top, American 1860-1880 . . . . **$400-800**

Label Under Glass – John H. Hamm / (motif of lady) / Rye Whiskey, Clear, 10", smooth base, tooled lip with original ground glass closure, American 1880-1900 . . . . **$1,100-1,300**

Label Under Glass – Fine Old / Port, Clear, 11", smooth base, tooled lip with original ground glass closure, American 1880-1900 . . . . **$375-500**

Label Under Glass – Brandy (motif of lady), Clear, 11", smooth base, tooled lip with original ground glass closure, American 1880-1900 . . . . **$1,600-1,800**

Large Rye (in gold lettering), Clear, 11", 12 panel base and cut-glass fluted shoulders, smooth base, applied top, American 1885-1900 . . . . **$275-375**

Magnet (motif of red and white magnet) Whiskey, Clear, 9", smooth base, tooled lip with original ground glass closure, American 1880-1900 . . . . **$500-700**

Pride Of Kentucky / (motif of "L" (Livingston) in diamond) / Sour Mash, Clear, 8", smooth base, tooled lip, applied handle, American 1895-1910 . . . . **$300-600**

Puritan Rye (white lettering), Clear, 11", swirled glass, smooth base, applied lip, American 1895-1900 . . . . **$250-400**

Rye, Deep cobalt blue, 11", smooth base, silver closure, American 1895-1900 . . . . **$250-300**

POTTERY AND STONEWARE WHISKEY JUGS

Blackbird Distillery (picture of blackbird on a branch) Guild Auld / Scotch Whiskey (pottery whiskey jug), Cream with brown glaze on neck and handle, 7-3/4", rare, American 1890-1915 . . . . **$400-500**

Chas. D. Moul / Wines / & Liquors / York, Pa, Cream color body with dark brown top, 4", smooth base, small open double handles, American 1885-1910 $150-250, Compliments / I.W. Harper / Nelson Co. / Kentucky, Brown and light brown pottery, 3", smooth base, American 1890-1915 . . . . **$75-100**

English Pub Jug – Henry White & Co's / Old Jamaica / Rum (inside a heart with an African Caribbean man on each side) London / Trade Mark, Cream color body with burnt orange glaze on neck, 6-3/8", smooth base (Frank Beardmore & Co), handled, American 1880-1920 . . . . **$275-375**

Helmet / Rye / Max Fruhauf & Co. / Cincinnati, O, Dark and light brown, 3", smooth base, American 1890-1915 . . . . . **$125-175**

Mark Twain / Hotel / Hannibal, Mo, Dark brown glaze, 2-3/4", smooth base (Hall / made in U.S.A.), handled, American 1905-1935, Hull Pottery, Crooksville, Ohio **$100-150**

Meredith's / Diamond Club / (motif of diamond) / Pure Rye / Whiskey / Expressly For Medicinal Use / East Liverpool Ohio, White, 4-1/2", smooth base reads "KT & K China" (Knowles, Taylor & Knowles Company; the word "China" on base refers to type of whiteware), handled jug, American, 1870-1900 .... **$50-100**

Meredith's / Diamond Club / (motif of diamond) / Pure Rye / Whiskey / Expressly For Medicinal Use / East Liverpool Ohio, White, 7", smooth base reads "KT & K China" (Knowles, Taylor & Knowles Company; the word "China" on base refers to type of whiteware), handled jug, American 1870-1900 .... **$75-100**

S. Harrison / Lincoln (stoneware whiskey flask), Gray, 6-1/2", smooth base, raised slab seal, English 1840-1860 .. **$350-550**

Spring Lake / Hand Made / Sour Mash / Bourbon, White, 7-3/4", smooth base reads "KT & K China" (Knowles, Taylor & Knowles Company; the word "China" on base refers to type of whiteware), handled jug, American 1870-1900 ..... **$75-100**

Wicklow Distillery (owl on branch) / Old Irish Whiskey / Guaranteed 1/4 Gallon (pottery whiskey jug), Cream with brown glaze neck, 7-3/4", handled, Irish 1890-1915 .... **$150-200**

NEW BOTTLES (POST-1900)

The bottles in this section have been listed by individual categories and/or type since the contents hold little interest for the collector. New bottles covered in this section are valued for their decorative, appealing, and unique designs.

The objective of most new-bottle collectors is to collect a complete set of items designed and produced by a favorite manufacturer. With reproductions, like the bottles Coca-Cola has released, or with new items, such as those made by Avon, the right time to purchase is when the first issue comes out on the retail market, or prior to retail release if possible. As with the old bottles, the following listings provide a representative cross section of new bottles in various price ranges and categories rather than listing only the rarest or most collectible pieces.

The pricing shown reflects the value of particular item listed. Newer bottles are usually manufactured in limited quantities without any reissues. Since retail prices are affected by factors such as source, type of bottle, desirability, condition, and the possibility the bottle was produced exclusively as a collectors' item, the pricing can fluctuate radically at any given time.

AVON BOTTLES

The cosmetic empire known today as Avon began as the California Perfume Company. It was the creation of D.H. McConnell, a door-to-door book salesman who gave away perfume samples to stop the doors from being slammed in his face. Eventually, McConnell gave up selling books and concentrated on selling perfumes instead. Although based in New York, the name "Avon" was used in 1929 along with the name California Perfume Company or C.P.C. After 1939, the name Avon was used exclusively. Bottles embossed with C.P.C. are very rare and collectible due to the small quantities issued and the even smaller number that have been well preserved.

Today, Avon offers collectors a wide range of products in bottles shaped like cars, people, chess pieces, trains, animals, sporting items (footballs, baseballs, etc.) and numerous other objects. The scarcest and most sought after pieces are the Pre-World War II figurals, since very few were well preserved.

To those who collect Avon items, anything Avon-related is considered collectible. That includes boxes, brochures, magazine ads, or anything else labeled with the Avon name. Since many people who sell Avon items are unaware of their value, collectors can find great prices at swap meets, flea markets, and garage sales.

While this book offers a good representation of Avon collectibles, I recommend that serious collectors obtain Bud Hastin's book *Avon Products & California Perfume Co. (CPC) Collector's Encyclopedia*, 18th Edition, which offers pricing and pictures of thousands of Avon & California Perfume Co. (CPC) products from 1886 to present.

A Man's World, Globe On Stand, 1969 . . . . **$7-10**

A Winner, Boxing Gloves, 1960 . . . . **$20-25**

Abraham Lincoln, Wild Country After Shave, 1970-1972 . . . **$3-5**

After Shave On Tap, Wild Country **$3-5**

Aladdin's Lamp, 1971 . . . . **$7-10**

Alaskan Moose, 1974 . . . . **$5-8**

Alpine Flask, 1966-1967 . . . . **$35-45**

American Belle, Sonnet Cologne, 1976-1978 . . . . **$5-7**

American Buffalo, 1975 . . . . **$6-8**

American Eagle Pipe, 1974-1975 . . . . **$6-8**

American Eagle, Windjammer After Shave, 1971-1972 . . . . . **$3-4**

American Ideal Perfume, California Perfume Comp., 1911
. . . . **$125-140**

American Schooner, Oland After Shave, 1972-1973 . . . . **$4-5**

American beauty fragrance jar, liquid, 4 oz, cork stopper, 1921, **$75-100.**

American Ideal Powder sachet, large size bottle with brass cap, 1912-1915, **$75-100.**

Aromatic bay rum, 4 oz, metal cork embossed stopper, 1927-1929, **$100-125.**

Andy Capp Figural (England), 1970 . . . . **$95-105**

Angler, Windjammer After Shave, 1970 . . . . **$5-7**

Apple Blossom Toilet Water, 1941-1942 . . . . **$50-60**

Apothecary, Lemon Velvet Moist Lotion,1973-1976. . . . . . . **$4-6**

Apothecary, Spicy After Shave, 1973-1974. . . . . **$4-5**

Aristocat Kittens Soap (Walt Disney). **$5-7**

Armoire Decanter, Charisma Bath Oil, 1973-1974 . . . . **$4-5**

Armoire Decanter, Elusive Bath Oil, 1972-1975 . . . . **$4-5**

Station wagon, 6 oz, green glass car with tan plastic top, 1971-1973, **$14.**

Auto Lantern, 1973 . . . . **$6-8**

Auto, Big Mack Truck, Windjammer After Shave, 1973-1975 . . . **$5-6**

Auto, Cord, 1937 Model, Wild Country After Shave, 1974-1978 . . . . **$7-8**

Auto, Country Vendor, Wild Country After Shave, 1973 . . . . . **$7-8**

Auto, Duesenberg, Silver, Wild Country After Shave, 1970-1972 . . . . **$8-9**

Auto, Dune Buggy, Sports Rally Bracing Lotion, 1971-1973 . . **$4-5**

Auto, Electric Charger, Avon Leather Cologne, 1970-1972 . . . **$6-7**

Auto, Hayes Apperson, 1902 Model, Avon Blend 7 After Shave, 1973-1974 . . . . **$5-7**

Auto, Maxwell 23, Deep Woods After Shave, 1972-1974 . . . . . **$5-6**

Auto, MG, 1936, Wild Country After Shave, 1974-1975 . . . . . **$4-5**

Auto, Model A, Wild Country After Shave, 1972-1974 . . . . . . **$4-5**

Auto, Red Depot Wagon, Oland After Shave, 1972-1973 . . . . **$6-7**

Auto, Rolls Royce, Deep Woods After Shave, 1972-1975 . . . . **$6-8**

Auto, Stanley Steamer, Windjammer After Shave, 1971-1972 . . . . **$6-7**

Auto, Station Wagon, Tai Winds After Shave, 1971-1973 . . . . **$7-8**

Auto, Sterling 6, Spicy After Shave, 1968-1970 . . . . **$6-7**

Auto, Sterling Six Ii, Wild Country After Shave, 1973-1974 . . . **$4-5**

Auto, Stutz Bearcat, 1914 Model, Avon Blend 7 After Shave, 1974-1977 . . . .**$5-6**

Auto, Touring T, Tribute After Shave, 1969-1970 . . . .**$6-7**

Auto, Volkswagen, Red, Oland After Shave, 1972 . . . .**$5-6**

Avon Calling, Phone, Wild Country After Shave, 1969-1970 . . . . **$15-20**

Avon Dueling Pistol Ii, Black Glass, 1972 . . . . **$10-15**

Avonshire Blue Cologne, 1971-1974 . . . .**$4-5**

Baby Grand Piano, Perfume Glace, 1971-1972 . . . .**$8-10**

Baby Hippo, 1977-1980 . . . .**$4-5**

Ballad Perfume, 3 Drams, 3/8 Ounce, 1939 . . . . **$100-125**

Bath Urn, Lemon Velvet Bath Oil, 1971-1973 . . . .**$4-5**

Beauty Bound Black Purse, 1964 . . . . **$45-55**

Bell Jar Cologne, 1973 . . . .**$5-10**

Benjamin Franklin, Wild Country After Shave, 1974-1976 . . . **$4-5**

Big Game Rhino, Tai Winds After Shave, 1972-1973 . . . .**$7-8**

Big Whistle, 1972 . . . .**$4-5**

Bird House Power Bubble Bath, 1969 . . . .**$7-8**

Bird Of Paradise Cologne Decanter, 1972-1974 . . . .**$4-5**

Blacksmith's Anvil, Deep Woods After Shave, 1972-1973 . . .**$4-5**

Bloodhound Pipe, Deep Woods After Shave, 1976 . . . .**$5-6**

Blue Blazer After Shave Lotion, 1964 . . . . $25-30

Blue Blazer Deluxe, 1965 . . . . $55-65

Blue Moo Soap On A Rope, 1972 . . . . $5-6

Blunderbuss Pistol, 1976 . . . . $7-10

Bon Bon Black, Field & Flowers Cologne, 1973 . . . . $5-6

Bon Bon White, Occur Cologne, 1972-1973 . . . . $5-6

Bon Bon White, Topaze Cologne, 1972-1973 . . . . $5-6

Boot Gold Top, Avon Leather After Shave, 1966-1971 . . . . . $3-4

Boot Western, 1973 . . . . $4-5

Boots And Saddle, 1968 . . . . $20-22

Brocade Deluxe, 1967 . . . . $30-35

Buffalo Nickel, Liquid Hair Lotion, 1971-1972 . . . . $4-5

Bulldog Pipe, Oland After Shave, 1972-1973 . . . . $4-5

Bunny Puff And Talc, 1969-1972 . . . . $3-4

Bureau Organizer, 1966-1967 . . . . $35-55

Butter Candlestick, Sonnet Cologne, 1974 . . . . $7-8

Butterfly Fantasy Egg, First Issue, 1974 . . . . $20-30

Butterfly, Unforgettable Cologne, 1972-1973 . . . . $4-5

Butterfly, Unforgettable Cologne, 1974-1976 . . . . $1-2

Cable Car After Shave, 1974-1975 . . . . $8-10

Camper, Deep Woods After Shave, 1972-1974 . . . . $6-7

Canada Goose, Deep Woods Cologne, 1973-1974 . . . . $4-5

Candlestick Cologne, Elusive, 1970-1971 . . . . $5-6

Car, Army Jeep, 1974-1975 . . . . **$4-5**

Casey's Lantern, Island Lime After Shave, 1966-1967 . . . **$30-40**

Catch A Fish, Field Flowers Cologne, 1976-1978 . . . . **$6-7**

Centennial Express 1876, Locomotive 1978 . . . . **$11-12**

Chevy '55, 1974-1975 . . . . **$6-8**

Christmas Ornament, Green or Red, 1970-1971 . . . . **$1-2**

Christmas Ornament, Orange, Bubble Bath, 1970-1971 . . . **$2-3**

Christmas Tree Bubble Bath, 1968 . . . . **$5-7**

Classic Lion, Deep Woods After Shave, 1973-1975 . . . . **$4-5**

Club Bottle, 1906 Avon Lady, 1977 . . . . **$25-30**

Club Bottle, 1st Annual, 1972 . . . . **$150-200**

Club Bottle, 2nd Annual, 1973 . . . . **$45-60**

Club Bottle, 5th Annual, 1976 . . . . **$25-30**

Club Bottle, Bud Hastin, 1974 . . . . **$70-95**

Club Bottle, CPC Factory, 1974 . . . . **$30-40**

Collector's Pipe, Windjammer After Shave, 1973-1974 . . . . . **$3-4**

Colt Revolver 1851, 1975-1976 . . . . **$10-12**

Corncob Pipe After Shave, 1974-1975 . . . . **$4-6**

Corvette Stingray '65, 1975 . . . . **$5-7**

Covered Wagon, Wild Country After Shave, 1970-1971 . . . . . **$4-5**

Daylight Shaving Time, 1968-1970 . . . . **$5-7**

Defender Cannon, 1966 . . . . **$20-24**

Dollar's 'N' Scents, 1966-1967 . . . . **$20-24**

Dutch Girl Figurine, Somewhere, 1973-1974 . . . . **$8-10**

Duck After Shave, 1971 . . . . **$4-6**

Dueling Pistol 1760, 1973-1974 . . . . **$9-12**

Dueling Pistol Ii, 1975 . . . . **$9-12**

Eight-ball Decanter, Spicy After Shave, 1973 . . . . **$3-4**

Electric Guitar, Wild Country After Shave, 1974-1975 . . . . . **$4-5**

Enchanted Frog Cream Sachet, Sonnet, 1973-1976 . . . . . . **$3-4**

Fashion Boot, Moonwind Cologne, 1972-1976 . . . . **$5-7**

Fashion Boot, Sonnet Cologne, 1972-1976 . . . . **$5-7**

Fielder's Choice, 1971-1972 . . . . **$4-6**

Fire Alarm Box, 1975-1976 . . . . **$4-6**

First Class Male, Wild Country After Shave, 1970-1971 . . . . **$3-4**

First Down, Soap On A Rope, 1970-1971 . . . . **$7-8**

First Down, Wild Country After Shave **$3-4**

First Volunteer, Tai Winds Cologne, 1971-1972 . . . . **$6-7**

Fox Hunt, 1966 . . . . **$25-30**

French Telephone, Moonwind Foaming Bath Oil, 1971
. . . . **$20-24**

Garnet Bud Vase, To A Wild Rose Colgone, 1973-1976 . . . . . **$3-5**

Gavel, Island Lime After Shave, 1967-1968 . . . . **$4-5**

George Washington, Spicy After Shave, 1970-1972 . . . . **$2-3**

George Washington, Tribute After Shave, 1970-1972 . . . . . . **$2-3**

Gold Cadillac, 1969-1973 . . . . **$7-10**

Gaylord Gator, 10" l., green and yellow rubber soap dish with yellow soap, 1967-1969, **$3** gator only, **$10** entire set.

First Class Male, 4-1/2" h., 4 oz, blue glass with red cap, 1970-1971 **$10**.

Gone Fishing, 1973-1974 . . . . **$5-7**

Grade Avon Hostess Soap, 1971-1972 . . . . **$6-8**

Hearth Lamp, Roses, Roses, 1973-1976 . . . . **$6-8**

Hobnail Decanter, Moonwind Bath Oil, 1972-1974 . . . . . . **$5-6**

Hunter's Stein, 1972 . . . . **$10-14**

Indian Chieftan, Protein Hair Lotion, 1972-1975 . . . . **$2-3**

Indian Head Penny, Bravo After Shave, 1970-1972 . . . . . . **$4-5**

Inkwell, Windjammer After Shave, 1969-1970 . . . . **$6-7**

Iron Horse Shaving Mug, Avon Blend 7 After Shave, 1974-1976
. . . . **$3-4**

Jack-in-the-box, Baby Cream, 1974 . . . . **$4-6**

Jaguar Car, 1973-1976 . . . . **$6-8**

Jolly Santa, 1978 .... **$6-7**

Joyous Bell, 1978 .... **$5-6**

King Pin, 1969-1970................................ **$4-6**

Kodiak Bear, 1977 .... **$5-10**

Koffee Klatch, Honeysuckle Foam Bath Oil, 1971-1974 .... **$5-6**

Liberty Bell, Tribute After Shave, 1971-1972 .... **$4-6**

Liberty Dollar, After Shave, 1970-1972 .... **$4-6**

Lincoln Bottle, 1971-1972 .... **$3-5**

Lip Pop Colas, Cherry, 1973-1974 .... **$1-2**

Lip Pop Colas, Cola, 1973-1974 .... **$1-2**

Lip Pop Colas, Strawberry, 1973-1974 .... **$1-2**

Longhorn Steer, 1975-1976.......................... **$7-9**

Looking Glass, Regence Cologne, 1970-1972............ **$7-8**

Mallard Duck, 1967-1968............................ **$8-10**

Mickey Mouse, Bubble Bath, 1969.................... **$10-12**

Mighty Mitt Soap On A Rope, 1969-1972 .... **$7-8**

Ming Cat, Bird Of Paradise Cologne, 1971.............. **$5-7**

Mini Bike, Sure Winner Bracing Lotion, 1972-1973 ...... **$3-5**

Nile Blue Bath Urn, Skin So Soft, 1972-1974 .... **$3-4**

Nile Blue Bath Urn, Skin So Soft, 1972-1974 .... **$4-6**

No Parking, 1975-1976............................. **$5-7**

Old Faithful, Wild Country After Shave, 1972-1973 ...... **$4-6**

One Good Turn, Screwdriver, 1976 .... **$5-6**

Opening Play, Dull Golden, Spicy After Shave, 1968-1969 ....**$8-10**

Opening Play, Shiny Golden, Spicy After Shave, 1968-1969 ....**$14-17**

Owl Fancy, Roses, Roses, 1974-1976 ....**$3-4**

Owl Soap Dish And Soaps, 1970-1971.................**$8-10**

Packard Roadster, 1970-1972........................**$4-7**

Pass Play Decanter, 1973-1975.......................**$6-8**

Peanuts Gang Soaps, 1970-1972......................**$8-9**

Pepperbox Pistol, 1976 ....**$5-10**

Perfect Drive Decanter, 1975-1976...................**$7-9**

Pheasant, 1972-1974 ....**$7-9**

Piano Decanter, Tai Winds After Shave, 1972...........**$3-4**

Pipe, Full, Decanter, Brown, Spicy After Shave, 1971-1972 . .**$3-4**

Pony Express, Avon Leather After Shave, 1971-1972.......**$3-4**

Pony Post "Tall", 1966-1967 ....**$7-9**

Pot Belly Stove, 1970-1971 ....**$5-7**

President Lincoln, Tai Winds After Shave, 1973 ....**$6-8**

President Washington, Deep Woods After Shave, 1974-1976 ....**$4-5**

Quail, 1973-1974 ....**$7-9**

Rainbow Trout, Deep Woods After Shave, 1973-1974 ......**$3-4**

Road Runner, Motorcycle **$4-5**

Thomas Jefferson handgun, 10" l., 2-1/2 oz, dark amber glass with gold and silver plastic cap, 1978-1979, **$11.**

Seahorse, clear glass, 6 oz, gold cap, 1970-1972, **$10.**

Rook, Spicy After Shave, 1973-1974 . . . . **$4-5**

Royal Coach, Bird Of Paradise Bath Oil, 1972-1973 . . . . . . **$4-6**

Scent With Love, Elusive Perfume, 1971-1972 . . . . **$9-10**

Scent With Love, Field Flowers Perfume, 1971-1972 . . . . . **$9-10**

Scent With Love, Moonwind Perfume, 1971-1972. . . . . . . **$9-10**

Side-Wheeler, Tribute After Shave, 1970-1971 . . . . **$4-5**

Side-Wheeler, Wild Country After Shave, 1971-1972. . . . . . **$3-4**

Small World Perfume Glace, Small World, 1971-1972. . . . **$3-4**

Snoopy Soap Dish Refills, 1968-1976 . . . . **$3-4**

Snoopys Bubble Tub, 1971-1972 . . . . **$3-4**

Spark Plug Decanter, 1975-1976 . . . . **$2-5**

Spirit Of St Louis, Excalibur After Shave, 1970-1972 . . . . . . **$3-5**

Stage Coach, Wild Country After Shave, 1970-1977 . . . . **$5-6**

Talcum powder, 3.5 oz, metal can, 1912-1915, **$300-360** (different caps on each can).

Sachet, glass bottle with metal cap, two-piece gold label, 1908, **$100-135.**

JIM BEAM BOTTLES

The James B. Beam distilling company was founded in 1778 by Jacob Beam in Kentucky and now bears the name of Col. James B. Beam, Jacob Beam's grandson. Beam whiskey was very popular in the South during the 19th and 20th century but was not produced on a large scale. Because of low production, the early Beam bottles are very rare, collectible, and valuable.

In 1953, the Beam company packaged bourbon in a special Christmas/New Year ceramic decanter—a rarity for any distiller. Because the decanters sold well, Beam decided to redevelop its packaging, leading to production of a number of decanter series in the 1950s. The first was the Ceramics Series in 1953. In 1955 the Executive Series was issued to commemorate the 160th anniversary of the corporation. In 1955, Beam introduced the Regal China Series, issued to honor significant people, places, and events with a focus on America and contemporary situations.

In 1956, political figures were introduced with the elephant and the donkey, as well as special productions for customer specialties made on commission. In 1957, the Trophy Series honored various achievements within the liquor industry. The State Series was introduced 1958 to commemorate the admission of Alaska and Hawaii into the Union. The practice has continued with Beam still producing decanters to commemorate all 50 states.

In total, over 500 types of Beam bottles have been issued since 1953. For further information, contact: International Association of Jim Beam Bottle and Specialties Clubs, PO Box 486, Kewanee, IL 61443, (309) 853-3370, www.beam-wade.org.

AC Spark Plug 1977, Replica of a spark plug in white, green, and gold **$22-26**

AHEPA 50th Anniversary 1972, Regal China bottle designed in honor of AHEPA'S (American Hellenic Education Progressive Association) 50th Anniversary. **$4-6**

Aida 1978, Figurine of character from the opera Aida . . . **$140-160**

Akron Rubber Capital 1973, Regal China bottle honoring Akron, Ohio. **$15-20**

Alaska 1958, Regal China, 9-1/2", star-shaped bottle . . . **$55-60**

Alaska 1964-1965, Re-issue of the 1958 bottle **$40-50**

Alaska Purchase 1966, Regal China, 10", blue and gold bottle **$4-6**

American Samoa 1973, Regal China, with the seal of Samoa. . . .**$5-7**

American Veterans. **$4-7**

Antique Clock. **$35-45**

Antioch 1967, Regal China, 10", commemorates Regal's Diamond Jubilee **$5-7**

Antique Coffee Grinder 1979, Replica of a box coffee mill used in mid-19th century. **$10-12**

Antique Globe 1980, Represents the Martin Behaim globe of 1492. . . . . **$7-11**

Antique Telephone (1897) 1978, Replica of an 1897 desk phone, second in a series **$50-60**

Antique Trader 1968, Regal China, 10-1/2", represents Antique Trader newspaper **$4-6**

Appaloosa 1974, Regal China, 10", represents favorite horse of the Old West. **$12-15**

Arizona 1968, Regal China, 12", represents the state of Arizona . . **$4-6**

Armadillo **$8-12**

Armanetti Award Winner 1969, Honors Aramnetti, Inc. of Chicago as "Liquor Retailer of the Year" **$6-8**

Armanetti Shopper 1971, Reflects the slogan "It's fun to Shop Armanetti - Self Service Liquor Store", 11-3/4" **$6-8**

Armanetti Vase 1968, Yellow toned decanter embossed with flowers. **$5-7**

Bacchus 1970, Issued by Armanetti Liquor Stores of Chicago, Illinois,11-3/4". **$6-9**

Barney's Slot Machine 1978, Replica of the world's largest slot machine. **$14-16**

Barry Berish 1985, Executive series **$110-140**

Barry Berish 1986, Executive series, bowl **$110-140**

Bartender's Guild 1973, Commemorative honoring the International Bartenders Assn. **$4-7**

Baseball 1969, Issued to commemorate the 100th anniversary of Baseball **$18-20**

Bean Pot 1980, Shaped like a New England bean pot; club bottle for the New England Beam Bottle and Specialties Club **$12-15**

Beaver Valley Club 1977, A club bottle to honor the Beaver Valley Jim Beam Club of Rochester **$8-12**

Bell Scotch 1970, Regal China, 10-1/2", in honor of Arthur Bell & Sons **$4-7**

Beverage Association, NLBA **$4-7**

The Big Apple 1979, Apple-shaped bottle with "The Big Apple" over the top **$8-12**

Bing's 31st Clam Bake Bottle 1972, Commemorates 31st Bing Crosby National Pro-Am Golf Tournament in January 1972 ..... **$25-30**

Bing Crosby National Pro-Am 1970 .... **$4-7**

Bing Crosby National Pro-Am 1971 .... **$4-7**

Bing Crosby National Pro-Am 1972 .... **$15-25**

Bing Crosby National Pro-Am 1973 .... **$18-23**

Bing Crosby National Pro-Am 1974 .... **$15-25**

Bing Crosby National Pro-Am 1975 .... **$45-65**

Bing Crosby 36th 1976 .... **$115-25**

Bing Crosby National Pro-Am 1977 . . . . **$12-18**

Bing Crosby National Pro-Am 1978 . . . . **$12-18**

Black Katz 1968, Regal China, 14-1/2" **$7-12**

Blue Cherub Executive 1960, Regal China, 12-1/2" **$70-90**

Blue Daisy 1967, Also know as Zimmerman Blue Daisy . . **$10-12**

Blue Gill, Fish **$12-16**

Blue Goose Order **$4-7**

Blue Jay 1969 . . . .**$4-7**

Blue Goose 1979, Replica of blue goose, authenticated by Dr. Lester Fisher, Dir. of Lincoln Park Zoological Gardens in Chicago . . **$7-9**

Blue Hen Club **$12-15**

Blue Slot Machine 1967 . . . . **$10-12**

Bobby Unser Olsonite Eagle 1975, Replica of the racing car used by Bobby Unser **$40-50**

Bob DeVaney **$8-12**

Bob Hope Desert Classic 1973, First genuine Regal China bottle created in honor of the Bob Hope Desert Classic **$8-9**

Bob Hope Desert Classic 1974 . . . .**$8-12**

Bohemian Girl 1974, Issued for the Bohemian Cafe in Omaha, Nebraska to honor the Czech and Slovak immigrants in the United States, 14-1/4" **$10-15**

Bonded Gold **$4-7**

Bonded Mystic 1979, Urn-shaped bottle, burgundy-colored **$4-7**

Bonded Silver **$4-7**

Boris Godinov, with Base 1978, Second in Opera series **$350-450**

Bourbon Barrel **$18-24**

Bowling Proprietors **$4-7**

Boys Town Of Italy 1973, Created in honor of the Boys Town of Italy **$7-10**

Bowl 1986, Executive series **$20-30**

Broadmoor Hotel 1968, To celebrate the 50th anniversary of this famous hotel in Colorado Springs, Colorado "1918-The Broadmoor-1968" **$4-7**

Buffalo Bill 1971, Regal China, 10-1/2", commemorates Buffalo Bill **$4-7**

Bull Dog 1979, Honors the 204th anniversary of the United States Marine Corps **$15-18**

Cable Car 1968, Regal China, 4-1/2" **$4-6**

Caboose 1980 . . . . **$50-60**

California Mission 1970, This bottle was issued for the Jim Beam Bottle Club of Southern California in honor of the 20th anniversary of the California Missions, 14" **$10-15**

California Retail Liquor Dealers Association 1973, Designed to commemorate the 20th anniversary of the California Retail Liquor Dealers Association **$6-9**

Cal-neva 1969, Regal China, 9-1/2" **$5-7**

Camellia City Club 1979, Replica of the cupola of the State Capitol building in Sacramento **$18-23**

Cameo Blue 1965, Also known as the Shepherd Bottle **$4-6**

Cannon 1970, Bottle issued to commemorate the 175th anniversary of the Jim Beam Co. Some of these bottles have a small chain shown on the cannon and some do not. Those without the chain are harder to find and more valuable, 8" Chain . . . **$2-4**
No Chain **$9-13**

Canteen 1979, Replica of the canteen used by the Armed Forces . **$8-12**

Captain And Mate 1980 . . . . **$10-12**

Cardinal (Kentucky Cardinal) 1968 . . . . **$40-50**

Carmen 1978, Third in the Opera series **$140-180**

Carolier Bull 1984, Executive series **$18-23**

Catfish **$16-24**

Cathedral Radio 1979, Replica of one of the earlier dome-shaped radios **$12-15**

Cats 1967, Trio of Cats; Siamese, Burmese, and Tabby **$6-9**

Cedars Of Lebanon 1971, Bottle issued in honor of the Jerry Lewis Muscular Dystrophy Telethon in 1971 . . . . **$5-7**

Charisma 1970, Executive series **$4-7**

Charlie McCarthy 1976, Replica of Edgar Bergen's puppet from the 1930s **$20-30**

Casey Jones with tender, 1989, **$50** / Casey Jones caboose, 1989, **$30**.

Cherry Hills Country Club 1973, Commemorating 50th anniversary of Cherry Hills Country Club. **$4-7**

Cheyenne, Wyoming 1977 . . . .**$4-6**

Chicago Cubs, Sports Series **$30-40**

Chicago Show Bottle 1977, Commemorates 6th Annual Chicago Jim Beam Bottle Show. **$10-14**

Christmas Tree **$150-200**

Churchill Downs – Pink Roses 1969, Regal China, 10-1/4" **$5-7**

Churchill Downs – Red Roses 1969, Regal China, 10-1/4" **$9-12**

Circus Wagon 1979, Replica of a circus wagon from the late 19th century. **$24-26**

Civil War North 1961, Regal China, 10-1/4". **$10-15**

Civil War South 1961, Regal China, 10-1/4". **$25-35**

Clear Crystal Bourbon 1967, Clear glass, 11-1/2" **$5-7**

Clear Crystal Scotch 1966. . . . .**$9-12**

Clear Crystal Vodka 1967 . . . .**$5-8**

Cleopatra Rust 1962, Glass, 13-1/4" **$3-5**

Cleopatra Yellow 1962, Glass, 13-1/4", rarer than Cleopatra Rust **$8-12**

Clint Eastwood 1973, Commemorating Clint Eastwood Invitational Celebrity Tennis Tournament in Pebble Beach. **$14-17**

Cocktail Shaker 1953, Glass, Fancy Diz. Bottle, 9-1/4". **$2-5**

Coffee Grinder **$8-12**

Coffee Warmers 1954, Four types are known: red, black, gold, and white **$7-12**

Coffee Warmers 1956, Two types with metal necks and handles **$2-5**

Coho Salmon 1976, Offical seal of the National Fresh Water Fishing Hall of Fame is on the back **$10-13**

Colin Mead **$180-210**

Cobalt 1981, Executive Series. **$18-23**

Collector's Edition 1966, Set of six glass famous paintings: The Blue Boy, On the Terrace, Mardi Gras, Austide Bruant, The Artist Before His Easel, and Laughing Cavalier (each) **$2-5**

Collectors Edition Volume II 1967, A set of six flask-type bottles with famous pictures: George Gisze, Soldier and Girl, Night Watch, The Jester, Nurse and Child,and Man on Horse (each) **$2-5**

Collectors Edition Volume III 1968, A set of eight bottles with famous paintings. On the Trail, Indian Maiden, Buffalo, Whistler's Mother, American Gothic, The Kentuckian, The Scout, and Hauling in the Gill Net (each). **$2-5**

Collectors Edition Volume IV 1969, A set of eight bottles with famous paintings: Balcony, The Judge, Fruit Basket, Boy with Cherries, Emile Zola, The Guitarist Zouave, and Sunflowers (each) . . .**$2-5**

Collectors Edition Volume V 1970, A set of six bottles with famous paintings: Au Cafe, Old Peasant, Boaring Party, Gare Saint Lazare, The Jewish Bride, and Titus at Writing Desk (each). **$2-5**

Collectors Edition Volume VI 1971, A set of three bottles with famous art pieces: Charles I, The Merry Lute Player, and Boy Holding Flute (each) **$2-5**

Collectors Edition Volume VII 1972, A set of three bottles with famous paintings: The Bag Piper, Prince Baltasor, and Maidservant Pouring Milk (each)....................**$2-5**

Collectors Edition Volume VIII 1973, A set of three bottles with famous portraits: Ludwig Van Beethoven, Wolfgang Mozart, and Frederic Francis Chopin (each).....................**$2-5**

Collectors Edition Volume IX 1974, A set of three bottles with famous paintings: Cardinal, Ring-Neck Pheasant, and the Woodcock (each)..............................**$3-6**

Collectors Edition Volume X 1975, A set of three bottles with famous pictures: Sailfish, Rainbow Trout, and Largemouth Bass (each) **$3-6**

Collectors Edition Volume XI 1976, A set of three bottles with famous paintings: Chipmunk, Bighorn Sheep, and Pronghorn Antelope (each)...............................**$3-6**

Collectors Edition Volume XII 1977, A set of four bottles with a different reproduction of James Lockhart on the front (each) **$3-6**

Collectors Edition Volume XIV 1978, A set of four bottles with James Lockhart paintings: Raccoon, Mule Deer, Red Fox, and Cottontail Rabbit (each) **$3-6**

Collectors Edition Volume XV 1979, A set of three flasks with Frederic Remington's paintings: The Cowboy 1902, The Indian Trapper 1902, and Lieutenant S.C.Robertson 1890 (each) **$2-5**

Collectors Edition Volume XVI 1980, A set of three flasks depicting duck scenes: The Mallard, The Redhead, and the Canvasback (each) **$3-6**

Collectors Edition Volume XVII 1981, A set of three flasks bottles with Jim Lockhart paintings: Great Elk, Pintail Duck, and the Horned Owl (each) **$3-6**

Colorado 1959, Regal China, 10-3/4" **$20-25**

Colorado Centennial 1976, Replica of Pike's Peak **$8-12**

Colorado Springs **$4-7**

Computer, Democrat 1984 . . . . **$12-18**

Computer, Republican 1984 . . . . **$12-18**

Convention Bottle 1971, Commemorate the first national convention of the National Association of Jim Beam Bottle and Specialty Clubs hosted by the Rocky Mountain Club, Denver, CO **$5-7**

Convention Number 2 – 1972, Honors the second annual convention of the National Association of Jim Beam Bottle and Specialty Clubs in Anaheim, CA **$20-30**

Convention Number 3 – Detroit 1973, Commemorates the third annual convention of Beam Bottle Collectors in Detroit, MI **$10-12**

Convention Number 4 – Pennsylvania 1974, Commemorates the annual convention of the Jim Beam Bottle Club in Lancaster, PA **$80-100**

Convention Number 5 – Sacramento 1975, Commemorates the annual convention of the Camellia City Jim Beam Bottle Club in Sacramento, CA **$5-7**

Convention Number 6 – Hartford 1976, Commemorates the annual convention of the Jim Beam Bottle Club in Hartford, CT **$5-7**

Convention Number 7 – Louisville 1978, Commemorates the annual convention of the Jim Beam Bottle Club in Louisville, KY **$5-7**

Convention Number 8 – Chicago 1978, Commemorates the annual convention of the Jim Beam Bottle Club in Chicago, IL. **$8-12**

Convention Number 9 – Houston 1979, Commemorates the annual convention of the Jim Beam Bottle Club in Houston, TX. **$20-30**

Cowboy, beige **$35-45**

Cowboy, in color **$35-45**

Convention Number 10 – Norfolk 1980, Commemorates the annual convention of the Jim Beam Bottle Club at the Norfolk Naval Base, VA **$18-22**

Waterman, pewter **$35-45**

Waterman, yellow. **$35-45**

Convention Number 11 – Las Vegas 1981, Commemorates the annual convention of the Jim Beam Bottle Club in Las Vegas, NV . . . **$20-22**

Showgirl, blonde **$45-55**

Showgirl, brunette **$45-55**

Convention Number 12 – New Orleans 1982, Commemorates the annual convention of the Jim Beam Bottle Club in New Orleans, LA. **$30-35**

Buccaneer, gold **$35-45**

Buccaneer, in color **$35-45**

Convention Number 13 – St. Louis 1983 (Stein), Commemorates the annual convention of the JIm Beam Bottle Club in St. Louis, MO **$55-70**

Gibson girl, blue................................ **$65-80**

Gibson girl, yellow **$65-80**

Convention Number 14 – Florida, King Neptune 1984, Commemorates the annual convention of the Jim Beam Bottle Club in Florida **$15-20**

Mermaid, blonde **$35-45**

Mermaid, brunette **$35-45**

Convention Number 15 – Las Vegas 1985, Commemorates the annual convention of the Jim Beam Bottle Club in Las Vegas, NV.................................... **$40-50**

Convention Number 16 – Pilgrim Woman, Boston 1986, Commemorates the annual convention of the Jim Beam Bottle Club in Boston, MA **$35-45**

Minuteman, color.............................. **$85-105**

Minuteman, pewter **$85-105**

Convention Number 17 – Louisville 1987, Commemorates the annual convention of the Jim Beam Bottle Club in Louisville, KY.................................. **$55-75**

Kentucky Colonel, blue ...... ,,,,,,,,, **$85-105**

Kentucky Colonel, gray **$85-105**

Convention Number 18 – Bucky Beaver, 1988 .... **$30-40**

Portland rose, red **$30-40**

Portland rose, yellow........................... **$30-40**

Convention Number 19 – Kansas City 1989, Commemorates the annual convention of the Jim Beam Bottle Club in Kansas City, MO **$40-50**

Cowboy 1979, Awarded to collectors who attended the 1979 convention for the International Association of Beam Clubs **$35-50**

CPO Open **$4-7**

Crappie 1979, Commemorates the National Fresh Water Fishing Hall of Fame **$10-14**

Dark Eyes Brown Jug 1978 . . . . **$4-6**

D-Day **$12-18**

Delaware Blue Hen Bottle 1972, Commemorates the state of Delaware **$4-7**

Delco Freedom Battery 1978, Replica of a Delco battery **$18-22**

Delft Blue 1963 . . . . **$3-5**

Delft Rose 1963 . . . . **$4-6**

Del Webb Mint 1970, Metal stopper, , ... **$10-12**

China stopper **$50-60**

Devil Dog **$15-25**

Dial Telephone 1980, Fourth in a series of Beam telephone designs **$40-50**

Dodge City 1972, Issued to honor the centennial of Dodge City . . **$5-6**

Doe 1963, Regal China, 13-1/2" **$10-12**

Doe – Reissued 1967 . . . . **$10-12**

Dog 1959, Regal China, 15-1/4" **$20-25**

Don Giovanni 1980, The fifth in the Opera series ... **$140-180**

Donkey And Elephant Ashtrays 1956, Regal China, 12" (pair) **$12-16**

Donkey And Elephant Boxers 1964 (pair) **$14-18**

Donkey And Elephant Clowns 1968, Regal China, 12" (pair) . **$4-7**

Donkey And Elephant Football Election Bottles 1972, Regal China, 9-1/2" (pair). **$6-9**

Donkey New York City 1976, Commemorates the National Democratic Convention in New York City. **$10-12**

Duck 1957, Regal China, 14-1/4". **$15-20**

Ducks And Geese 1955 . ... **$5-8**

Ducks Unlimited Mallard 1974. .... **$40-50**

Ducks Unlimited Wood Duck 1975 . ... **$45-50**

Ducks Unlimited 40th Mallard Hen 1977 .... **$40-50**

Ducks Unlimited Canvasback Drake 1979. .... **$30-40**

Ducks Unlimited Blue-Winged Teal 1980, The sixth in a series, 9-1/2". **$40-45**

Ducks Unlimited Green-Winged Teal 1981 .... **$35-45**

Ducks Unlimited Wood Ducks 1982 .... **$35-45**

Ducks Unlimited American Widgeon Pair 1983 ...... **$35-45**

Ducks Unlimited Mallard 1984. .... **$55-75**

Ducks Unlimited Pintail Pr 1985 . ... **$30-40**

Ducks Unlimited Redhead 1986 . ... **$15-25**

Ducks Unlimited Blue Bill 1987 . ... **$40-60**

Ducks Unlimited (American widgeon pair), 1989, **$65** / Football, 1989, **$50** / American Brands, 1989, **$300.**

Nutcracker, 1989, **$50** / Nutcracker, 1989, **$100.**

Ducks Unlimited Black Duck 1989 . . . . **$50-60**

Eagle 1966, Regal China, 12-1/2" **$10-13**

Eldorado 1978 . . . .**$7-9**

Election, Democrat 1988 . . . . **$30-40**

Election, Republican 1988 . . . . **$30-40**

Elephant And Donkey Supermen, 1980 (set of two) . . . **$10-14**

Elephant Kansas City 1976, Commemorates the National Democratic Convention in New York City **$8-10**

Elks **$4-7**

Elks National Foundation **$8-12**

Emerald Crystal Bourbon 1968, Green glass, 11-1/2" **$3-5**

Emmett Kelly 1973, Likeness of Emmett Kelly as sad-faced Willie the Clown **$18-22**

Emmett Kelly, Native Son **$50-60**

Ernie's Flower Cart 1976, In honor of Ernie's Wines and Liquors of Northern California **$24-28**

Evergreen, Club Bottle **$7-10**

Expo 1974, Issued in honor of the World's Fair held at Spokane, WA **$5-7**

Falstaff 1979, Second in Australian Opera series, Limited edition of 1,000 bottles **$150-160**

Fantasia Bottle 1971 . . . .**$5-6**

Fathers Day Card **$15-25**

Female Cardinal 1973 . . . .**$8-12**

Fiesta Bowl, Glass. **$8-12**

Fiesta Bowl 1973, The second bottle created to commemorate the Fiesta Bowl. **$9-11**

Figaro 1977, Character Figaro from the opera Barber of Seville **$140-170**

Fighting Bull. **$12-18**

Fiji Islands **$4-6**

First National Bank Of Chicago 1964, Commemorates the 100th anniversary of the Firt National Bank of Chicago. Approximatley 130 were issued with 117 being given as momemtos to the bank directors with none for public distribution. This is the most valuable Beam Bottle known. Also beware of reproductions. **$1,900-2,400**

Fish 1957, Regal China, 14". **$15-18**

Fish Hall Of Fame **$25-35**

Five Seasons 1980, Club bottle for the Five Seasons Club of Cedar Rapids honors the state of Iowa **$10-12**

Fleet Reserve Association 1974, Issued by the Fleet Reserve Association to honor the Career Sea Service on their 50th anniversary. . . **$5-7**

Florida Shell 1968, Regal China, 9" **$4-6**

Floro De Oro 1976 . . . . **$10-12**

Flower Basket 1962, Regal China, 12-1/4" **$30-35**

Football Hall Of Fame 1972, Reproduction of the new Professional Football Hall of Fame building. **$14-18**

Foremost – Black And Gold 1956, First Beam bottle issued for a liquor retailer, Foremost Liquor Store of Chicago. . . . **$225-250**

Foremost – Speckled Beauty 1956, The most valuable of the Foremost bottles **$500-600**

Fox 1967, Blue Coat **$65-80**

Fox 1971, Gold Coat **$35-50**

Fox, Green Coat........................... **$12-18**

Fox, White Coat........................... **$20-30**

Fox, On A Dolphin........................ **$12-15**

Fox, Uncle Sam **$5-6**

Fox, Kansas City, Blue, Miniature **$20-30**

Fox, Red Distillery........................ **$1,100-1,300**

Franklin Mint........................ **$4-7**

French Cradle Telephone 1979, Third in the Telephone Pioneers of America series **$20-22**

Galah Bird 1979 .... **$14-16**

Gem City, Club Bottle **$35-45**

George Washington Commemorative Plate 1976, Commemorates the U.S. Bicentennial, 9-1/2" **$12-15**

German Bottle – Weisbaden 1973 .... **$4-6**

German Stein **$20-30**

Germany 1970, Issued to honor the American Armed Forces in Germany **$4-6**

Glen Cambell 51st 1976, Honors the 51st Los Angeles Open at the Riviera Country Club in February 1976 .... **$7-10**

Golden Chalice 1961 .... **$40-50**

Golden Jubilee 1977, Executive Series. **$48-12**

Golden Nugget 1969, Regal China, 12-1/2". **$35-45**

Golden Rose 1978 . . . . **$15-20**

Grand Canyon 1969, Honors the Grand Canyon National Park 50th Anniversary. **$7-9**

Grant Locomotive 1979. . . . . **$55-65**

Gray Cherub 1958, Regal China, 12". **$240-260**

Great Chicago Fire Bottle 1971, Commemorates the great Chicago fire of 1871 and to salute Mercy Hospital, which helped the fire victims. **$18-22**

Great Dane 1976 . . . . **$7-9**

Green China Jug 1965, Regal Glass, 12-1/2". **$4-6**

Hank Williams, Jr. **$40-50**

Hannah Dustin 1973, Regal China, 14-1/2" **$10-12**

Hansel And Gretel Bottle 1971,. **$44-50**

Harley Davidson 85th Anniversary Decanter **$175-200**

Harley Davidson 85th Anniversary Stein. **$180-220**

Harolds Club – Man-in-a-Barrel 1957, First in a series made for Harolds Club in Reno, Nevada **$380-410**

Harolds Club – Silver Opal 1957, Commemorates the 25th anniversary of Harolds Club **$20-22**

Harolds Club – Man-in-a-Barrel 1958. . . . . **$140-160**

Harolds Club – Nevada (Gray) 1963, Created for the "Nevada Centennial - 1864-1964 as a state bottle. This is a rare and valuable bottle. **$90-110**

Harolds Club – Nevada (Silver) 1964 . . . . **$90-110**

Harolds Club – Pinwheel 1965 . . . . **$40-45**

Harolds Club – Blue Slot Machine 1967 . . . . **$10-14**

Harolds Club – VIP Executive 1967, Limited quantity issued
. . . . **$50-60**

Harolds Club – VIP Executive 1968 . . . . **$55-65**

Harolds Club – Gray Slot Machine 1968 . . . .**$4-6**

Harolds Club – VIP Executive 1969, This bottle was used as a
Christmas giftv to the casino's executives **$260-285**

Harolds Club – Covered Wagon 1969-1970 . . . .**$4-6**

Harolds Club 1970 . . . . **$40-60**

Harolds Club 1971 . . . . **$40-60**

Harolds Club 1972 . . . . **$18-25**

Harolds Club 1973 . . . . **$18-24**

Harolds Club 1974 . . . . **$12-16**

Harolds Club 1975 . . . . **$12-18**

Harolds Club VIP 1976 . . . . **$18-22**

Harolds Club 1977 . . . . **$20-30**

Harolds Club 1978 . . . . **$20-30**

Harolds Club 1979 . . . . **$20-30**

Harolds Club 1980 . . . . **$25-35**

Harolds Club 1982 . . . . **$110-145**

Harp Seal **$12-18**

Harrahs Club Nevada – Gray 1963, This is the same bottle used for the Nevada Centennial and Harolds Club **$500-550**

Harry Hoffman **$4-7**

Harveys Resort Hotel At Lake Tahoe **$6-10**

Hatfield 1973, The character of Hatfield from the stor of the Hatfield and McCoy feud **$15-20**

Hawaii 1959, Tribute to the 50th state. **$35-40**

Hawaii – Reissued 1967 . . . . **$40-45**

Hawaii 1971 . . . .**$6-8**

Hawaii Aloha 1971 . . . .**$6-10**

Hawaiian Open Bottle 1972, Honors the 1972 Hawaiian Open Golf Tournament. **$6-8**

Hawaiian Open 1973, Second bottle created in honor of the United Hawaiian Open Golf Classic **$7-9**

Hawaiian Open 1974, Commemorates the 1974 Hawaiian Open Golf Classic **$5-8**

Hawaiian Open Outrigger 1975 . . . .**$9-11**

Hawaiian Paradise 1978, Commemorates the 200th anniversary of the landing of Captain Cook. **$15-17**

Hemisfair 1968, Commemorates the "Hemisfair 68-San Antonio". **$8-10**

Herre Brothers. **$22-35**

Hobo, Australia **$10-14**

Hoffman 1969 . . . .**$4-7**

Holiday - Carolers **$40-50**

Holiday - Nutcracker **$40-50**

Home Builders 1978, Commemorates the 1979 convention of the Home Builders **$25-30**

Hone Heke **$200-250**

Honga Hika 1980, First in a series of Maori warrior bottles. Honga Hika was a war-chief of the Ngapuke tribe **$220-240**

Horse (Appaloosa) **$8-12**

Horse (Black) **$18-22**

Horse (Black) Reissued 1967 . . . . **$10-12**

Horse (Brown) **$18-22**

Horse (Brown) Reissued 1967 . . . . **$10-12**

Horse (Mare And Foal) **$35-45**

Horse (Oh Kentucky) **$70-85**

Horse (Pewter) **$12-17**

Horse (White) **$18-20**

Horse (White) Reissued 1967 . . . . **$12-17**

Horseshoe Club 1969 . . . .**$4-6**

Hula Bowl 1975 . . . .**$8-10**

Hyatt House – Chicago **$7-10**

Hyatt House – New Orleans **$8-11**

Idaho 1963 . . . . **$30-40**

Illinois 1968, Honors Illinois Sesquicentennial 1818-1968 . . **$4-6**

Julian McShane bottle, 1983, **$60** / Noel Executive, 1983, **$50** / Stein, 1983, **$19** / Zimmerman Liquors 50th Anniversary, 1983, **$25** / 1904 "100 Digit" dial telephone, 1983, **$46.**

Kaiser International Open Bottle 1971, Commemorates the 5th Annual Kaiser International Open Golf Tournament **$5-6**

Kangaroo 1977 . . . . **$10-14**

Kansas 1960, Commemorates the "Kansas 1861-1961 Centennial" **$35-45**

Kentucky Black Head – Brown Head 1967, Black Head . . . **$12-18**

Brown Head **$20-28**

White Head **$18-23**

Kentucky Derby 95th, Pink, Red Roses 1969 . . . . **$4-7**

Kentucky Derby 96th, Double Rose 1970 . . . . **$15-25**

Kentucky Derby 97th 1971 . . . . **$4-7**

Kentucky Derby 98th 1972 . . . . **$4-6**

Kentucky Derby 100th 1974 . . . . **$7-10**

Key West 1972, Honors the 150th anniversary of Key West, Florida **$5-7**

King Kamehameha 1972, Commemorates the 100th anniversary of King Kamehameha Day **$8-11**

King Kong 1976, Commemorates Paramount's movie release in December 1976 . . . . **$8-10**

Kiwi 1974 . . . . **$5-8**

Koala Bear 1973 . . . . **$12-14**

Laramie 1968, Commemorates the "Centennial Jubilee Laramie Wyo. 1868-1968" **$4-6**

Largemouth Bass Trophy Bottle 1973, Honors the National Fresh Water Fishing Hall of Fame. **$10-14**

Las Vegas 1969, Bottle used for Customer Specials, Casino series
....**$4-6**

Light Bulb 1979, Honors Thomas Edison **$14-16**

Lombard 1969, Commemorates "Village of Lombard, Illinois-
1869 Centennial 1969" **$4-6**

London Bridge **$4-7**

Louisville Downs Racing Derby 1978 ....**$4-6**

Louisiana Superdome **$8-11**

LVNH Owl **$20-30**

Madame Butterfly 1977, Figurine of Madame Butterfly, music
box plays "One Fine Day" from the opera **$340-370**

The Magpies 1977, Honors an Australian football team. **$18-20**

Maine 1970 ....**$4-6**

Majestic 1966 ....**$20-24**

Male Cardinal **$18-24**

Marbled Fantasy 1965 ....**$38-42**

Marina City 1962, Commemorates modern apartment complex
in Chicago...................................**$10-15**

Marine Corps **$25-35**

Mark Antony 1962 ....**$18-20**

Martha Washington 1976 ....**$5-6**

McCoy 1973, Character of McCoy from the story of the Hatfield
and McCoy feud................................**$14-17**

McShane – Mother-of-Pearl 1979, Executive series... **$85-105**

McShane – Titans 1980 .... **$85-105**

McShane – Cobalt 1981, Executive series.......... **$115-135**

McShane – Green Pitcher 1982, Executive series **$80-105**

McShane – Green Bell 1983, Executive series **$80-110**

Mephistopheles 1979, Figurine depicts Mephistopheles from the opera Faust, Music box plays Soldier's Chorus..... **$160-190**

Michigan Bottle 1972 ....**$7-9**

Milwaukee Stein **$30-40**

Minnesota Viking 1973 ....**$9-12**

Mint 400 1970 .... **$80-105**

Mint 400 1970 ....**$5-6**

Mint 400 1971 ....**$5-6**

Mint 400 1972, Commemorates the 5th annual Del Webb Mint 400 ....**$5-7**

Mint 400 1973, Commemorates the 6th annual Del Webb Mint 400...**$6-8**

Mint 400 1974 ....**$4-7**

Mint 400 7th Annual 1976 ....**$9-12**

Mississippi Fire Engine 1978 .... **$120-130**

Model A Ford 1903 (1978)   ,,,,,,,,,,,, **$38-42**

Model A Ford 1928 (1980) **$65-75**

Montana 1963, Tribute to "Montana, 1864 Golden Years Centennial 1964".............................. **$50-60**

Monterey Bay Club 1977, Honors the Monterey Bay Beam Bottle and Specialty Club. **$9-12**

Mortimer Snerd 1976 . . . . **$24-28**

Mother-of-Pearl 1979 . . . . **$10-12**

Mount St. Helens 1980, Depicts the eruption of Mount St. Helens **$20-22**

Mr. Goodwrench 1978 . . . . **$24-28**

Musicians On A Wine Cask 1964 . . . . **$4-6**

Muskie 1971, Honors the National Fresh Water Fishing Hall of Fame **$14-18**

National Tobacco Festival 1973, Commemorates the 25th anniversary of the National Tobacco Festival **$7-8**

Nebraska 1967 . . . . **$7-9**

Nebraska Football 1972, Commemorates the University of Nebraska's national championship football team of 1970-1971 . . . . **$5-8**

Nevada 1963 . . . . **$34-38**

New Hampshire 1967 . . . . **$4-8**

New Hampshire Eagle Bottle 1971 . . . . **$18-23**

New Jersey 1963 . . . . **$40-50**

New Jersey Yellow 1963 . . . . **$40-50**

New Mexico Bicentennial 1976 . . . . **$8-12**

New Mexico Statehood 1972, Commemorates New Mexico's 60 years of statehood **$7-9**

New York World's Fair 1964 . . . . **$5-6**

North Dakota – 1965 .... **$45-55**

Northern Pike 1977, The sixth in a series designed for the National Fresh Water Fishing Hall of Fame **$14-18**

Nutcracker Toy Soldier 1978 .... **$90-120**

Ohio 1966 .... **$5-6**

Ohio State Fair 1973, In honor of the 120th Ohio State Fair...**$5-6**

Olympian 1960 .... **$2-4**

One Hundred First Airborne Division 1977, Honors the division known as the Screaming Eagles **$8-10**

Opaline Crystal 1969 .... **$4-6**

Oregon 1959, Honors the centennial of the state **$20-25**

Oregon Liquor Commission **$25-35**

Osco Drugs **$12-17**

Panda 1980 .... **$20-22**

Paul Bunyan **$4-7**

Pearl Harbor Memorial 1972, Honoring the Pearl Harbor Survivors Association............................ **$14-18**

Pearl Harbor Survivors Association 1976 .... **$5-7**

Pennsylvania 1967 .... **$4-6**

Pennsylvania Dutch, Club Bottle..................... **$8-12**

Permian Basin Oil Show 1972, Commemorates the Permian Basin Oil Show in Odessa, Texas **$4-6**

Petroleum Man **$4-7**

Pheasant 1960 .... **$14-18**

Pheasant 1961 Re-issued; Also '63, '66, '67, '68 . . . .**$8-11**

Phi Sigma Kappa (Centennial Series) 1973, Commemorates the 100th anniversary of this fraternity **$3-4**

Phoenician 1973 . . . .**$6-9**

Pied Piper Of Hamlin 1974 . . . .**$3-6**

Ponderosa 1969, A replica of the Cartwrights of the Bonanza TV show. **$4-6**

Ponderosa Ranch Tourist 1972, Commemorates the one millionth tourist to the Ponderosa Ranch **$14-16**

Pony Express 1968 . . . .**$9-12**

Poodle – Gray And White 1970. . . . .**$5-6**

Portland Rose Festival 1972, Commemorates the 64th Portland, Oregon Rose Festival. **$5-8**

Portola Trek 1969, Bottle was issued to celebrate the 200th anniversary of San Diego **$3-6**

Poulan Chain Saw 1979 . . . . **$24-28**

Powell Expedition 1969, Depicts John Wesley Powell's survey of the Colorado River. **$3-5**

Preakness 1970, Issued to honor the 100th anniversary of the running of the Preakness **$5-6**

Preakness Pimlico 1975 . . . .**$4-7**

Presidential 1968, Executive series. **$4-7**

Prestige 1967, Executive series **$4-7**

Pretty Perch 1980, 8th in a series, this fish is used as the official seal of the National Fresh Water Fishing Hall of Fame **$13-16**

Republican Convention 1972 .... **$500-700**

Republican Football 1972 .... **$350-450**

Richard Hadlee **$110-135**

Richards – New Mexico 1967, Created for Richards Distributing
Co. of Alburquerque New Mexico **$8-10**

Robin 1969 .... **$5-6**

Rocky Marciano 1973 .... **$14-16**

Rocky Mountain, Club Bottle..................... **$10-15**

Royal Crystal 1959 .... **$3-6**

Royal Di Monte 1957 .... **$45-55**

Royal Emperor 1958 .... **$3-6**

Royal Gold Diamond 1964 .... **$30-35**

Royal Gold Round 1956 .... **$80-90**

Royal Opal 1957 .... **$5-7**

Royal Porcelain 1955 .... **$380-420**

Royal Rose 1963 .... **$30-35**

Ruby Crystal 1967 .... **$6-9**

Ruidoso Downs 1968, Pointed ears................ **$24-26**

Flat ears **$4-6**

Sahara Invitational Bottle 1971, Introduced in honor of the Del
Webb 1971 Sahara Invitational Pro-Am Golf Tournament **$6-8**

San Bear – Donkey 1973, Political series **$1,500-2,000**

Samoa **$4-7**

San Diego 1968, Issued by the Beam Co. for the 200th anniversary of its founding in 1769 .... **$4-6**

San Diego – Elephant 1972 .... **$15-25**

Santa Fe 1960.............................. **$120-140**

SCCA, Etched................................. **$15-25**

SCCA, Smoothed.............................. **$12-18**

Screech Owl 1979 .... **$18-22**

Seafair Trophy Race 1972, Commemorates the Seattle Seafair Trophy Race................................. **$5-6**

Seattle World's Fair 1962 .... **$10-12**

Seoul – Korea 1988............................ **$60-75**

Sheraton Inn **$4-6**

Short Dancing Scot 1963 .... **$50-65**

Santa Claus, 1983, **$60** / Santa Claus paperweight, 1983, **$30** / Gibson Girl (blonde), 1983, **$60** / Gibson Girl (brunette), 1983, **$60** / Thirteenth Convention stein, 1983, **$60**.

Short-timer 1975............................... $15-20

Shriners 1975................................. $10-12

Shriners – Indiana $4-7

Shriners Pyramid 1975, Issued by the El Kahir Temple of Cedar Rapids, Iowa $10-12

Shriners Rajah 1977........................... $24-28

Shriners Temple 1972 .... $20-25

Shriners Western Association..................... $15-25

Sierra Eagle $15-22

Sigma Nu Fraternity 1977........................$9-12

Sigma Nu Fraternity – Kentucky $8-12

Sigma Nu Fraternity – Michigan $18-23

Smiths North Shore Club 1972, Commemorating Smith's North Shore Club, at Crystal Bay, Lake Tahoe $10-12

Smoked Crystal 1964 ....$6-9

Snow Goose 1979 ....$8-10

Snowman $125-175

South Carolina 1970, In honor of celebrating its Tri-centennial 1670-1970 ....$4-6

South Dakota – Mouth Rushmore 1969 ....$4-6

South Florida – Fox On Dolphin 1980, Bottled sponsored by the South Florida Beam Bottle and Specialties Club $14-16

Sovereign 1969, Executive series.....................$4-7

Spengers Fish Grotto 1977 .... $18-22

Sports Car Club Of America $5-7

Statue Of Liberty 1975 . . . .$8-12

Statue Of Liberty 1985 . . . . $18-20

St. Bernard 1979 . . . . $30-35

St. Louis, Club Bottle $10-15

St. Louis Arch 1964 . . . . $10-12

St. Louis Arch – Reissue 1967 . . . . $16-18

St. Louis Statue 1972 . . . .$8-10

Sturgeon 1980, Exclusive issue for a group that advocates the preservation of sturgeons $14-17

Stutz Bearcat 1914 1977 . . . . $45-55

Submarine – Diamond Jubilee $35-45

Submarine Redfin 1970, Issued for Manitowoc Submarine Memorial Association $5-7

Superdome 1975, Replica of the Louisiana Superdome $5-8

Swagman 1979, Replica of an Australian hobo called a swagman who roamed that country looking for work during the Depression $10-12

Sydney Opera House 1977 . . . .$9-12

Tall Dancing Scot 1964 . . . .$9-12

Tavern Scene 1959 . . . . $45-55

Telephone No. 1 1975, Replica of a 1907 phone of the magneto wall type. $25-30

Telephone No. 2 1976, Replica of an 1897 desk set $30-40

Telephone No. 3 1977, Replica of a 1920 cradle phone . **$15-20**

Telephone No. 4 1978, Replica of a 1919 dial phone . . . **$40-50**

Telephone No. 5 1979, Replica of a pay phone **$25-35**

Telephone No. 6 1980, Replica of a battery phone **$20-30**

Telephone No. 7 1981, Replica of a digital dial phone . . **$35-45**

Ten-Pin 1980 . . . . **$8-11**

Texas Hemisfair **$7-11**

Texas Rose 1978, Executive Series **$14-18**

Thailand 1969 . . . . **$4-6**

Thomas Flyer 1907 1976 . . . . **$60-70**

Tiffiny Poodle 1973, Created in honor of Tiffiny, the poodle mascot of the National Association of the Jim Beam Bottle and Specialties Clubs **$20-22**

Tiger – Australian. .$14-18, The Tigers 1977, Issued in honor of an Australian football team **$20-24**

Titian 1980 . . . . **$9-12**

Tobacco Festival **$8-12**

Tombstone **$4-7**

Travelodge Bear **$4-7**

Treasure Chest 1979 . . . . **$8-12**

Trout Unlimited 1977, To honor the Trout Unlimited Conservation Organization **$14-18**

Truth Or Consequences Fiesta 1974, Issued in honor of Ralph Edwards radio and televison show **$14-18**

Turquoise China Jug 1966 . . . . **$4-6**

Twin Bridges Bottle 1971, Commemorates the largest twin bridge between Delaware and New Jersey **$40-42**

Twin Cherubs 1974, Executive series. **$8-12**

Twin Doves 1987, Executive series. **$18-23**

US Open 1972, Honors the US Open Golf Tourney at Pebble Beach, CA. **$9-12**

Vendome Drummers Wagon 1975, Honored the Vendomes of Beverly IIIlls, CA **$60-70**

VFW Bottle 1971, Commemorates the 50th anniversary of the Department of Indana VFW. **$5-6**

Viking 1973 . . . . **$9-12**

Volkswagen Commemorative Bottle – Two Colors 1977, Commemorates the Volkswagen Beetle. **$40-50**

Vons Market **$28-35**

St. Louis Glass Convention bottles (bourbon, vodka, scotch, gin, brandy, tequila, Canadian whiskey), 1983, **$5 each.**

Walleye Pike 1977, Designed for the National Fresh Water Fishing Hall of Fame **$12-15**

Walleye Pike 1987 .... **$17-23**

Washington 1975, A state series bottle to commemorate the Evergreen State **$5-6**

Washington – The Evergreen State 1974, The club bottle for the Evergreen State Beam Bottle and Specialties Club.... **$10-12**

Washington State Bicentennial 1976 .... **$10-12**

Waterman 1980 .... **$100-130**

Western Shrine Association 1980, Commemorates the Shriners convention in Phoenix, Arizona **$20-22**

West Virginia 1963......................... **$130-140**

White Fox 1969, Issued for the 2nd anniversary of the Jim Beam Bottle and Specialties Club in Berkley, CA **$25-35**

Wisconsin Muskie Bottle 1971 .... **$15-17**

Woodpecker 1969 .... **$6-8**

Wyoming 1965 .... **$40-50**

Yellow Katz 1967, Commemorates the 50th anniversay of the Katz Department Stores......................... **$15-17**

Yellow Rose 1978, Executive series **$7-10**

Yellowstone Park Centennial **$4-7**

Yosemite 1967 .... **$4-6**

Yuma Rifle Club **$18-23**

Zimmerman – Art Institute **$5-8**

Zimmerman Bell 1976, Designed for Zimmerman Liquor Store of Chicago **$6-7**

Zimmerman Bell 1976 . . . . **$6-7**

Zimmerman – Blue Beauty 1969 . . . . **$9-12**

Zimmerman – Blue Daisy **$4-6**

Zimmerman Cherubs 1968 . . . . **$4-6**

Zimmerman – Chicago **$4-6**

Zimmerman – Eldorado **$4-7**

Zimmerman – Glass 1969 . . . . **$7-9**

Zimmerman Oatmeal Jug **$40-50**

Zimmerman – The Peddler Bottle 1971 . . . . **$4-6**

Zimmerman Two-Handled Jug 1965 . . . . **$45-60**

Zimmerman Vase, Brown. **$6-9**

Zimmerman Vase, Green **$6-9**

Zimmerman – 50th Anniversary **$35-45**

Automobile and Transportation Series
CHEVROLET

1957 Convertible, Black, New **$85-95**

1957 Convertible, Red, New. **$75-85**

1957, Black **$70-80**

1957, Dark Blue, PA **$70-80**

1957, Red **$80-90**

1957, Sierra Gold **$140-160**

1957, Turquoise **$50-70**

1957, Yellow Hot Rod **$65-75**

Camaro 1969, Blue. **$55-65**

Camaro 1969, Burgundy **$120-140**

Camaro 1969, Green **$100-120**

Camaro 1969, Orange **$55-65**

Camaro 1969, Pace Car **$60-70**

Camaro 1969, Silver. **$120-140**

Camaro 1969, Yellow, PA **$55-65**

Corvette 1986, Pace Car, Yellow, New **$60-85**

Corvette 1984, Black **$70-80**

Corvette 1984, Bronze **$100-200**

Corvette 1984, Gold **$100-120**

Corvette 1984, Red. **$55-65**

Corvette 1984, White **$55-65**

Corvette 1978, Black **$140-170**

Corvette 1978, Pace Car. **$135-160**

Corvette (black), 1989, **$95** / Corvette (bronze), 1989, **$110** / Corvette (gold), 1989 **$110** /
Nineteenth Convention bottle, 1989, **$40.**

Corvette 1978, Red **$50-60**

Corvette 1978, White **$40-50**

Corvette 1978, Yellow **$40-50**

Corvette 1963, Black, PA **$75-85**

Corvette 1963, Blue, NY **$90-100**

Corvette 1963, Red **$60-70**

Corvette 1963, Silver **$50-60**

Corvette 1955, Black, New **$110-140**

Corvette 1955, Copper, New **$90-100**

Corvette 1955, Red, New **$110-140**

Corvette 1954, Blue, New **$90-100**

Corvette 1953, White, New **$100-120**

DUESENBERG

Convertible, Cream **$130-140**

Convertible, Dark Blue **$120-130**

San Francisco cable car, 1983, **$60** / Duesenberg convertible coupe, 1983, **$250-275**.

Convertible, Light Blue. **$80-100**

Convertible Coupe, Gray **$160-180**

FORD

International Delivery Wagon, Black. **$80-90**

International Delivery Wagon, Green **$80-90**

Fire Chief 1928 . . . . **$120-130**

Fire Chief 1934 . . . . **$60-70**

Fire Pumper Truck 1935. . . . . **$45-60**

Model A, Angelos Liquor. **$180-200**

Model A, Parkwood Supply. **$140-170**

Model A 1903, Black. **$35-45**

Model A 1903, Red **$35-45**

Model A 1928 . . . . **$60-80**

Model A Fire Truck 1930 . . . .**$130-170**

Model T 1913, Black. **$30-40**

Ford Fire Engine (1930 Model A) 1983, **$205.**

Model T 1913, Green **$30-40**

Mustang 1964, Black **$100-125**

Mustang 1964, Red. **$35-45**

Mustang 1964, White **$25-35**

Paddy Wagon 1930 . . . . **$100-120**

Phaeton 1929 . . . . **$40-50**

Pickup Truck 1935 . . . . **$20-30**

Police Car 1929, Blue. **$75-85**

Police Car 1929, Yellow **$350-450**

Police Patrol Car 1934 . . . . **$60-70**

Police Tow Truck 1935 . . . . **$20-30**

Roadster 1934, Cream, PA, New. **$80-90**

Thunderbird 1956, Black. **$60-70**

Thunderbird 1956, Blue, PA **$70-80**

Thunderbird 1956, Gray **$50-60**

Thunderbird 1956, Green **$60-70**

Ford Woodie (1929) 1983, **$90** / Police Patrol Wagon (1931) 1983, **$155.**

Thunderbird 1956, Yellow **$50-60**

Woodie Wagon 1929 . . . . **$50-60**

MERCEDES

1974, Blue **$30-40**

1974, Gold **$60-80**

1974, Green **$30-40**

1974, Mocha **$30-40**

1974, Red **$30-40**

1974, Sand Beige, PA **$30-40**

1974, Silver, Australia **$140-160**

1974, White **$35-45**

TRAINS

Baggage Car **$40-60**

Box Car, Brown **$50-60**

Box Car, Yellow **$40-50**

Bumper **$5-8**

Caboose, Gray **$45-55**

Caboose, Red **$50-60**

Casey Jones With Tender **$65-80**

Casey Jones Caboose **$40-55**

Casey Jones Accessory Set **$50-60**

Coal Tender, No Bottle **$20-30**

Combination Car **$55-65**

Dining Car **$75-90**

Flat Car **$20-30**

General Locomotive **$60-70**

Grant Locomotive **$50-65**

Log Car **$40-55**

Lumber Car **$12-18**

Observation Car **$15-23**

Passenger Car **$45-53**

Tank Car **$15-20**

Track **$4-6**

Turner Locomotive **$80-100**

Watertower **$20-30**

Wood Tender **$40-45**

Wood Tender, No Bottle **$20-25**

OTHER

Ambulance	$18-22
Army Jeep	$18-20
Bass Boat	$12-18
Cable Car	$25-35
Circus Wagon	$20-30
Ernie's Flower Cart	$20-30
Golf Cart	$20-30
HC Covered Wagon 1929	$10-20
Jewel Tea	$70-80
Mack Fire Truck 1917	$120-135
Mississippi Pumper Firetruck 1867	$115-140
Oldsmobile 1903	$25-35
Olsonite Eagle Racer	$40-35
Police Patrol Car 1934, Yellow	$110-140
Space Shuttle	$20-30
Stutz 1914, Gray	$40-50
Stutz 1914, Yellow	$40-50
Thomas Flyer 1909, Blue	$60-70
Thomas Flyer 1909, Ivory	$60-70
Vendome Wagon	$40-50
Volkswagen, Blue	$40-50
Volkswagen, Red	$40-50

MINIATURE BOTTLES

When a discussion on bottle collecting begins, it's clear that most collectors focus their attention on the physically large bottles such as beer, whiskey, or maybe bitters. But there is a distinct group of collectors who eschew big finds and set their sights on the small. Their quest for that special find leads them into the world of miniatures. Until I started bottle collecting, the only miniature bottles that I knew of were the ones passengers bought on airplanes. Today, there is tremendous enthusiasm for miniature bottle collecting. Not only are there specialty clubs

and dealers across the United States but throughout the world in the Middle East, Japan, England, Scotland, Australia, and Italy to name just a few. The new collector will soon discover that all miniatures are unique and fascinating in their own way. Because of the low average cost of one dollar to five dollars per bottle, and the relatively small amount of space required storing them, it's easy to start a collection. As is the case with the larger bottles, there are some rare and expensive miniatures.

While a number of miniatures were manufactured in the 1800s, most were produced from the late 1920 to the 1950s with peak production in the 1930s. While miniatures are still made today, some of the most interesting and sought after are those produced before 1950. The state of Nevada legalized the sale of miniatures in 1935, Florida in 1935, and Louisiana in 1934.

If you are looking for a nineteenth century miniature, you might seek out miniature beer bottles. They are a good example of a bottle that was produced for more than one use. Most of the major breweries produced them as advertisements, novelties, and promotional items. In fact, most of the bottles did not contain beer. A number of these bottles came with perforated caps so that they could be used as salt and pepper shakers. The Pabst Blue Ribbon Beer Company was the first brewery to manufacture a beer bottle miniature commemorating the Milwaukee Convention of Spanish American War Veterans. Pabst's last miniature was manufactured around 1942. Most of the miniature beers you'll find today date from before World War II. In 1899 there were as many as 1,507 breweries, all of which produced miniatures.

Beyond the whiskey, beer, and soda pop bottles identified in this chapter, don't overlook earlier chapters, such as Barsottini, Garnier, Lionstone, and Luxardo, which also list miniatures.

Collecting miniature liquor bottles has become a special interest for other than bottle collectors. A number of the state liquor stamps from the early 1930s and 1940s have specific series numbers that sought by stamp collectors. As a reference for pricing, I have consulted Robert E. Kay's *Miniature Beer Bottles & Go-Withs* price guide and reference manual with corresponding pricing codes (CA-1, California, MN-1, Minnesota, etc).

Beer Bottles

Pre-Prohibition – Circa 1890-1933

Grand Rapids – Brewing Co. Silver Foam – Grand Rapids, Mich., (MI-2), 1900, Embossed and paper label, 5-1/8", Grand Rapids, MI **$100-150**

Indianapolis Brewing Co., (IN-2), 1890, Paper label, embossed, 4-1/2", Indianapolis, IN. **$30-50**

Pabst Brewing Co – Milwaukee, (WI-4), 1900, Paper label, 5-1/2", Milwaukee, WI. **$100-150**

Pre-War, Old Rams Head, 1923, **$50-75.**   Atherton, 1932, **$25-35.**

Post Prohibtion – Circa 1933-present

A-1 Pilsner Beer, Arizona Brewing Co., (AZ-3), 1958, Foiled paper label, 4", Phoenix, AZ **$5-10**

Acme Beer, Acme Breweries, (CA-6), 1940, Decal paper label, 3", San Francisco, CA **$10-20**

Acme Beer, Acme Breweries, (CA-10), 1950, Paper label, 4 1/4", San Francisco, CA **$5-10**

Budweiser Lager Beer – Anheuser-Busch, Inc., (MO-17), 1950, Paper label, 4-1/4", St. Louis, MO **$10-20**

Black Gold, 1933, **$25-35.**

Bond & Lillard, 1933, **$25-35.**

Camden Pilsner Beer – Camden County Beverage Co., (NJ-1), 1940, Decal paper label, 3", Camden, NJ **$75-100**

Canadian Brand Cream Ale – George F. Stein Brewery, Inc., (NY-17), 1950, Decal paper label, 4", Buffalo, NY **$10-20**

Carling Black Label Beer – Brewing Corp. of America, (OH-16), 1950, Paper label, 4-1/4", Cleveland, OH **$5-10**

Citizens Beer, Joliet Citizens Brewing Co., (IL-32), 1940, Decal paper label, 3", Joilet, IL **$100-150**

Deep Springs – Tennessee Whisky, 1935; Old McCall's, 1940; Ben Franklin, 1933, **$20-30 each.**

Mount Vernon, 1933, **$35-45.**

Congress Beer – Haberle Congress Brewing Co., Inc., (NY-40), 1940, Decal paper label, 4-1/4", Syracuse, NY **$100-150**

Country Club Pilsener Beer – M.K. Goetz Brewing Co., (MO-6), 1940, Decal paper label, 4-1/4", St. Joseph, MO **$5-10**

Crystal Rock Beer – Cleveland & Sandusky Brewing Co., (OH-23), 1935, Decal paper label, 4-1/4", Sandusky, OH . . . **$50-75**

Doerschuck Beer – North American Brewing Co., (NY-28), 1940, Decal paper label, 3", Brooklyn, NY **$75-100**

Drewrys Beer, Drewrys Ltd. U.S.A. Inc., (IN-6), 1955, Paper label, 4-1/4", South Bend, IN **$30-50**

Drewrys Beer, Drewrys Ltd. U.S.A. Inc., (IL-31), 1952, Decal paper label, 4-1/4", Chicago, IL. **$20-30**

Goebel 22 Beer – Goebel Brewing Co., (MI-9), 1952, Foiled paper label, 4-1/4", Detroit, MI **$5-10**

Gold Bond Beer – Cleveland Sandusky Brewing Co., (OH-22), 1935, Decal paper label, 4-1/4", Cleveland, OH **$10-20**

Gluek's Pilsener Pale Beer – Gluck Brewing Co., (MN-10), 1945, Decal paper label, 4", Minneapolis, MN **$10-20**

Falstaff Beer, Falstaff Brewing Company, (CA-16), 1953, Foiled paper label, 3", San Jose, CA **$5-10**

Falstaff Pale Beer – Falstaff Brewing Corp., (MO-23), 1936, Decal paper label, 4-1/4", St. Louis,MO **$10-20**

Fleck's Beer – Ernst Fleckenstein Brewing Co., (MN-2), 1936, Decal paper label, 4-1/4", Faribault, MN. **$10-20**

Hamm's Preferred Stock Beer – Theodore Hamm Brewing Co., (MN-17), 1950, Paper label, 4-1/4", St. Paul, MN **$10-20**

Three Musketeers, 1933, **$25-35**; Crown's Old Camel Brand, 1933, **$35-45**; Nite Club Special, 1933, **$25-35**.

Meister Brau – Peter Hand Brewery Co., (IL-16), 1952, Foiled paper label, 4", Chicago, IL.......................**$5-10**

Prager Beer – Atlas Brewing Co., (IL-25), 1950, Paper label, 4-1/4", Chicago, IL............................**$5-10**

Primo Lager Beer – Hawaii Brewing Corp, (HA-1), 1940, Decal paper label, 3", Honolulu, HI **$100-150**

Ruppert Knickerbocker Beer – Jacob Ruppert, (NY-31), 1955, Foiled paper label, 4", Brooklyn, NY..............**$10-20**

Schmidt's Beer – Jacob Schmidt Brewing Co., (MN -23), 1955, Foiled paper label, 4-1/4", St. Paul, MN **$5-10**

Old Rip Van Winkle, "Many Years in the Woods", 1933, **$40-50.**

Gallant Knight, 1933, **$35-45.**

Schaefer Beer – The F. & M. Schaefer Brewing Co., (NY-26), 1950, Foiled paper label, 4-1/4", Brooklyn, NY........**$5-10**

Schmidt's – The Schmidt Brewing Co., (MI-6), 1950, Paper label, 4-1/4", Detroit, MI.....................**$5-10**

Stein's Ale – George F. Stein Brewery, Inc., (NY-10), 1940, Decal paper label, 3", Buffalo, NY.....................**$10-20**

Stein's Canandaigua Light Ale – Geo. F. Stein Brewery, Inc., (NY-4), 1950, Paper label, 4", Buffalo, NY.............**$10-20**

Tip Top Bohemian Brand Beer – The Sunrise Brewing Co., (OH-25), 1939, Decal paper label, 3", Cleveland, OH......**$10-20**

Trophy Beer, Birk Bros. Brewing Co., (IL-23), 1950, Paper label, 4", Chicago, IL..................................**$5-10**

Whiskey Nipper, Happy Voyage, 1930s, **$45-55.**

Whiskey Nipper – Make Him Happy – Give Him A Little Scotch, 1930s, **$40-50.**

Foreign Beer Bottles

Milwaukee Brew Cerveza – German Pacific Brewery, (Pan-1) 1940, Decal paper label, 3", Panama **$75-100**

Castle Ale – Rhodesian Breweries Ltd., (RHOD-1), 1960, Paper Label, 4-1/4", Rhodesia **$10-20**

Castle Golden Pilsener – South African Breweries Ltd., (RHOD-6), 1960, Paper label, 4-1/2", South Africa **$10-20**

Chivo Clausen – Columbia, (COLM-1), 1957, Paper label, 4-1/4", Columbia, South America **$10-20**

Superior, (Mex – 5), 1958, Enamel label, 4-1/4", Mexico **$10-20**

Whiskey Flasks (Circa 1928-1936)

Antique Straight Whiskey (1934) **$100**

Barclay's Gold Label (1936) **$125**

Bourbon De Luxe (1932) **$90**

Brigadier (1930) **$80**

Calvert's "Reserve" (1935) **$100**

Cedar Arms (1930) **$125**

Cobbs Creek (1936) **$75**

Daniel Webster (1933) **$100**

Four Seasons Brand (1936) **$75**

Golden Oak (1935) **$125**

Green Mill (1936) **$75**

Kentucky Boy (1934) **$100**

Kentucky Tavern (1936) **$75**

Major Paul's (1934) **$75**

Mattingly & Moore (1934) **$100**

Old "73" - 93 Proof – Straight Whiskey (1934) **$200**

Old 3-G Brand – Straight Bourbon Whiskey **$100**

Old Underproof – Kentucky Straight Bourbon Whiskey . . **$80**

Rosemont – Kentucky Straight Bourbon Whiskey **$125**

Royal Oak (1936) **$80**

"Old Barbee", 1930, **$45-50.**

Scotch Whiskey

Auld Nicholas	$90-175
Beverages Finest Liqueur	$130-175
Black Horse	$130-175
Black Rod – Grand North Country	$90-175
Campbells	$45-90
Campbelltown	$175-255
Cardow	$250-350
Clangrant	$90-175
Daire's	$130-175
Dalmore – 12 Years Old	$90-175
Gayscot	$175-255
Glencory	$250-350
Glen Grant	$45-90
Golden Drop	$250-350
Henekeys – H R H. – Henekeys Ltd	$45-90
Iliska	$90-175
Johnny Lauder's	$130-175
Kingburn	$130-175
Linkwood – 5 Years Old	$90-175
MacLagan's	$175-255
Offiler's	$175-255
Old Argyll	$175-255

Rothsay. **$90-175**

Royal No. 1 . . . . **$90-175**

Strathglass House **$175-255**

Soda Pop Bottles
(3" To 5", Circa 1930s-1950s)

Applied Color Painted Label (ACL)

Canada Dry Water **$10**

Double Cola **$10**

Hires (RB) **$18**

Nesbitt's. **$10**

O-So Beverages. **$10**

Pepsi-Cola. **$40**

Pioneer Valley **$15**

Royal Crown Cola **$15**

SODA BOTTLES - APPLIED COLOR LABEL

Anyone who has ever had a cold soda on a hot summer day from a bottle with a painted label probably didn't realize that the bottle would become rare and collectible. Today, collecting Applied Color Label (ACL) Soda Bottles has become one of the fastest growing and most affordable areas of bottle collecting. This rapid growth has resulted in the Painted Soda Bottle Collectors Association, which is the national collectors group dedicated to the promotion and preservation of ACL Soda Bottles.

So, what is an Applied Color Label soda bottle? The best description is this excerpt from an article written by Dr. J.H. Toulouse, a noted expert on bottle collecting and glass manufacturing in the late 1930s:

"One of the developments of the last few years has been that of permanent fused on labels on glass bottles. The glass in a glass furnace is homogenous in character, all of one color and composition. When the bottles are ready for decoration, the color design is printed on them in the process that superficially resembles many printing or engraving processes. The color is applied in the form of a paste-like material, through a screen of silk, in which the design has been formed. The bottles which contain the impression of that design must then be dried and then fired by conducting it thorough a lehr, which is long, tunnel-like enclosure through which the bottles pass at a carefully controlled rate of speed and in which definite zones of temperature are maintained. The maximum temperature chosen is such that the glass body will not melt, but the softer glass involved in the color will melt and rigidly fuse on the glass beneath it."

The first commercially sold soda, Imperial Inca Cola—whose name was inspired by the Native American Indian—promoted medical benefits. Coca-Cola was developed in 1886 by Dr. John Stith Pemberton of Atlanta, Georgia, and became the first truly successful cola drink. Carbonated water was added in 1887, and by 1894 bottled Coca-Cola was in full production. The iconic shape of the Coke bottle, the hobbleskirt design, was created in 1915 by Alex Samuelson. Numerous inventors attempted to ride on the coattails of Coke's success. The most successful of these inventors was Caleb Bradham, who started Brad's drink in 1890 and in 1896 changed its name to Pep-Kola. In 1898, it was changed to Pipi-Cola and by 1906 to Pepsi-Cola.

The ACL soda bottle was conceived in the 1930s when Prohibition forced numerous brewing companies to experiment with soda. What started out as a temporary venture saved many brewing companies from bankruptcy, and some companies never looked back. From the mid-1930s to the early 1960s, with the peak production in the 1940s and 1950s, many small, local bottlers throughout the United States created bottle labels that will forever preserve unique moments in American history. The labels featured Western scenes, cowboys, Native Americans, aircraft from biplanes to jets, clowns, famous figures, birds, bears, boats, Donald Duck, and even Las Vegas (Vegas Vic).

Since Native Americans and cowboys were popular American figures, these bottles are among the most popular and collectible. In fact, the Big Chief ACL sodas are the most popular bottles, even more than the embossed types. The small bottlers actually produced most of the better-looking labels. in contrast to the largely uniform bottles by major bottlers such as Coca-Cola and Pepsi-Cola. Because these bottles were produced in smaller quantities, they are rarer and, hence, more valuable. While rarity will affect value, a bottle with a larger label is even more desirable for collectors. The most sought-after bottles are those with a two-color label, each color adding more value to the bottle.

Unless noted otherwise, all ACL soda bottles listed have a smooth base and a crown top:

Applied Color Label Bottles

A Treat, Allentown, PA, White, 12 oz., 1952 . . . . **$35**

Aircraft Beverages, Stratford, CT, White and red, 24 oz., 1958 . . . . **$43**

Arrowhead Famous Beverages, Los Angeles, CA, White, 10 oz., 1953 . . . . **$15**

Bauneg Beg Beverages, Springvale, ME, Green and white, 7-1/2 oz., 1944 . . . . **$15**

Belfast Sparkling Beverages, San Francisco, CA, White, 10 oz., 1957...................................... **$10**

Big Boy Beverages, Cleveland, OH, Red and white, 7 oz., 1947......**$15**

Big Chief Soda Water, Natchitoches, LA, Red and white, 8 oz., 1951...................................... **$20**

Big Chief Beverages, Modesto, CA, Green bottle with red label, 10 oz., 1956.................................. **$300-400**

Blue Jay Beverages, Junction City, KN, Blue and white, 9 oz., 1956...................................... **$45**

Capitol Club Beverages, Norristown, PA, White, 7 oz., 1954. **$15**

Champ of Thirst Quenchers, Philadelphia, PA, Brown, white and yellow, 8 oz., 1960........................... **$25**

Chase Flavors, Jackson / Memphis, TN, Brown and white, 10 oz., 1952...................................... **$15**

Simba **$10**; Sperky **$5**; Smile **$27**; Smile **$23**; Smarty **$12**; Son-E- Boy **$11**; Setzler's **$5**; Stevens **$17**.

Cherry River Beverages, Richmond, WV, Red and white, 10 oz., 1958 . . . . **$20**

Chief Muskogee Fine Beverages, Muskogee, OK, Red, black and white, 8-1/2 oz., 1950-52 . . . . **$30**

Clipper Old Fashioned Root Beer, New Castle, ME, Amber glass with black and white label, 10 oz., 1953 . . . . **$35**

Daniel Boone Mix, Spencer, NC, Black and white, 7 oz., 1946 . **$12**

Drink–O Delicious, Knoxville, TN, Green and white, 10 oz., 1955-56 . . . . **$40**

Duke Beverages, Alton, IL, Red and white, 12 oz., 1954 . . . . **$75**

Dumpy Wumpy Beverages, Dunbar, WV, Purple and white, 6 oz., 1948 . . . . **$150**

Excel, Breese, IL, Red and white, 10 oz., 1961 . . . .$7

Fawn Beverage Co., Elmira, NY, White, 12 oz., 1951 . . . . . . **$36**

Fontinalis Berverages, Grayling, MI, Red and white, 8 oz., 1946 . . . . **$125**

TIP **$5**; Top's **$10**; Tecumseh **$19**; Tom Tucker **$41**; Ted's Root Beer **$20**; Tiny Tim **$16**; Tiny Tim **$10**; TNT **$22**.

Fox Beverages, Fremont, OH, Red and white, 10 oz., 1963-68 . . **$5**

Frontier Beverages, North Platte, NE, Brown and white, 8 oz., 1948 . . . . **$250**

Gholson Bros. Beverages, Albuquerque, NM, White, 7 oz., 1953-58 . . . . **$10**

Go – For Brand, Austin, MN, Orange and white, 7 oz., 1948 . . **$15**

Golden Dome Ginger Ale, Montpelier, VT, Yellow and white, 28 oz., 1948 . . . . **$15**

Grantman Beverages, Antigo, WI, Red and white, 7 oz., 1965 . . . . **$10**

Hamakua, Paauilo, HI, White, 12 oz., 1941 . . . . **$15**

Harris Springs Ginger Ale, Waterloo, SC, Green glass with white label, 12 oz., 1938-48 . . . . **$70**

Harrison's – Heart –O-Orange, Globe, AZ, Orange and white, 10 oz., 1941 . . . . **$16**

Heep Good Beverages – Wenatchee Bottling Works, Wenatchee, WA, Green, 7 oz., 1937 . . . . **$80**

Hy-Plane Beverages, Connersville, IN, Yellow, white, and red, 7 oz., 1945 . . . . **$35**

Indian Mound Springs Quality Beverages – Ace of Them All, Bridgeville, PA, Red and white, 7 oz., 1966 . . . . **$18**

Iwana Beverages, Dover, OH, Black and white, 8 oz., 1944-50 . . **$25**

Jacks – Up, Gillespie, IL, Green glass with white label, 7 oz., 1954 . . . . **$45**

Jay Cola Sparkling Beverages, Oklahoma City, OK, Red, black, and yellow, 10 oz., 1947 . . . . **$320**

Jet Up Space-Age Beverages, Grove City, PA, Red and black, 7 oz., 1960 . . . . **$15**

Johnny Bull Root Beer, Wheeling, WV, Green glass with red and white label, 7-1/2 oz., squat shape 1952-56 . . . . **$170**

K.C. Beverages – Kit Carson Love, Muskogee, OK, Red and white, 10 oz., 1957 . . . . **$35**

K's Fruit Beverages, Los Angeles, CA, Blue and white, 7 oz., 1944 . **$20**

Kelly's Cream-Top Root Beer, Mishawaka, IN, Red and white, 10 oz., 1953 . . . . **$45**

King Orange Soda, W. Barrington, RI / Buff, NY, Red, blue, and white, 12 oz., 1941 . . . . **$15**

Lammi Beverages, Iron Mountain, MI, Red and white, 7 oz., 1959-1960 . . . . **$20**

Land – O – Lakes Beverages, Paris, MI, White, 7 oz., 1948 . . . **$10**

Lazy-B Beverages, Fremont, OH, Red and white, 8 oz., 1957 . . **$15**

LIX **$33**; Lane's **$5**; Lucky Club **$25**; Lincoln **$75**; Lemmy **$25**; Lift **$11**; Little Joe **$11**; Long Tom **$8**.

Lincoln, Chicago, IL, Blue and red, 12 oz., Abe Lincoln with cabin in background, 1957 .... **$75**

Little Joe, Perry, IA, Green glass with red and white label, 7 oz., 1947 .... **$20**

Mac Fuddy Beverages, Flint, MI, Green, red, and white, 10 oz., 1963 .... **$25**

Magic City Beverages, Birmingham, AL, Red and white, 7 oz., 1947 .... **$150**

Maple Spring Beverages, E. Wareham, MA, Red, green, and white, 7 oz., 1962-67 .... **$15**

Mingo Beverages, Williamson, WV, Black and orange, 9 oz., 1922 and 1950 .... **$75**

Mixer Man Beverages, Elkins, WV, White and green, 16 oz., 1955 .... **$65**

Ma's **$6**; Mayville **$8**; Mid-Valley **$13**; Mix-Up **$7**; Mission **$6**; Oscar's **$8**.

Nemasket Springs Beverages, Middleboro, MA, Red and white, 8 oz., 1948. . . . . **$70**

New Yorker Beverages, Detroit, MI, White, 7 oz., 1947. . . . . **$25**

Nezinscot Beverages, Turner, ME, Red, white, and black, 6 oz., 1941. . . . . **$10**

Nu-Life Grape – For Better Life, New Orleans, LA, Black and white, 7 oz., 1947. . . . . **$75**

Old Jamaica Beverages, Waldoboro, ME, Red, 7 oz., 1964 . . **$20**

Old Nassua – Pale Dry – Ginger Ale, Mineola, NY, Green and white, 7 oz., 1947. . . . . **$20**

Old Smoky Beverages, Greenville, TN, Red and white, 10 oz., 1952-58 . . . . **$35**

Out West Beverages, Colorado Springs, CO, White, 10 oz., 1959-1956. . . . . **$150**

PA-Poose Root Beer, Coshocton, OH, Red and yellow, 12 oz., 1941-43 . . . . **$50**

Pacific (Surfer and Surfer Girl), Honolulu, HI, Green and white, 6-1/2 oz., 1950-53 . . . . **$50**

Pelican Beverages, Alexandria, LA, Red and white, 10 oz., 1964-70. . . . . **$30**

Peter Pan – Delicious – Refreshing, Buffalo, NY, Red and white, 7 oz., 1948. . . . . **$30**

Polar Pak Beverages, San Diego, CA, Green and white, 7 oz., 1944-46 . . . . **$25**

Quality Flower's Beverages, Charlotte, NC, Blue and white, 10 oz., 1969. . . . . **$7**

Ralph's Beverages, Zanesville, OH, Red and yellow, 10 oz., 1961 . . **$30**

Red Arrow Beverages – Taste Better, Detroit, MI, Red and white, 7 oz., 1946-47 . . . . **$15**

Red Lodge Beverage Company, Red Lodge, MT, Red and white, 7 oz., 1950. . . . . **$44**

Rocket Beverages, Greeley, CO, White, 10 oz., 1965 . . . . **$50**

Royal Palm, Ft. Myers, FL, Red and white, 8 oz., 1955-58. . . **$10**

Sioux Beverages, Sioux Falls, SD, Red and white, 7 oz., 9148-52. **$80**

Sno-Maid, Reading, PA, Green and white, 7 oz., 1966. . . . . . **$25**

Snow White Beverages, Saxton, PA, Green and white, 12 oz., 1961. . . . . **$10**

T & T Beverages, Gipsy, PA, White, 7 oz., 1957 . . . . **$30**

Tasty Maid, Madera, CA, White, 10 oz., 1968 . . . . **$20**

Devil Shake **$80**; Dew **$8**; Diamond **$15**; Diet-Way **$6**; Dodger **$6**; Double Cola **$20**; Double Cola **$7**; Double Cola **$5**.

Uncle Tom's Root Beer, San Bernardino, CA, Red, white, and yellow, 10 oz., 1955 . . . . **$520**

Variety Club Junior Beverages, Columbus, OH, Red and white, 7-1/2 oz., 1943. . . . . **$60**

Vino – Pride of Florida – Punch, Wildwood, FL, Red and white, 7 oz., 1960 . . . . **$25**

Walker's Root Beer, Melrose, MA, White, 12 oz., 1949 . . . . . **$35**

Western Beverages, Albuquerque, NM, White, 8 oz., 1947 . . **$50**

Zeeh's Beverages, Kingston, NY, Red and white, 12 oz., 1949 **$35**

Zills's Best Soda, Rapid City, SD, Yellow, 7 oz., 1948 . . . . **$20**

7-UP – Star Beverage Co. (lady in bathing suit around bubbles), Amber, 7 oz., crown top, American 1920-1930 . . . . . . **$100-150**

Embossed

All bottles have a smooth base unless noted otherwise

Coca-Cola

Coca-Cola – Los Angeles (embossed around lower part of bottle), Aqua, 7", crown top, American 1910-1925 . **$100-150**

Coca-Cola – Los Angeles, Amber, 7", crown top, American 1910-1920. . . . . **$150-200**

Coca-Cola – Richfield, Utah, Clear, 9", crown top, American 1910-1925. . . . . **$100-150**

Coca-Cola Co. – Seattle, Aqua, 8", crown top, American 1910-1925. . . . . **$75-100**

Coca-Cola – Ten Fl. Oz. – Bottling Works – Rochester NY – 10 Fl. Oz., Amber, 8", crown top, American 1910-1925 . **$300-400**

Coca-Cola – Trade Mark Registered – Boise Idaho, Aqua, 7", crown top, American 1910-1925 . . . . **$100-200**

Coca-Cola – Trade Mark Registered – Crown – Bottling Works – Contents 6 Fl. Oz – Cheyenne Wyo, Clear, 7-3/4", crown top, American 1910-1930 . . . . **$750-950**

Coca-Cola – Trade Mark Registered – Dr. J.C. Bogue – Sherman, Texas, Clear, 8", crown top, American 1915-1930. . . **$100-150**

Coca-Cola – Trade Mark Registered – Pueblo Coca-Cola – Pueblo Colo. – Bottling Works, Clear, 7", crown top, American 1910-1925 . . . . **$100-150**

Coca-Cola Bottling Co – Las Cruces – Deming – New Mexico, Clear, 8", ABM top, 6 panel arches, American 1900-1915 . . . . . **$100-120**

Coca-Cola Bottling Works – Los Angeles (embossed around the base), Clear, 8-1/2", CCBW on base, tooled crown top, American 1905-1915 . . . . **$100-160**

Coca-Cola – Denver, Clear, 8-3/4", crown top, American 1905-1916 . . . . **$150-200**

Coca-Cola – San Francisco Cal., Clear, 8", tooled top, American 1905-1925 . . . . **$200-250**

Colorado – Coca-Cola (in script) – Springs, Clear, 9", crown top, American 1910-1925 . . . . **$150-230**

Indian Rock – Ginger Ale – Coca-Cola – Bottling Co. – Washington N.C., Light green aqua, 7 3/4", ten-pin shape, crown top, American 1910-1930 . . . . **$300-500**

Property of Salt Lake Coca-Cola – Bottling Co. – Coca-Cola (in script) – Salt Lake City – Registered, Clear, 8", tooled top, American 1905-1925 . . . . **$100-150**

Property of – Salt Lake – Coca-Cola (in script) – Bottling Co. – Salt Lake City Utah, Blue aqua, 10", tooled top, American 1905-1920 .... **$325-425**

The Best By A Dam Site – Boulder – Products – Las Vegas Nev (Las Vegas Coke), Clear, 7-1/2", ABM top, American 1905-1920 .... **$150-200**

The – Coca-Cola – Trade Mark Registered – Bottling Co. – Denver, Colo, Clear, 7", crown top, American 1905-1920 .... **$75-100**

The Salt Lake Coca-Cola Bottling Co. – Red Seal Brand, Aqua, 7-1/2", ABM top, American 1905- 1915 .... **$50-100**

Pepsi-Cola

Indian Rock – Ginger Ale – Richmond – Pepsi-Cola Co. – Richmond VA – 7 Fluid Ounces, Clear, 7-3/4", ten-pin shape, crown top, American 1910-1930 .... **$300-500**

Pepsi-Cola (prototype bottle), Clear, 7", crown top, American 1906-1910 .... **$900-1,000**

Registered – Pepsi Cola (In script on four of the eight panels), Clear, 8", ABM top, base reads: Ideal Bottling Works – L.A. Calif., American 1906-1920 .... **$200-400**

VIOLIN AND BANJO BOTTLES

While roaming the aisles of bottle and antique shows, I have often seen a violin- or banjo-shaped bottle on a table, admired its shape and color, then set it back down and moved on to whiskey and medicine bottles. I didn't fully appreciate these uniquely shaped bottles until I attended the June 1999

National Bottle Museum Antique Bottle Show in Saratoga, NY, to participate in a book signing. Before the show, a silent auction was held that included a spectacular display of violin and banjo bottles. At that time, I had the pleasure of meeting several knowledgeable collectors and members of the Violin Bottle Collectors Association and received a short lesson about the characteristics and history of violin bottles. With the help of many dedicated members of the Violin Bottle Collectors Association, we've written a chapter that will assist both the veteran and the novice collector with understanding the fun and collecting of violin and banjo bottles.

While gathering the information for this chapter, it became clear that most bottle and antique collectors and dealers (including this collector) had very little knowledge about violin and banjo bottles and their beginnings. Are they considered antiques? How old are violin bottles? Why and where were they manufactured?

First, most were manufactured in the 20th century, with heavy production beginning in the 1930s. Interestingly, violin and banjo bottles are completely original designs and not copied from any earlier bottle forms such as historic flasks or bitters. This makes these bottles antique in that they are the first of their design and style.

As with other specialty groups, violin and banjo bottles have specific categories, and specific classes and codes within each category. For the serious collector, I recommend *The Classification of Violin Shaped Bottles*, 2nd Edition 1999, and 3rd Edition 2004, by Robert A. Linden and *Violin Bottles, Banjos, Guitars, and Other Novelty Glass*, 1st Edition 1995, by Don and Doris Christensen. Information on the association can be obtained by writing to:

Violin Bottle Collector's Association,
1210 Hiller Road,
McKinleyville, CA 95519

or by contacting Frank Bartlett, Membership Chairman,
at e-mail fbviobot@hotmail.com.

VIOLIN BOTTLES

Category 1: American Styles

LV: Large Violin-Shaped Bottle (Figure 1)

Eight molds have been identified:

- Molds 1, 4, and 6: Produced at Clevenger Brothers Glass Works
- Molds 2, 3, and 7: Produced at Dell Glass Company
- Mold 5: Maker unidentified
- Mold 8: Produced in Japan

- Bottles had no contents and were made only for decorative purposes.
- Production began in the 1930s; first identified in the marketplace in the 1940s.
- Height range of 9" to 10-1/4"; body width 4-1/4" to 4-3/8"; 1-1/2" thick near base.
- Colors: amber, amberina, amethyst, blue, cobalt, green, yellowish, and vaseline.

Figure 1

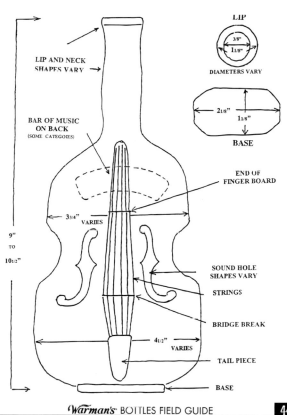

LIP

3/8"

1 1/8"

DIAMETERS VARY

LIP AND NECK
SHAPES VARY →

2 1/8"

1 1/8"

BASE

BAR OF MUSIC
ON BACK
(SOME CATEGOIES)

END OF
FINGER BOARD

3 3/4" VARIES

9"
TO
10 1/2"

SOUND HOLE
SHAPES VARY

STRINGS

BRIDGE BREAK

4 1/2" VARIES

TAIL PIECE

BASE

SV: SMALL VIOLIN-SHAPED BOTTLE (FIGURE 2)

Three molds have been identified:

- Mold 1: Produced at Clevenger Brothers Glass Works and Old Jersey Glass Co (a Dell Glass Company)
- Mold 2: Produced at Dell Glass Company
- Mold 3: Produced at Clevenger Brothers Glass Works

- Less common than large violin bottles.
- Bottles had no contents and were made only for decorative purposes.
- First identified in the marketplace in the 1940s.
- Height range of 7-1/4"; body width 3"; 1-1/4" thick near base.
- Colors: cobalt, clear, blue, green, amber, and amethyst.

FIGURE 2

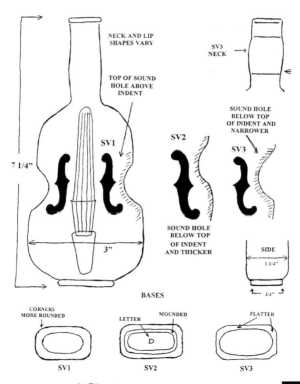

NECK AND LIP
SHAPES VARY

TOP OF SOUND
HOLE ABOVE
INDENT

SV1

SV2

SV3
NECK

SOUND HOLE
BELOW TOP
OF INDENT AND
NARROWER

SV3

7 1/4"

SOUND HOLE
BELOW TOP
OF INDENT
AND THICKER

3"

SIDE

1 1/4"

3/4"

BASES

CORNERS
MORE ROUNDED

LETTER   MOUNDED

FLATTER

D

SV1   SV2   SV3

EV: Violin-Shaped Bottle with Tuning Pegs or "Ears" on the neck. (Figure 3)

Four molds have been identified. Four neck shapes represent four mold patterns and numerals 1-7 are cavity numbers (Figure 4).

- EVA1 up to EVA7: Each has an "A" neck shape.
- EVB1 up to EVB7: Each has a "B" neck shape.
- EVC1 up to EVC7: Each has a "C" neck shape.
- EVD1 up to EVD7: Each has a "D" neck shape.

- Produced at Maryland Glass Company.
- ABM product (mold line goes up through neck, ears, and lip).
- Bottles had contents such as cosmetic lotion.
- Labeled as flasks, figurals, vases, and cosmetic bottles.
- Production began in the mid-1930s and lasted through the mid-1950s.
- Height 8"; body width 4".
- Colors: blue, amber, and clear.

Figure 4

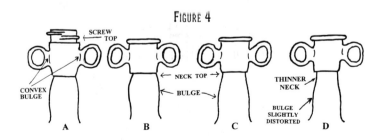

Figure 3

FACE

BASE

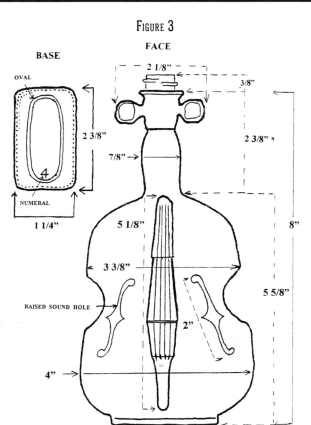

OVAL

2 1/8"

3/8"

2 3/8"

2 3/8" "

NUMERAL

7/8" →

1 1/4"

5 1/8"

8"

3 3/8"

RAISED SOUND HOLE

2"

5 5/8"

4" →

Violin bottles (EV) with "ears" or "tuning pegs", cobalt blue, amber, **$10-20 each.**

BV: Bardstown Violin-Shaped Whiskey Bottle (Figures 5 and 6)

During the late 1930s, bourbon whiskey was distilled in Bardstown, Kentucky, and distributed throughout the Eastern United States and Canada. Bardstown used several sizes of violin-shaped bottles with attractive labels that became a common identifier until production ceased in 1940. Interestingly, the violin bottle molds spanned 16 years, but the molds were only used for four years. Due to the limited production, Bardstown bottles with full labels are very difficult to find.

Two molds have been identified (Produced at Owens-Illinois and Anchor-Hocking)
- Mold 1 – Cork Top
  - BVC1: 11", quart
  - BVC2: 11", 4/5 quart
  - BVC3: 10-1/8", pint
  - BVC4: 9-5/8", pint
  - BVC5: 8-1/8", 1/2 pint
- Mold 2 – Screw Top
  - BVS1: 14", half gallon
  - BVS2: 9-1/2" to 10", pint
  - BVS3: 7-3/4" to 8-1/8", half pint
  - BVS4: 4-3/4" to 4-7/8", nip
- Only American violin figural designed and patented specifically with alcoholic content.
- Production began in the 1930s and lasted until 1940 when production ceased.
- Color: amber.

FIGURE 5

Dec. 7, 1937.

H. D. HENSHEL

BOTTLE

Filed Oct. 19, 1937

Des. 107,353

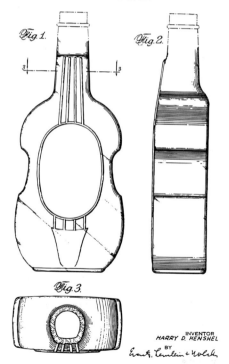

Fig.1.

Fig.2.

Fig.3.

INVENTOR
HARRY D. HENSHEL
BY

Figure 6

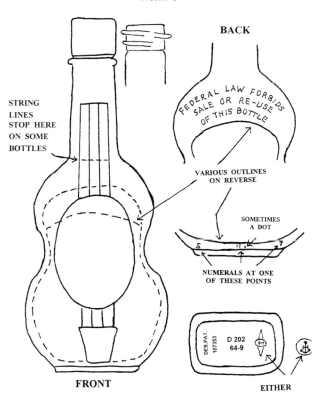

BACK

STRING
LINES
STOP HERE
ON SOME
BOTTLES

FEDERAL LAW FORBIDS
SALE OR RE-USE
OF THIS BOTTLE

**VARIOUS OUTLINES
ON REVERSE**

**SOMETIMES
A DOT**

5   11   7

**NUMERALS AT ONE
OF THESE POINTS**

DES. PAT.
107353

D 202
64-9

FRONT

EITHER

Category 2: European Styles

DV: Definitive violin-shaped bottles.

FV: Violin-shaped bottle embossed "Bottles Made in France" on base.

CV: Violin-shaped bottle etched "Czecho" and "Slovakia" on base.

Category 3: Special Styles

OV: Other violin-shaped bottles, including miniatures.

Category 4: Banjo-Shaped Bottles (Figure 7)

LB: Large Banjo-Shaped Bottles

Six molds have been identified.

- LB1: Does not have a base (mold line goes all around the body) and has no embossing
- LB2: Plain oval base and no embossing. Possible prototype for future models.
- LB3: Only type produced to contain alcohol. LB3 bottles have the following embossed legend "Federal Law Forbids Sale or Reuse of this Bottle," which was required from 1933 (repeal of prohibition) to 1966.
- LB4: Minor changes with a "new" face and a clean reverse side.
- LB5: Same as LB4 with a pontil mark but with the famous base embossing removed.
- LB6: No pontil marks, since snap case tools were used. Finer and more delicate string and sound hole embossing.

FIGURE 7

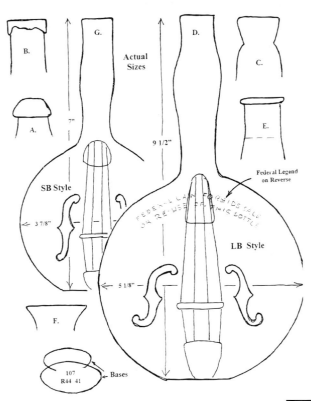

Actual Sizes

7"

9 1/2"

SB Style

3 7/8"

Federal Legend on Reverse

FEDERAL LAW FORBIDS SALE OR RE-USE OF THIS BOTTLE

LB Style

5 1/8"

Bases

107
R44 41

- All large banjos have the same discus body shape, approximate height, width, and neck measurements. (Height 9-1/2"; diameter 5-1/4"; thickness 1-5/8" ; oval base 1-1/2" long by 3/4" wide)
- Production began in 1942 and continued until 1975.
- Produced at Clevenger Brothers Glass Works, Dell Glass Company, and the Maryland Glass Company.
- Colors: amber, green, blue, and amethyst.

SB: Small Banjo-Shaped Bottles

Two molds have been identified:

- SB1: Smaller version of LB; height 7"; discus diameter 3-7/8"; lady's neck 3-1/8"; oval base 1-1/8" by 3/4".
- SB2: Squared sides; height 7-7/8"; discus diameter 4-1/2"; straight neck 3-1/2"; oval base 2" by 1-1/8" with 1" kickup in center of bottle (scarce).
- Produced at Clevenger Brothers Glass Works, Dell Glass Company, and the Maryland Glass Company.
- Colors: amber, green, blue, amethyst

OB: Other Banjo-Shaped Bottles

Three molds have been identified:

- OB1: cork stopped whiskey measuring 10-3/4" tall; 5-5/8" wide; and 2-1/2" thick. Embossed on back is "Medley Distilling Company, Owensboro, Kentucky 4/5 Quart." Color: clear
- OB2: Produced in Italy for 8" to 12" liquor bottles. Base embossing with "Patent Nello Gori." Color: clear
- OB3: Possible miniature, 4-1/2" tall, cobalt salt and pepper shakers in the image of a banjo. Produced by Maryland Glass Company in the 1930s.

Violin Bottle Pricing

LV1a1 (United Church Bandstand)
    Amethyst **$150-250**
LV1a2 (Auburn Die Company)
    Amethyst **$250-350**
LV1a3 (VBCA 1997)
    Cobalt **$50-100**
LV1a4 (VBCA 1999)
    Amethyst **$50-150**

Large violin bottle (LV1a3), cobalt blue, **$50-100.**

Large violin bottle (LV1), amber, **$40-50.**

LV1 (Clevenger)

Blue.................................. **$20-30**
Green................................. **$20-30**
Amethyst.............................. **$30-45**
Jersey green.......................... **$30-45**
Amber................................. **$40-50**
Cobalt................................ **$50-100**
Amberina.............................. **$400-550**

LV2 (Dell)

Blue.................................. **$15-25**
Green................................. **$15-25**
Amethyst.............................. **$30-45**

Large violin bottle (LV3), amethyst, **$30-45.**

Large violin bottle (LV5), yellow, **$100-120.**

LV3 (Dell)
  Blue. **$15-25**
  Green **$15-25**
  Amethyst. **$30-45**

LV4 (Clevenger)
  Green **$50-60**
  Amethyst. **$50-60**
  Amber **$50-60**
  Cobalt **$80-100**

LV5 (Dell Glass)
  Royal blue. **$50-70**
  Clear **$50-70**
  Deep green **$90-110**
  Golden amber. **$100-120**
  Yellow **$100-120**
  Florescing green **$250-350**

LV6 (Clevenger)
  Blue. **$20-30**
  Green **$20-30**
  Jersey green. **$25-40**
  Amethyst. **$30-45**
  Amber **$40-50**
  Clear **$40-50**
  Cobalt **$50-100**
  Vaseline. **$250-350**

LV7 (Dell glass)
  Light blue **$25-35**
  Light green **$25-35**
  Light amethyst **$30-45**
  Milk glass . . . . **$400+**

Large violin bottle (LV6), blue **$20-30**, green **$20-30**, amber **$40-50.**

LV8 (Japan)
Light blue	**$60-80**
Dark blue	**$60-80**
Dark green	**$60-80**
Dark amethyst	**$60-80**

SV1 (Clevenger)
Blue	**$25-35**
Green	**$25-35**
Amethyst	**$35-45**
Jersey green	**$35-45**
Amber	**$45-60**
Clear	**$45-60**
Cobalt	**$45-60**

Large violin bottle (LV7), light amethyst, **$30-45.**

Large violin bottle (LV8), light blue, **$60-80.**

Small violin bottles (SV1), green **$25-35**, clear **$45-60**, cobalt blue **$45-60**, blue **$25-35**, amber **$45-60**.

SV2 (Dell)
Blue	**$15-25**
Green	**$15-25**
Amethyst	**$20-30**

SV3 (Clevenger)
Blue	**$25-35**
Green	**$25-35**
Amethyst	**$35-45**
Amber	**$45-60**
Cobalt	**$45-60**

SV3app (Pairpoint Glass)

Ruby red . . . . **$60+**

EVs (Maryland Glass Company)

Light cobalt. **$10-20**

Dark cobalt. **$10-20**

Amber **$10-20**

Clear **$10-20**

DV1 (Unknown)

Blue. **$30-50**

Green **$30-50**

Clear **$30-50**

Amber **$40-60**

Red **$80-100**

Small violin bottle (SV2), amethyst, **$20-30.**

Violin bottle (EV) with "ears" or "tuning pegs", cobalt blue, **$10-20.**

Definitive violin bottles (DV1), blue, **$30-50.**

DV2 (Unknown)

Clear **$15-25**
Blue. **$20-30**
Green **$20-30**
Amber **$25-40**
Red **$60-100**

DV3 (Unknown)

Clear **$15-25**
Blue. **$20-30**
Green **$20-30**
Amber **$25-40**
Red **$60-100**

FV1-3 (French)

Clear **$15-30**
Blue tint **$40-60**
Green tint **$40-60**
Light peach **$50-75**

OV2 (Wheaton)

Clear **$5-10**
Blue. **$5-10**
Green **$5-10**

OV12 (George West)

Amber **$150-250**
Cobalt . . . . **$500+**

OV14 (Stumpy)

Light blue **$40-60**
Green **$50-80**
Amethyst **$50-80**

Definitive violin bottles (DV 2 & 3), ruby red, **$60-100 each.**

Special style violin bottle, amber, **$150-250.**

French violin bottle (FV1-3), blue tint **$40-60**, green tint **$40-60**, light peach **$50-75.**

OV16 (Decanter)

Light blue	**$150-300**
Green	**$150-300**
Amethyst	**$150-300**
Clear	**$150-300**

Banjo Bottle Pricing

LB1: 9"- No base or embossing, mottled glass, small applied tooled lip. Unknown origin.

Green .... **$75-$125**

LB2: 9-1/2" - Oval base, no embossing. Unknown origin.

Blue.................................... **$40-$70**

Amethyst .... **$40-$70**

Green .... **$60-$100**

LB3: 9-1/2" - 107 R44 41 embossed on base. "FEDERAL LAW FORBIDS SALE OR REUSE OF THIS BOTTLE" embossed on reverse. Maryland Glass pre-1966.

Blue.................................... **$60-$100**

Large banjo (LB1, 9"), green, **$75-125.**

LB4: 9-1/2" - 107 R44 41 embossed on base, strings, and soundholes. Dell Glass 1940s.

Blue...................................... **$25-$40**
Amethyst................................ **$25-$40**
Green .... **$25-$40**

LB5: 9-1/2" - No embossing on base, strings, and soundholes. Dell Glass 1940s.

Blue...................................... **$25-$40**
Amethyst................................ **$25-$40**
Green .... **$25-$40**

Large banjo (LB4 & 5, 9-1/2"), blue, amethyst, green,
$25-40 each.

LB6: 9-1/2" - No embossing on base, strings, and soundholes. Clevenger 1940s.

Type E Neck

Blue	**$25-$50**
Amethyst	**$25-$50**
Green	**$25-$50**
Cobalt	**$75-$100**

Flared Lip

Blue	**$75-$100**
Amethyst	**$50-$75**
Green	**$50-$75**
Amber	**$150-$200**

LB6: 9-1 2" – Embossed Slug plate Commemoratives. No embossing on base, strings, and sound holes. Clevenger 1970s.

LB6a: Depiction of East Bridgewater Church.

Amber	**$150-$250**

LB6b: Just the words "American Handmade, Clevenger Brothers Glass Works, Clayton, NJ."

Amber	**$100-$150**

LB6c: Depiction of two glassblowers and the words "Clevenger Brothers Glass Works American Made Mouth Blown."

Blue	**$75-$100**
Amethyst	**$75-$100**
Green	**$75-$100**
Amber	**$75-$100**

LB6d: Bicentennial "Celebrating 200 Years of Freedom 1776-1976."
Green .... **$50-$100**

LB6: 9-1/2" – Embossed slug plate commemoratives. No embossing on base, strings, and sound holes. Pairpoint Glass 2001.

LB6e: VBCA 2000 Commemorative.
Cobalt .... **$45-$65**

Small banjo (SB1, 7"), blue **$25-50**, amethyst **$25-50**, green, **$75-100**.

LB6f: VBCA blank slug plate.

    Cobalt . . . . **$45-$65**

LB6g: Chelmsford Historical Society/Ezekial Byam Commemorative.

    Teal . . . . **$30-$50**

SB1: 7" - Embossed strings and sound holes. Old Jersey Glass/Dell 1940s.

    Blue. . . . . **$25-$50**

    Amethyst . . . . **$25-$50**

    Green . . . . **$75-$100**

SB2: 7-7/8" with 4-1/2" diameter disk body, embossed strings, no sound holes. Origin unknown.

    Blue. . . . . **$35-$60**

    Amethyst . . . . **$35-$60**

    Green . . . . **$75-$100**

Large banjo (LB6b), amber, **$100-150.**

TRADEMARKS

Trademarks are very helpful for determining the identification, age, and value of a bottle. In addition, researching trademarks will give the bottle collector a deeper knowledge of the companies that made the bottles and their contents.

What is a trademark? It's a word, name, letter, number, symbol, design, phrase, or a combination of all of these items that identifies and distinguishes a product from its competitors. Usually, the markings appear on the bottom of the bottle. A trademark only protects the symbol that represents the product, not the product itself.

Trademarks have been around for a long time. The first glass makers to use identification marks were Ennion of Sidon who lived in the first century, and two of his students, Jason and Aristeas, who imprinted their identification into the sides of the molds.

In the 1840s, English glass manufacturers continued this practice by identifying their flasks with side lettering inside the molds in a similar fashion. Identifying marks have been found on antique Chinese porcelain, on pottery from ancient Greece and Rome, and on items from India dating back to 1300 BC.

In Medieval times, the craft and merchant owners also relied upon the marks to distinguish their products from makers of inferior goods to gain buyers' loyalties. Trademarks then were applied to just about everything; watermarks on paper, bread, leather goods, and weapons. Goldsmiths and silversmiths also began to rely on trademarks. In the late 1600s, bottle manufacturers began to mark their products with a glass seal that was applied to the bottle while still hot. Because the concept of trademarks had their roots in Europe, they were widely adopted in North America as immigrants flooded the new land.

For many early trademark owners, protection for the trademark owner was almost non-existent. While the United States Constitution provided rights of ownership in copyrights and patents, Congress didn't enact the first federal trademark law until 1870.

If you're able to determine the owner of the mark, and when it might have been used, you will usually be able to determine the date of a bottle. If the mark was not used for long, it will be easy to pinpoint the age of the bottle. If the mark was used for a long time, however, you'll have to rely on other references to help with the dating process.

Very few companies used identical marks, which is amazing, considering the vast number of manufacturers. Unfortunately, most numbers appearing with trademarks are not part of the trademark and are not useful for dating bottles.

While more than 1,200 trademarks have been created for bottles and fruit jars, only a sampling are included in this chapter.

The words and letters in bold are the company's trademarks as they appear on the bottle. Each trademark is followed by the complete name and location of the company and the approximate period of time during which the trademark was used.

United States Trademarks

- A -

A: Adams & Co., Pittsburgh, PA, 1861-1891

A: John Agnew & Son, Pittsburgh, PA, 1854-1866

A: Arkansas Glass Container Corp., Jonesboro, AR, 1958 to date (if machine made)

A (in a circle): American Glass Works, Richmond, VA and Paden City, WV, 1908-1935.

A & B together (AB): Adolphus Busch Glass Manufacturing Co., Belleville, IL, and St. Louis, MO, 1904-1907

ABC: Atlantic Bottle Co., New York City, NY, and Brackenridge, PA, 1918-1930

ABCo.: American Bottle Co., Chicago, IL, 1905-1916; Toledo, OH, 1916-1929

ABCO (in script): Ahrens Bottling Company, Oakland, CA, 1903-1908

A B G M Co.: Adolphus Busch Glass Manufacturing Co., Belleville, IL, 1886-1907; St. Louis, MO, 1886-1928

A & Co.: John Agnew and Co., Pittsburgh, PA, 1854-1892

A C M E: Acme Glass Co., Olean, NY, 1920-1930

A & D H C - A. & D.H.: Chambers, Pittsburgh, PA, Union Flasks, 1843-1886

AGCo: Arsenal Glass Co. (or Works), Pittsburgh, PA, 1865-1868

AGEE and Agee (in script): Hazel Atlas Glass Co., Wheeling, WV, 1919-1925

AGNEW & CO.: Agnew & Co., Pittsburgh, PA, 1876-1886

AGWL, PITTS PA: American Glass Works, Pittsburgh, PA 1865-1880, American Glass Works Limited, 1880-1905

AGW: American Glass Works, Richmond, VA, & Paden City, WV, 1908-1935

AMF & Co.: Adelbert M. Foster & Co., Chicago, IL, Millgrove, Upland, and Marion, IN, 1895-1911

Anchor figure (with H in center): Anchor Hocking Glass Corp., Lancaster, OH, 1955

A. R. S.: A. R. Samuels Glass Co., Philadelphia, PA, 1855-1872

A S F W W Va.: A.S. Frank Glass Co., Wellsburg, WV, 1859

ATLAS: Atlas Glass Co., Washington, PA, and later Hazel Atlas Glass Co., 1896-1965

- B -

B: Buck Glass Co., Baltimore, MD, 1909-1961

B (in circle): Brockway Machine Bottle Co., Brockway, PA, 1907-1933

Ball and Ball (in script): Ball Bros. Glass Manufacturing Co., Muncie, IN, and later Ball Corp., 1887-1973

Baker Bros. Balto. MD: Baker Brothers, Baltimore, MD, 1853-1905

BAKEWELL: Benjamin P. Bakewell Jr. Glass Co., 1876-1880

BANNER: Fisher-Bruce Co., Philadelphia, PA, 1910-1930

BB Co: Berney-Bond Glass Co., Bradford, Clarion, Hazelhurst, and Smethport, PA, 1900

BB & Co: Berney-Bond Glass Co., Bradford, Clarion, Hazelhurst, and Smethport, PA, 1900

BB48: Berney-Bond Glass Co., Bradford, Clarion, Hazelhurst, and Smethport, PA, 1920-1930

BBCo: Bell Bottle Co., Fairmount, IN, 1910-1914

Bennett's: Gillinder & Bennett (Franklin Flint Glass Co.) Philadelphia, PA, 1863-1867

Bernardin (in script): W. J. Latchford Glass Co., Los Angeles, CA, 1932-1938

The Best: Gillender & Sons, Philadelphia, PA, 1867-1870

B F B Co.: Bell Fruit Bottle Co., Fairmount, IN, 1910

B. G. Co.: Belleville Glass Co., IL, 1882

Bishop's: Bishop & Co., San Diego and Los Angeles, CA, 1890-1920

BK: Benedict Kimber, Bridgeport and Brownsville, PA, 1825-1840

BLUE RIBBON: Standard Glass Co., Marion, IN, 1908

BOLDT: Charles Boldt Glass Manufacturing Co., Cincinnati, OH, and Huntington, WV, 1900-1929

Boyds (in script): Illinois Glass Co., Alton, IL, 1900-1930

BP & B: Bakewell, Page & Bakewell, Pittsburgh, PA, 1824-1836

Brelle (in script) Jar: Brelle Fruit Jar Manufacturing Co., San Jose, CA, 1912-1916

Brilliante: Jefferis Glass Co., Fairton, NJ and Rochester, PA, 1900-1905

- C -

C (in a circle): Chattanooga Bottle & Glass Co. and later Chattanooga Glass Co., 1927-Present

C (in a square): Crystal Glass Co., Los Angeles, CA, 1921-1929

C (in a star): Star City Glass Co., Star City, WV, 1949-Present

C (in upside-down triangle): Canada Dry Ginger Ale Co., N.Y.C., 1930-1950

Canton Domestic Fruit Jar: Canton Glass Co., Canton, OH, 1890-1904

C & Co. or C Co: Cunninghams & Co., Pittsburgh, PA, 1880, 1907

CCCo: Carl Conrad & Co., St. Louis, MO, (beer), 1860-1883

C.V.Co. No. 1 & No 2: Milwaukee, WI, 1880-1881

C C Co.: Carl Conrad & Co., St. Louis, MO, 1876-1883

C C G Co.: Cream City Glass Co., Milwaukee, WI, 1888-1894

C.F.C.A.: California Fruit Canners Association, Sacramento, CA, 1899-1916

CFJCo: Consolidated Fruit Jar Co., New Brunswick, NJ, 1867-1882

C G I: California Glass Insulator Co., Long Beach, CA, 1912-1919

C G M Co: Campbell Glass Manufacturing Co., West Berkeley, CA, 1885

C G W: Campbell Glass Works, West Berkeley, CA, 1884-1885

C & H: Coffin & Hay, Hammonton, NJ, 1836-1838, or Winslow, NJ, 1838-1842

C L G Co.: Carr-Lowrey Glass Co., Baltimore, MD, 1889-1920

CLARKE: Clarke Fruit Jar Co., Cleveland, OH, 1886-1889

CLOVER LEAF (in arch with picture of a clover leaf), marked on ink and mucilage bottles, 1890.

Clyde, N.Y.: Clyde Glass Works, Clyde, NY, 1870-1882

The Clyde (in script): Clyde Glass Works, Clyde, NY, 1895

C Milw: Chase Valley Glass Co., Milwaukee, WI, 1880-1881

Cohansey: Cohansey Glass Manufacturing Co., Philadelphia, PA, 1870-1900

CO-SHOE: Coshocton Glass Corp., Coshocton, OH, 1923-1928

C R: Curling, Robertson & Co., Pittsburgh, PA, 1834-1857 or Curling, Ringwalt & Co., Pittsburgh, PA, 1857-1863

CRYSTO: McPike Drug Co., Kansas City, MO, 1904

- D -

D 446: Consolidated Fruit Jar Co., New Brunswick, NJ, 1871-1882

DB: Du Bois Brewing Co., Pittsburgh, PA, 1918

Dexter: Franklin Flint Glass Works, Philadelphia, PA, 1861-1880

Diamond (plain): Diamond Glass Co., 1924-Present

The Dictator: William McCully & Co., Pittsburgh, PA, 1855-1869

Dictator: William McCully & Co., Pittsburgh, PA, 1869-1885

D & O: Cumberland Glass Mfg. Co., Bridgeton, NJ, 1890-1900

D O C: D. O. Cunningham Glass Co., Pittsburgh, PA, 1883-1937

DOME: Standard Glass Co., Wellsburg, WV, 1891-1893

D S G Co.: De Steiger Glass Co., LaSalle, IL, 1879-1896

Duffield: Dr. Samuel Duffield, Detroit, MI, 1862-1866 and Duffield, Parke & Co, Detroit, MI, 1866-1875

Dyottsville: Dyottsville Glass Works, Philadelphia, PA, 1833-1923

- E -

E4: Essex Glass Co., Mt. Vernon, OH, 1906-1920

Economy (in script) TRADE MARK: Kerr Glass Manufacturing Co., Portland, OR, 1903-1912

Electric Trade Mark (in script): Gayner Glass Works, Salem, NJ, 1910

Electric Trade Mark: Gayner Glass Works, Salem, NJ, 1900-1910

Erd & Co., E R Durkee: E. R. Durkee & Co., New York, NY, post-1874

The EMPIRE: Empire Glass Co., Cleveland, NY, 1852-1877

E R Durkee & Co: E. R. Durkee & Co., New York, NY, 1850-1860

Eureka 17: Eurkee Jar Co., Dunbar, WV, 1864

Eureka (in script): Eurkee Jar Co., Dunbar, WV, 1900-1910

Everett and EHE: Edward H. Everett Glass Co., (Star Glass Works) Newark, OH, 1893-1904

Everlasting (in script) JAR: Illinois Pacific Glass Co., San Francisco, CA, 1904

E W & Co: E. Wormser & Co., Pittsburgh, PA, 1857-1875

Excelsior: Excelsior Glass Co., St. John, Quebec, Canada, 1878-1883

- F -

F (inside a jar outline or keystone): C. L. Flaccus Glass Co., Pittsburgh, PA, 1900-1928

F WM. Frank & Sons: WM. Frank & Co., Pittsburgh, PA, 1846-1966, WM. Frank & Sons, Pittsburgh, PA, 1866-1876

F & A: Fahnstock & Albree, Pittsburgh, PA, 1860-1862

FERG Co: F.E. Reed Glass Co., Rochester, NY, 1898-1947

FF & Co: Fahnstock, Fortune & Co., Pittsburgh, PA, 1866-1873

F G: Florida Glass Manufacturing Co., Jacksonville, FL, 1926-1947

FL or FL & Co.: Frederick Lorenz & Co., Pittsburgh, PA, 1819-1841

FLINT – GREEN: Whitney Glass Works, Glassborough, NJ, 1888

FOLGER, JAF&Co., Pioneer, Golden Gate: J. A. Folger & Co., San Francisco, CA, 1850-Present

- G -

G (in circle with bold lines): Gulfport Glass Co., Gulfport, MS, 1955-1970

G E M: Hero Glass Works, Philadelphia, PA, 1884-1909

G & H: Gray & Hemingray, Cincinnati, OH, 1848-1851; Covington, KY, 1851-1864

G & S: Gillinder & Sons, Philadelphia, PA, 1867-1871 and 1912-1930

Gillinder: Gillinder Bros., Philadelphia, PA, 1871-1930

Gilberds: Gilberds Butter Tub Co., Jamestown, NY, 1883-1890

GLENSHAW (G in a box underneath name): Glenshaw Glass Co., Glenshaw, PA, 1904

GLOBE: Hemingray Glass Co., Covington, KY (The symbol "Parquet-Lac" was used beginning in 1895), 1886

Greenfield: Greenfield Fruit Jar & Bottle Co., Greenfield, IN, 1888-1912

G W K & Co.: George W. Kearns & Co., Zanesville, OH, 1848-1911

- H -

H and H (in heart): Hart Glass Manufacturing Co., Dunkirk, IN, 1918-1938

H (with varying numerals): Holt Glass Works, West Berkeley, CA, 1893-1906

H (in a diamond): A.H. Heisey Glass Co., Oakwood Ave., Newark, OH, 1893-1958

H (in a triangle): J. T. & A. Hamilton Co., Pittsburgh, PA, 1900

Hazel: Hazel Glass Co., Wellsburg, WV, 1886-1902

H.B.Co: Hagerty Bros. & Co., Brooklyn, NY, 1880-1900

Helme: Geo. W. Helme Co., Jersey City, NJ, 1870-1895

Hemingray: Hemingray Brothers & Co. and later Hemingray Glass Co., Covington, KY, 1864-1933

H. J. Heinz: H.J. Heinz Co., Pittsburgh, PA, 1860-1869

Heinz & Noble: H. J. Heinz Co., Pittsburgh, PA, 1869-1872

F. J. Heinz: H.J. Heinz Co., Pittsburgh, PA, 1876-1888

H. J. Heinz Co.: H. J. Heinz Co., Pittsburgh, PA, 1888-Present

HELME: Geo. W. Helme Co., N.J., 1870-1890

HERO: Hero Glass Works, Philadelphia, PA, 1856-1884 and Hero Fruit Jar Co., Philadelphia, PA, 1884-1909

HS (in a circle): Twitchell & Schoolcraft, Keene, NH, 1815-1816

- I -

IDEAL: Hod C. Dunfee, Charleston, WV, 1910

I G Co.: Ihmsen Glass Co., Pittsburgh, PA, 1855-1896

I. G. Co: Ihmsen Glass Co., 1895

I. G. Co.: Monogram, Ill. Glass Co. on fruit jar, 1914

IPGCO: Ill. Pacific Glass Company, San Francisco, 1902-1926

IPGCO (in diamond): Ill. Pacific Glass Company, San Francisco, CA, 1902-1926

IG: Illinois Glass, F inside of a jar outline, C. L. Flaccus 1/2 glass 1/2 co., Pittsburgh, PA, 1900-1928

Ill. Glass Co.: 1916-1929

I G: Illinois Glass Co., Alton, IL, before 1890

I G Co. (in a diamond): Illinois Glass Co., Alton, IL, 1900-1916

Improved G E M: Hero Glass Works, Philadelphia, PA, 1868

I P G: Illinois Pacific Glass Co., San Francisco, CA, 1902-1932

I X L: I X L Glass Bottle Co., Inglewood, CA, 1921-1923

- J -

J (in keystone): Knox Glass Bottle Co., of Mississippi, Jackson, MS, 1932-1953

J (in a square): Jeannette Glass Co., Jeannette, PA, 1901-1922

JAF & Co., Pioneer and Folger: J.A. Folger & Co., San Francisco CA, 1850 Present

J D 26 S: Jogn Ducan & Sons, New York, NY, 1880-1900

J. P. F.: Pitkin Glass Works, Manchester, CT, 1783-1830

J R: Stourbridge Flint Glass Works, Pittsburgh, PA, 1823-1828

JBS monogram: Joseph Schlitz Brewing Co., Milwaukee, WI, 1900

JT: Mantua Glass Works and later Mantua Glass Co., Mantua, OH, 1824

JT & Co: Brownsville Glass Works, Brownsville, PA, 1824-1828

J. SHEPARD: J. Shepard & Co., Zanesville, OH, 1823-1838

- K -

K (in a keystone): Knox Glass Bottle Co., Knox, PA, 1924-1968

Kensington Glass Works: Kensington Glass Works, Philadelphia, PA, 1822-1932

Kerr (in script): Kerr Glass Manufacturing Co. and later Alexander H. Kerr Glass Co., Portland, OR; Sand Spring, OK; Chicago, IL; Los Angeles, CA, 1912-Present

K H & G: Kearns, Herdman & Gorsuch, Zanesville, OH, 1876-1884

K & M: Knox & McKee, Wheeling, WV, 1824-1829

K & O: Kivlan & Onthank, Boston, MA, 1919-1925

KO – HI: Koehler & Hinrichs, St. Paul, MN, 1911

K Y G W and KYGW Co: Kentucky Glass Works Co., Louisville, KY, 1849-1855

- L -

L (in a keystone): Lincoln Glass Bottle Co., Lincoln, IL, 1942-1952

L: W. J. Latchford Glass Co., Los Angeles, CA, 1925-1938

Lamb: Lamb Glass Co., Mt. Vernon, OH, 1855-1964

LB (B inside L): Long Beach Glass Co., Long Beach, CA 1920-1933

L & W: Lorenz & Wightman, PA, 1862-1871

LGW: Laurens Glass Works, Laurens, SC, 1911- 1970

L G Co: Louisville Glass Works, Louisville, KY, 1880

Lightning: Henry W. Putnam, Bennington, VT, 1875-1890

LP (in a keystone): Pennsylvania Bottle Co., Wilcox, PA, 1940-1952

L K Y G W: Louisville Kentucky Glass Works, Louisville, KY, 1873-1890

- M -

Mascot, Mason and M F G Co.: Mason Fruit Jar Co., Philadelphia, PA, 1885-1890

Mastadon: Thomas A. Evans Mastadon Works, and later Wm. McCully & Co. Pittsburgh, PA, 1855-1887

MB Co: Muncie Glass Co., Muncie, IN, 1895-1910

M B & G Co: Massillon Bottle & Glass Co., Massillon, OH, 1900-1904

M B W: Millville Bottle Works, Millville, NJ, 1903-1930

McL (in circle): McLaughlin Glass Co., Vernon, CA, 1920-1936, Gardena, CA, 1951-1956

MEDALLION: M.S. Burr & Co., Boston, MA (manufacturer of nursing bottles), 1874

M (in keystone): Metro Glass Bottle Co., Jersey City, NJ, 1935-1949

MG: straight letters 1930-1940; slant letters 1940-1958; Maywood Glass, Maywood, CA

M.G. CO.: Modes Glass Co., Cicero, IN, 1895-1904

M.G.W.: Middletown Glass Co., NY, 1889

Moore Bros.: Moore Bros., Clayton, NJ, 1864-1880

MOUNT VERNON: Cook & Bernheimer Co., New York, NY, 1890

- N -

N (in a keystone): Newborn Glass Co., Royersford, PA, 1920-1925

N: H. Northwood Glass Co., Wheeling, WV, 1902-1925

N (bold N in bold square): Obear-Nester Glass Co., St. Louis, MO, and East St. Louis, IL, 1895

N B B G Co: North Baltimore Bottle Glass Co., North Baltimore, OH, 1885-1930

N G Co: Northern Glass Co., Milwaukee, WI, 1894-1896

N - W: Nivison-Weiskopf Glass Co., Reading, OH, 1900-1931

- O -

O (in a square): Owen Bottle Co., 1911-1929

O B C: Ohio Bottle Co., Newark, OH, 1904-1905

O-D-1-O & Diamond & I: Owens Ill. Pacific Coast Co., CA, 1932-1943. Mark of Owen-Ill. Glass Co. merger in 1930

O G W: Olean Glass Co. (Works), Olean, NY, 1887-1915

Oil City Glass Co.: Oil City, PA, 1920-1925

OSOTITE (in elongated diamond): Warren Fruit Jar Co., Fairfield, IA, 1910

O-U-K I D: Robert A Vancleave, Philadelphia, PA, 1909

- P -

P (in keystone): Wightman Bottle & Glass Co., Parker Landing, PA, 1930-1951

PCGW: Pacific Coast Glass Works, San Francisco, CA, 1902-1924

PEERLESS: Peerless Glass Co., Long Island City, NY, 1920-1935 (was Bottler's & Manufacturer's Supply Co.), 1900-1920

P G W: Pacific Glass Works, San Francisco, CA, 1862-1876

Picture of young child in circle: M. S. Burr & Co., Boston, MA (manufacturer of nursing bottles), 1874

Premium: Premium Glass Co., Coffeyville, KS, 1908-1914

P (in square) or Pine (in box): Pine Glass Corp., Okmulgee, OK, 1927-1929

P S: Puget Sound Glass Co., Anacortes, WA, 1924-1929

Putnam Glass Works (in a circle): Putnam Flint Glass Works, Putnam, OH, 1852-1871

P & W: Perry & Wood and later Perry & Wheeler, Keene, NH, 1822-1830

- Q -

Queen (in script) Trade Mark (all in a shield): Smalley, Kivian & Onthank, Boston, MA, 1906-1919

- R -

Rau's: Fairmount Glass Works, Fairmount, IN, 1898-1908

R & C Co: Roth & Co., San Francisco, CA, 1879-1888

Red (with a key through it): Safe Glass Co., Upland, IN, 1892-1898

R G Co.: Renton Glass Co., Renton, WA, 1911

Root: Root Glass Co., Terre Haute, IN, 1901-1932

- S -

S (inside a star): Southern Glass Co., LA, 1920-1929

S (in a triangle): Schloss Crockery Co., San Francisco, CA, 1910

SB & GCo: Stretor Bottle & Glass Co., Streator, IL, 1881-1905

SF & PGW: San Francisco & Pacific Glass Works, 1876-1900

S & C: Stebbins & Chamberlain or Coventry Glass Works, Coventry, CT, 1825-1830

S F G W: San Francisco Glass Works, San Francisco, CA, 1869-1876

SIGNET (blown-in bottom): Chicago Heights Bottle Co., Chicago, Heights, IL, 1913

Squibb: E.R. Squibb, M.D., Brooklyn, NY, 1858-1895

Standard (in script, Mason): Standard Coop. Glass Co. and later Standard Glass Co., Marion, IN, 1894-1932

Star Glass Co: Star Glass Co., New Albany, IN, 1867-1900

Swayzee: Swayzee Glass Co. Swayzee, IN, 1894-1906

- T -

T C W: T.C. Wheaton Co. Millville, NJ, 1888-Present

THE BEST (in an arch): Gotham Co., New York, NY, 1891

TIP TOP: Charles Boldt Glass Co., Cincinnati, OH, 1904

T W & Co.: Thomas Wightman & Co., Pittsburgh, PA, 1871-1895

T S: Coventry Glass Works, Coventry, CT, 1820-1824

- U -

U: Upland Flint Bottle Co., Upland, Inc., 1890-1909

U (in a keystone): Pennsylvania Bottle Co., Sheffield, PA, 1929-1951

U S: United States Glass Co., Pittsburgh, PA, 1891-1938, Tiffin, OH, 1938-1964

- W -

WARRANTED (in an arch) FLASK: Albert G. Smalley, Boston, MA, 1892

W & CO: Thomas Wightman & Co., Pittsburgh, PA, 1880-1889

W C G Co: West Coast Glass Co., Los Angeles, CA, 1908-1930

WF & S MILW: William Franzen & Son, Milwaukee, WI, 1900-1929

W G W: Woodbury Glass Works, Woodbury, NJ, 1882-1900

WYETH: a drug manufacturer, 1880-1910

W T & Co: Whitall-Tatum & Co., Millville, NJ, 1857-1935

W T R Co.: W. T. Rawleigh Manufacturing Co., Freeport, IL, 1925-1936

Foreign Trademarks

A (in a circle): Alembic Glass, Industries Bangalore, India

Big A in center GM: Australian Glass Mfg. Co., Kilkenny, So. Australia

A.B.C.: Albion Bottle Co., LTD., Oldbury, Worcs., England, 1928-1969

A.G.W.: Alloa Glass Limited, Alloa, Scotland

A G B Co.: Albion Glass Bottle Co., England, trademark is found under Lea & Perrins, 1880-1900

AVH: A. Van Hoboken & Co., Rotterdam, the Netherlands, 1800-1898

B & C Co. L: Bagley & Co. Ltd., England, established 1832 and still operating

Beaver: Beaver Flint Glass Co., Toronto, Ontario, Canada, 1897-1920

Bottle (in frame): Veb Glasvoerk Drebkau Drebkau, N.L. Germany

Crown (with three dots): Crown Glass, Waterloo, N.S.. Wales

Crown (with figure of a crown): Excelsior Glass Co., St. Johns, Quebec and later Diamond Glass Co., Montreal, Quebec, Canada, 1879-1913

CS & Co.: Cannington, Shaw & Co., St. Helens, England, 1872-1916

CSTS (in center of hot air balloon): C. Stolzles Sohne Actiengeselischaft fur Glasfabrikation, Vienna, Austria, Hungary, 1905

D (in center of a diamond): Dominion Glass Co., Montreal, Quebec, Canada

D.B. (in a book frame): Dale Brown & Co., Ltd., Mesborough, Yorks, England

Fish: Veb Glasvoerk Stralau, Berlin

Excelsior: Excelsior Glass Co., St. John, Quebec, Canada, 1878-1883

HH: Werk Hermannshutte, Czechoslovakia

Hamilton: Hamilton Glass Works, Hamilton, Ontario, Canada, 1865-1872

Hat: Brougba, Bulgaria

Hunyadi Janos: Andreas Saxlehner, Buda-Pesth, Austria-Hungary, 1863-1900

IYGE (all in a circle): The Irish Glass Bottle, Ltd. Dublin, Ireland

KH: Kastrupog Holmeqaads, Copenhagen

L (on a bell): Lanbert S.A., Belgium

LIP: Lea & Perrins, London, England, 1880-1900

LS: In a circle, Lax & Shaw, Ltd., Leeds, York, England

M (in a circle): Cristales Mexicanos, Monterey, Mexico

N (in a diamond): Tippon Glass Co., Ltd., Tokyo, Japan

NAGC: North American Glass Co., Montreal, Quebec, Canada, 1883-1890

NP: Imperial Trust for the Encouragement of Scientific and Industrial Research, London, England, 1907

NS (in middle of bottle shape): Edward Kavalier of Neu Sazawa, Austria-Hungary, 1910

P & J A: P. & J. Arnold, LTD., London, England, 1890-1914

PRANA: Aerators Limited, London, England, 1905

PG: Verreries De Puy De Dome, S. A. Paris, France

R: Louit Freres & Co., France, 1870-1890

S (in a circle): Vetreria Savonese, A. Voglienzone, S.A. Milano, Italy

S.A.V.A. (all in a circle): Asmara, Ethiopia

S & M: Sykes & Macvey, Castleford, England, 1860-1888.

T (in a circle): Tokyo Seibin, Ltd., Tokyo, Japan

vFo: Vidreria Ind., Figuerras Oliveiras, Brazil

VT: Ve.Tri S.p.a., Vetrerie Trivemta Vicenza, Italy

VX: Usine de Vauxrot, France

WECK (in a frame): Weck Glaswerk G. mb.H, ofigen, in Bonn, Germany

Y (in a circle): Etaria Lipasmaton, Athens, Greece

GLOSSARY

ABM (Automatic Bottle Machine): The innovation of Michael Owens in 1903 to allow an entire bottle to be made in one step.

ACL: Applied Color Label created by pyroglaze or enameled lettering, usually used with soda pop bottles from 1920 to 1960.

Agate Glass: A glass made from mix incorporating blasting furnace slag. Known in tints of chocolate brown, caramel brown, natural agate, tanned leather, showing striations of milk glass in off-white tints. Made from 1850 to 1900s.

Amethyst-Colored Glass: A clear glass that, when exposed to the sun or bright light for a long period of time, will turn various shades of purple. Only glass containing manganese turns purple.

Amber-Colored Glass: Nickel was added in glass production to obtain this common bottle color. The dark color was believed to prevent the sun from ruining the contents of the bottle.

Annealing: The gradual cooling of hot glass in a cooling chamber or an annealing oven.

Applied Color Labeling: Method of decorating a bottle by applying glass with a low melting point to a bottle through a metal screen and then baking it.

Applied Lip/Top: On pre-1880s bottles, the neck was applied after removal from the blow-pipe. This type of top may be consist of only a ring of glass trailed around the neck.

Aqua-Colored Glass: A natural color of glass. Its shade depends on the amount of ion oxide contained in the raw materials. Produced until the 1930s.

Bail: Wire clamp consisting of a wire that goes over the top of the lid or lip, and a "locking" wire that is pushed down to cause pressure on the bail and the lid, resulting in an airtight closure.

Barber Bottle: In the 1880s, these colorful bottles decorated the shelves of barbershops and usually were filled with bay rum.

Batch: A mixture of the ingredients necessary in the manufacturing of glass.

Battledore: A wooden paddle used to flatten the bottom or sides of a bottle.

Bitters: An herbal medicine, medicinal and flavoring, which contains a great quantity of alcohol, usually corn whiskey.

Black Glass: This type of glass produced between 1700 and 1875 is actually a dark olive green caused by the carbon in the glass production.

Blob Seal: A coin-shaped blob of glass applied to the shoulder of a bottle, into which a seal with the logo or name of the distiller, date, or product name was impressed. The information contained on the blob seal provides a way of identifying an unembossed bottle.

Blob Top: A large thick blob of glass placed around the lip of soda or mineral water bottles. A wire held the stopper, which was seated below the blob and anchored the wire when the stopper was closed, to prevent the carbonation from escaping.

Blown in Mold, Applied Lip (Bimal): The process by which a gather of glass is blown into a mold to take the shape of the mold. The lip on these types were added later and the bases often have open pontil scars.

Blowpipe: A hollow iron tube wider and thicker at the gathering end than at the blowing end. It is used by the blower to pick up the molten glass, which is then blown-in mold or free-blown outside the mold. The pipe can vary from 2-1/2 ft. to 6 ft. long.

Blow-Over: A bubble-like extension of glass above a jar or bottle lip blown so the blowpipe could be broken free from the jar after blowing. The blow-over was then chipped off and the lip was ground.

Borosilicate: A type of glass originally formulated for making scientific glassware.

Calabash: A type of flask with a rounded bottom. This type of bottle is known as a "Jenny Lind" flask and was common in the 19th century.

Camphor Glass: A white cloudy glass that resembles refined gum camphor. Bottles made with this glass are known in blown, blown-mold, and pressed forms.

Carboys: Cylindrical bottles with short necks.

Clapper: A glassmaker's tool used in shaping and forming the footing of an object.

Cobalt Colored Glass: This color was used with patented medicines and poisons to distinguish them from regular bottles. Excessive amounts resulted in the familiar "cobalt blue" color.

Codd: A bottle enclosure patented in 1873 by Hiram Codd of England. A small ball is blown inside of the bottle. The ball is forced to the top of the neck by pressure, creating a method of sealing the contents from the outside air.

Crown Cap: A metal cap formed from a tin plate to slip tightly over the rolled lip of a bottle. The inside of the cap was filled with a cork disk to create an airtight seal.

Cullet: Clean, broken glass added to a batch to bring about rapid fusion to produce new glass.

Date Line: The mold seam or mold line on a bottle. The line helps estimate the approximate date in which the bottle was manufactured.

De-Colorizer: A compound added to natural aquamarine-colored bottle glass to render the glass clear.

Dip Mold: A one-piece mold open at the top.

Embossed Lettering: Raised or embossed letter on a bottle denoting the name of the product.

Fire Polishing: The reheating of glass to eliminate unwanted blemishes.

Flared Lip: Bottles produced prior to 1900 have lips that were worked out or flared out to reinforce the strength of the opening.

Flashing: A method of coloring glass by dipping a bottle into a batch of colored glass.

Flint Glass: Glass composed of a silicate of potash and lead. Commonly referred to as "lead crystal" in present terminology.

Free Blown Glass: Glass produced with a blowpipe rather than a mold.

Frosted Glass: A textured surface produced when a bottle's surfaced is sandblasted.

Gaffer: A master blower in early glass houses.

Gather: A gob of molten glass adhering to the blowpipe.

Glass Pontil: The earliest type of pontil, in which a sharp glass ring remains.

Glory Hole: The small furnace used for the frequent re-heating necessary during the making of a bottle. The glory hole was also used in fire polishing.

Green Glass: Refers to a composition of glass and not a color. The green color was caused by the iron impurities in the sand which could not be controlled by the glass makers.

Ground Pontil: When a rough pontil scar has been ground off, the remaining smooth circle is a ground pontil.

Hobbleskirt: The paneled shape used to describe Coca-Cola bottles.

Hobnail: A pattern of pressed glass characterized by an all-over pattern of bumps that resemble hobnail heads.

Hutchinson: A spring-type internal closure that seals soda bottles patented by Charles Hutchinson in 1879.

Imperfections: Bubbles (tears) of all sizes and shapes, bent shapes and necks, imperfect seams, and errors in spelling and embossing.

Improved Pontil: Bottles having an improved pontil have reddish or blackish tinges on their base.

ISP (Inserted Slug Plate): Special or unique company names or names of people were sometimes embossed on ale, whiskey, and wine bottles with a plate inserted into the mold.

Iron Pontil: The solid iron rod heated and affixed to the bottle's base creates a scar as a black circular depression often turning red upon oxidation.

Kick-Up: A deep indentation in the bottom of many bottles. This is formed by placing a projected piece of wood or metal in the base of the mold while the glass is still hot. The kickup is common on wine bottles and calabash flasks.

Laid-On Ring: A bead of glass trailed around the neck opening to reinforce the opening.

Lady's Leg: Bottles shaped like long curving necks.

Lightning Closure: A closure that used an intertwined wire bale configuration to hold the lid on fruit jars. This closure was also common with soda bottles.

Lipper: A wood tool used to widen lips and form rims and spouts of pitchers, carafes, and wide-mouthed jars.

Manganese: Used as a decolorizer between 1850 and 1910, manganese will cause glass to turn purple under extreme heat.

Melting Pot: A clay pot used to melt silicate in the process of making glass.

Metal: Molten glass.

Milk Glass: A white-colored glass created by adding tin to the glass batch during glass production. Milk glass was used primarily for cosmetic bottles.

Mold, Full-Height, Three-Piece: A mold that formed an entire bottle. The two seams run the height of the bottle to below the lip on both sides.

Mold, Three-Piece Dip: In this mold, the bottom part of the bottle mold was one piece and the top, from the shoulder up, was two separate pieces. Mold seams appear circling the bottle at the shoulder and on each side of the neck.

Opalescence: This is seen on the frosty bottle or variated color bottle that has been buried in the earth in mud or silt. The minerals in these substances have interacted with the glass to created these effects.

Open Pontil: The blowpipe was affixed to the base instead of a separate rod with a scar that is a depressed or raised circle called a moile.

Painted Label: Another name for Applied Color Label (ACL), which is baked on the outside of the bottle. ACLs were commonly used on soda pop bottles and milk bottles.

Panelled: A bottle that isn't circular or oval, but rather is formed from four to twelve panels.

Paste Mold: A mold made from two or more pieces of iron that were coated with a paste to prevent scratches on the glass. The mold eliminated seams, as the glass was turned in the mold.

Pattern Mold: A designation for a type of glass "patterned" before completed blowing.

Plate Glass: Pure glass comprised of lime and soda silicate.

Pontil, Puntee, or Punty Rod: The iron rod attached to the base of a bottle by a gob or glass to hold the bottle during the finishing.

Pontil Marks: To remove the bottle from the blowpipe, an iron rod with a small amount of molten glass was applied to the bottom of the bottle after the neck and lip were finished. A sharp tap removed the bottle from the pontil leaving a jagged glass scar called a pontil mark.

Potstone: Impurities in the glass batch that, when blown into a piece of finished glass, resemble a white stone.

Pressed Glass: Glass that has been pressed into a mold to take the shape of the mold or the pattern within the mold.

Pucellas: A tool that is essential in shaping both the body and opening in blown bottles.

Pumpkinseed: A small round flat flask, often found in areas of the American West. Generally made of clear glass, the shape resembles the seed of the grown pumpkin. These bottles are also known as "Mickies," "Saddle Flasks," and "Two-Bit Ponies."

Ribbed: A bottle with vertical or horizontal lines embossed into the bottle.

Round Bottom: A soda bottle made of heavy glass in the shape of a torpedo. The bottle is designed to lie on its side, keeping the liquid in contact with the cork to prevent the cork from drying and popping out of the bottle.

Satin Glass: Smooth glass manufactured by exposing the surface of the glass to hydrofluoric acid vapors.

Seal: A circular or oval slug of glass applied to the shoulder of a bottle with an imprint of the manufacturer's name, initials, or mark.

Seam: The mark on a bottle caused by glass assuming the shape of the mold where the two halves meet.

Sheared Lip: After a bottle was blown, a pair of scissor-like shears clipped the hot glass from the blowpipe. No top was applied and sometimes a slight flange was created.

Sick Glass: Glass bearing a superficial decay or deterioration that takes on a grayish tinge caused by erratic firing.

Slug Plate: A metal plate about 2 inches by 4 inches with a firm's name on it was inserted into a mold so the glass house could use the same mold for many companies.

Smooth Base: Bottles that do not have a pontil.

Snap Case: A tool that replaced the pontil rod. The snap case's vertical arms curved out from a central stem to grip a bottle firmly during finishing of the neck and lip, thus eliminating pontil scars or marks on the bottom of the bottle. The snap case may leave grip marks on the side however.

Squat: A form of bottle used to contain beer, porter, and soda.

Tooled Top: A top formed in a bottle mold, rather than added separately. These molded tops were made after 1885.

Torpedo: A beer or soda bottle with a rounded base meant to lie on its side to keep the cork wet.

Turn-Mold Bottles: Bottles that were turned while forming in a mold using special solvents. The continuous turning with the solvent eventually erased all of the seams and mold marks. This also resulted in a distinct luster to the bottle.

Wetting Off: Marking the neck of a hot bottle with water so that it can easily be broken from the blow pipe.

Whittle Marks: Bottles with small irregularities created by forming them in wood-carved molds. These flaws were also caused by forming glass in cold early morning molds, creating "goose pimples" on the surface of these bottles. As the molds warmed, later bottles became smoother.

BIBLIOGRAPHY

Books

Barnett, R.E. *Western Whiskey Bottles*, 4th Edition. Bend, OR: Maverick Publishing, 1997.

Ham, Bill. *Bitters Bottles*. Self Published, 1999, Supplement 2004, P.O. Box 427, Downieville, CA 95936.

Hastin, Bud. *Avon Products & California Perfume Co. Collector's Encyclopedia,* 17th Edition, Kansas City, MO: Bud Hastin Publications, 2003.

Kovill, William E. Jr. *Ink Bottles and Ink Wells*. Taunton, MA: William L. Sullwold, 1971.

Leybourne, Doug. *Red Book #9, Fruit Jar Price Guide*, Privately Published, North Muskegon, MI, 2001.

Linden, Robert A. *The Classification of Violin Shaped Bottles*, 2nd Edition, Privately Published, 1999.

———. *Collecting Violin & Banjo Bottles, A Practical Guide*, 3rd Edition, Privately Published, 2004.

McCann, Jerry. *2007 Fruit Jar Annual*. Chicago, IL: J. McCann Publisher, 2007.

McKearin, Helen and George S. *American Glass*. New York, NY: Crown Publishers, 1956.

———. *Two Hundred Years of American Blown Glass*. New York, NY: Crown Publishers, 1950.

McKearin, Helen and Kenneth M. Wilson. *American Bottles and Flasks and Their Ancestry*. New York, NY: Crown Publishers, 1978.

Polak, Michael. *Antique Trader-Bottles: Identification and Price Guide*, 5th Edition. Krause Publications, Iola, WI, 2006.

————. *Official Price Guide to American Patriotic Memorabilia*, 1st Edition. House of Collectibles, New York, NY, 2002.

Rensselaer, Stephen Van. *Early American Bottles and Flasks*. Stratford, CT: J. Edmund Edwards Publisher, 1969.

Sweeney, Rick. *Collecting Applied Color Label Soda Bottes, 3rd Edition*. La Mesa, CA: Painted Soda Bottles Collectors Assoc., 2002.

Toulouse, Julian Harrison. *Bottle Makers and Their Marks*. Camden, NJ: Thomas Nelson Incorporated, 1971.

Zumwalt, Betty. *Ketchup, Pickles, Sauces*. Sandpoint, ID: Mark West Publishers, 1980.

Periodicals

Ale Street News, P.O. Box 1125, Maywood, NJ 07607, E-Mail: JamsOD@aol.com, Web Site: www.AleStreetNews.com

Antique Bottle & Glass Collector, Jim Hagenbuch, 102 Jefferson Street, P.O. Box 187, East Greenville, PA 18041

Antique Bottle Collector UK Limited, Llanerch, Carno, Caersws, Powys SY17 5JY, Wales

Australian Antique Bottles and Collectibles, AABS, Box 235, Golden Square, 3555, Australia

BAM (Bottles and More) *Magazine*, P.O. Box #6, Lehighton, PA 18235

Bottles & Bygones, 30 Brabant Rd, Cheadle Hulme, Cheadlek, Cheshire, SKA 7AU, England

Bottles & Extra Magazine, 1966 King Springs Road, Johnson City, TN 37601

British Bottle Review (BBR), Elsecar Heritage Centre, Barnsley, S. York, S74, 8HJ England

Canadian Bottle & Stoneware Collector Magazine, 102 Abbeyhill Drive, Kanata, ON K2L 1H2, Canada, Web site: www.cbandsc.com

Crown Jewels of the Wire, P.O. Box 1003, St. Charles, IL 60174-1003

Fruit Jar Newletter, FJN Publishers, 364 Gregory Avenue, West Orange, NH 07052-3743

Root Beer Float, P.O. Box 571, Lake Geneva, WI 53147

The Miniature Bottle Collector, P.O. Box 2161, Palos Verdes Peninsula, CA 92074, Brisco Publications

The Soda Spectrum, A Publication by Soda Pop Dreams, P.O Box 23037, Krug Postal Outlet, Kitchener, Ontario, Canada N2B 3V1

Treasure Hunter's Gazette (Collector's Newsletter), 14 Vernon St., Keene, NH, 03431, George Streeter - Publisher & Editor

WEB SITES

American Bottle Auctions: www.americanbottle.com

Antique Bottle Forum: www.antique-bottles.net

Antique Fruit Jars: www.antiquebottles.com

Antique Pottery/Stoneware Auctions:

www.antiques-stoneware.com

The "Bottle Bible": www.bottlebible.com

The Bottle Den: www.bottleden.com

Breweriana: www.brewerygems.com

Canadian Bottles: www.glassco.com

Digger Odell Bottle Price Guides: www.bottlebooks.com

Federation of Historical Bottle Collectors: www.fohbc.com

Glass Works Auctions: www.glswrk-auction.com

Norman C. Heckler Auctions: www.hecklerauction.com

Painted Soda Bottle Collectors Association:

www.psbca.thesodafizz.com

Rich Penn Auctions: www.richpennauctions.com

Showtime Auction Services: www.showtimeauction.com

PHOTO INDEX

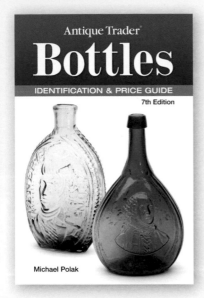